Grade 1

Jumbo Workbook

This workbook belo

....

Use pencils, crayons, and stickers to complete the activities in this book. When there is a sticker missing, you will see this pattern:

Dear Parents and Families,

Welcome to the *Grade 1 Jumbo Workbook*!

Here are some tips to help ensure that your child gets the most from this book.

- ★ Look at the pages with your child, ensuring they know what to do before starting.
- ★ Plan short, regular sessions, only doing one or two pages at a time.
- ★ Praise your child's efforts and improvements.
- ★ Encourage your child to assess their own efforts in a positive way. For example, say: "You've written some great F's there. Which one do you think you did best?"
- ★ Make the learning sessions positive experiences. Give prompts where they might help. If a section is too hard for your child, leave those pages until they are ready for them.
- ★ Relate the learning to things in your child's world. For example, if your child is working on a page about three-dimensional shapes, ask them to find some 3D shapes in your home.
- ★ There are stickers to use throughout the book. They help build your child's hand–eye coordination and observation skills. Encourage your child to place the stickers on each page before starting the other activities. There are also reward stickers to help increase motivation.
- ★ At the back of the workbook is an answer section. Encourage your child to attempt the activities and check them over before looking at the answers. Some activities have open questions with no right or wrong answer. Help your child to recognize these activities and to use self-expression.

Together, the activities in the workbook help build a solid understanding of core learning concepts and topics to ensure your child is ready for second grade.

We wish your child hours of enjoyment with this fun workbook!

Scholastic Early Learning

Picture credits: All photos courtesy of **Shutterstock,** unless noted as follows: **Andrey Lobachev/Shutterstock.com:** 140mr (brown car); **bh-2/Shutterstock.com:** 227tl (fire station); **Claudio Divizia/Shutterstock.com:** 140tr (red car); **Dmitry Dven/Shutterstock.com:** 140cl (black car); **Erena.Wilson/Shutterstock.com:** 140cl (white car); **Evannovostro/Shutterstock.com:** 140tl (purple car); **MBI Images:** 26br (hand icing cake), 27bm (boys playing football), 27mr (girl on horse), 29mr (hand), 30br (dinosaur), 66bl (sock), 80br (boy walking dog), 89bl (dinosaur toy), 90br (bunny), 106bl (lion cub), 108ml (stone), 111tl (boy king), 115mr (building block), 130tc (rabbit), 160tl (pencils), 160br (red apple), 161br (purple rose), 181br (blocks), 191br (crayons), Sticker sheet 2tr (10 on book); (9 on book); (4 on book); (2 on book); (plus on book); (minus on book); green ruler), 2ml (plate and cutlery), Sticker sheet 4m (jeans), Sticker sheet 5tm (flower), 5m (sock), Sticker sheet 6tl (log), Sticker sheet 9tl (blue shell), 9tl (purple shell).

Contents

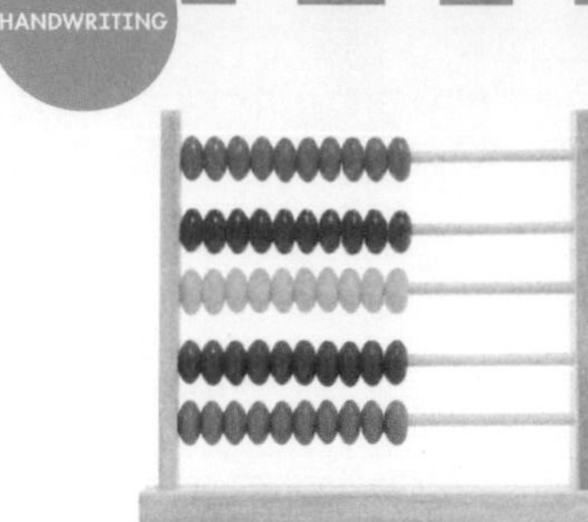

abacus

alpaca

Trace and write **a**'s.

Write these words in alphabetical order.

ape **aardvark** **April** **avocado**

Write this sentence.

Ava ate an awesome apricot.

bulb

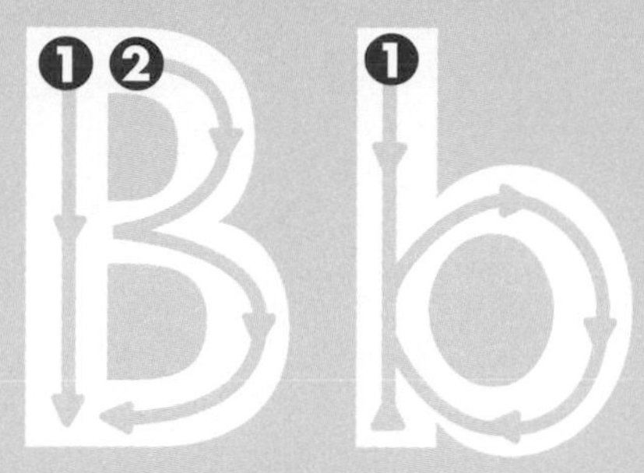

bumblebee

Trace and write **b**'s.

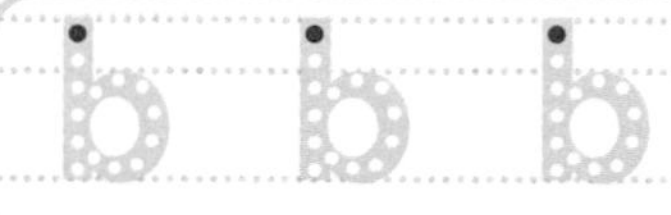

Write these words in alphabetical order.

Boston bubble bamboo bluebird

Write this sentence.

Ben bought Bella a big balloon.

cactus

chick

Trace and write **c**'s.

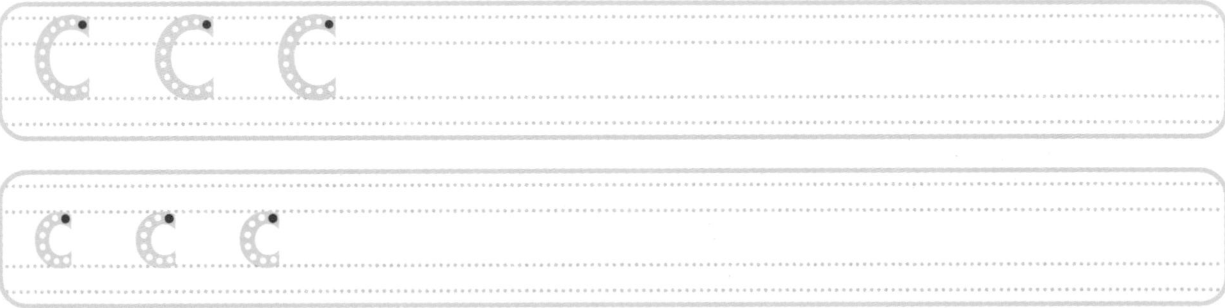

Write these words in alphabetical order.

circle clock castle Canada

Write this sentence.

Cora camps in a cool canyon.

dribble

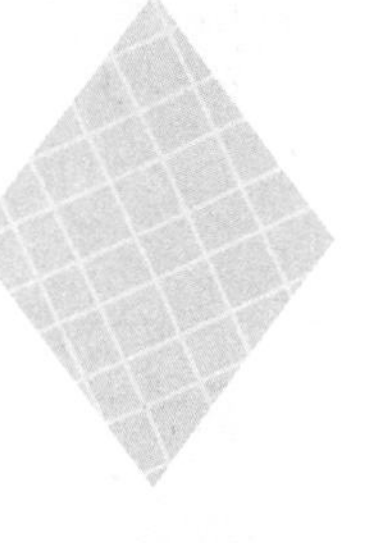

diamond

Trace and write **d**'s.

Write these words in alphabetical order.

dragon dodge December dad

Write this sentence.

Dan does a dazzling disco dance.

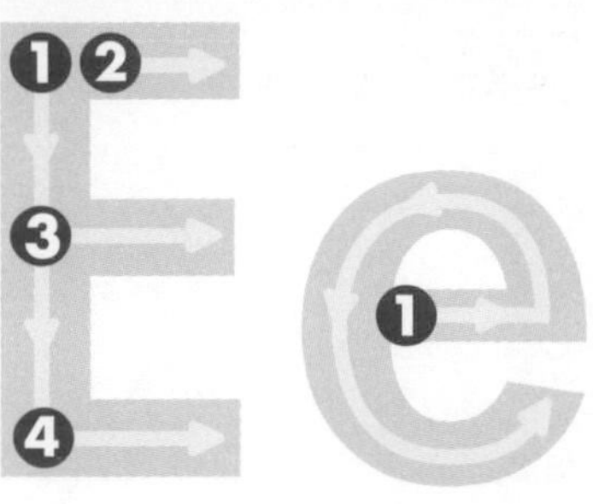

Trace and write **e**'s.

Write these words in alphabetical order.

energy **Earth** **eel** **elephant**

Write this sentence.

Emma eats eggs every evening.

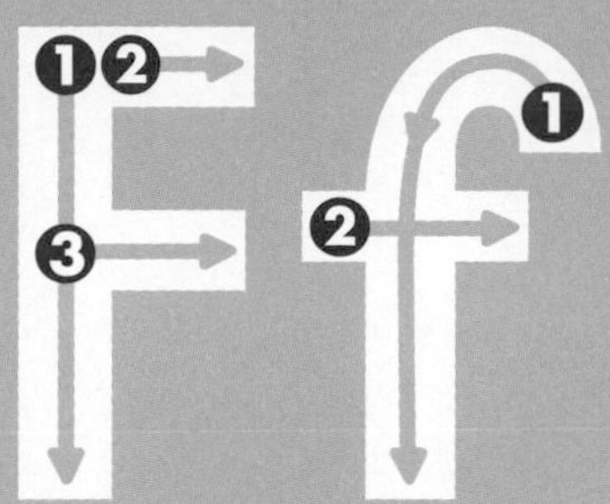

Trace and write **f**'s.

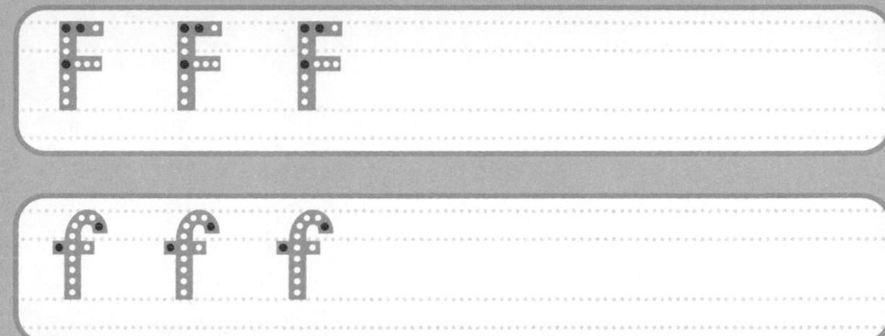

Write this sentence.

Fido and Fifi are fun friends.

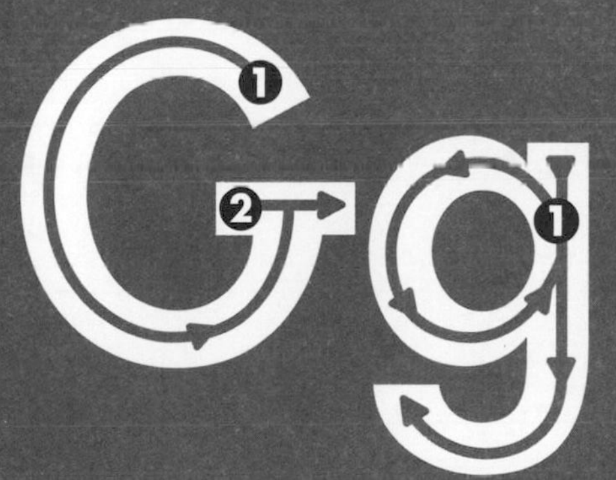

Trace and write **g**'s.

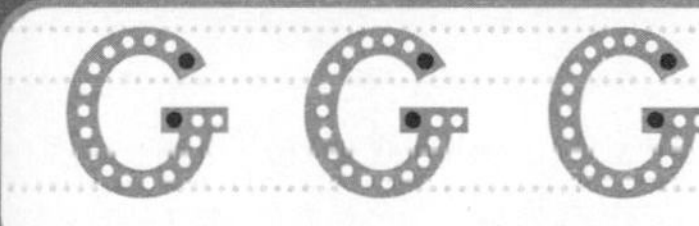

Write this sentence.

A greedy goat grazes on green grass.

hatch

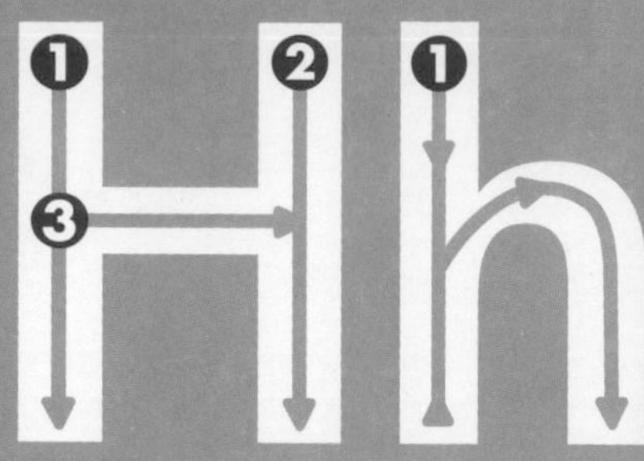

hedgehog

Trace and write **h**'s.

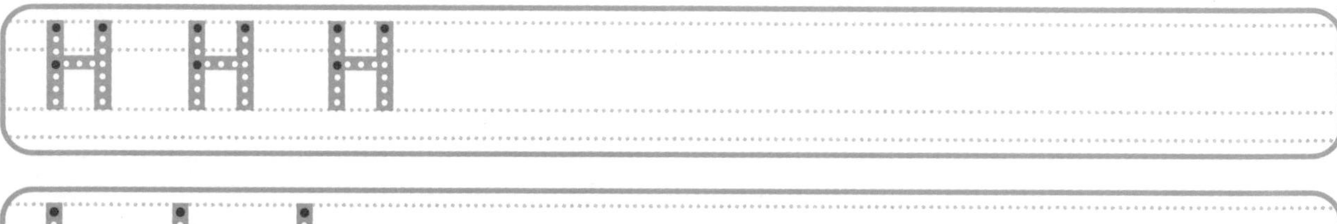

Write these words in alphabetical order.

high hero hip-hop Hawaii

Write this sentence.

Hilda the horse hunts for hay.

insect

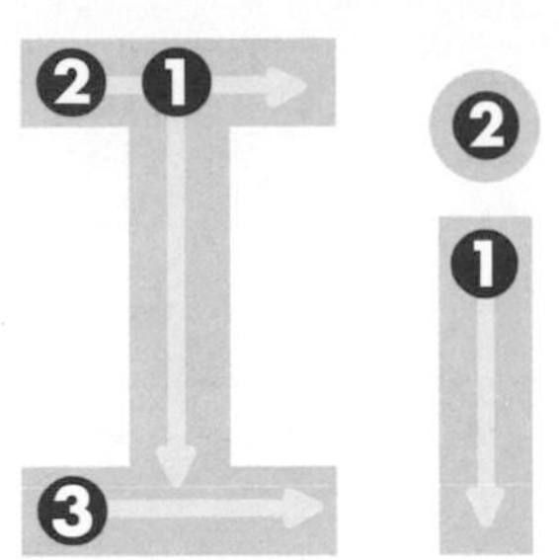

identical

Trace and write **i**'s.

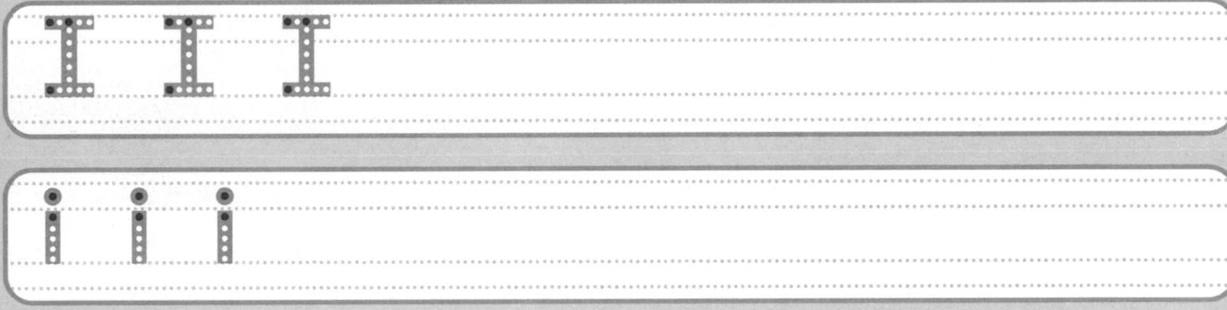

Write these words in alphabetical order.

icing inside India island

Write this sentence.

Isaac is inside his icy igloo.

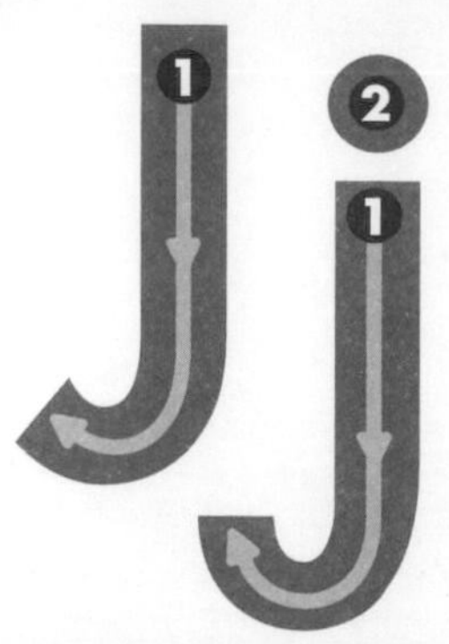

Trace and write **j**'s.

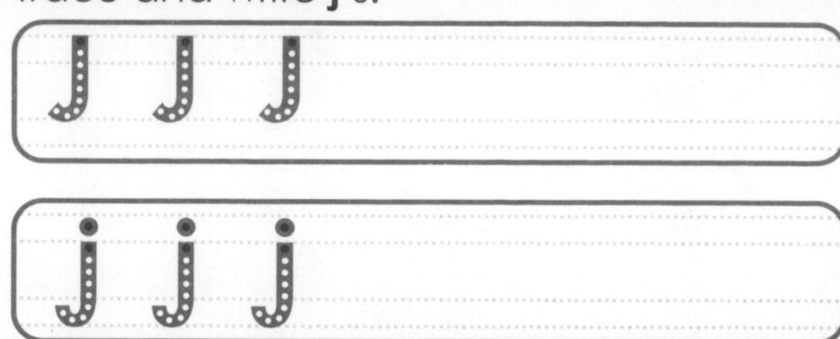

Write this sentence.

Judy juggles in June and July.

Trace and write **k**'s.

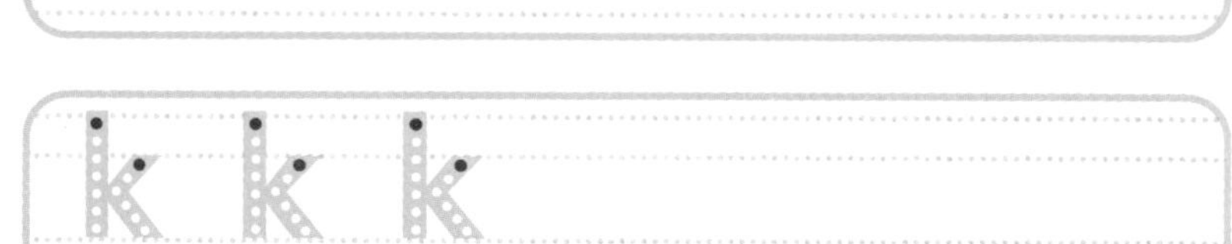

Write this sentence.

Kevin the koala knows karate.

lily

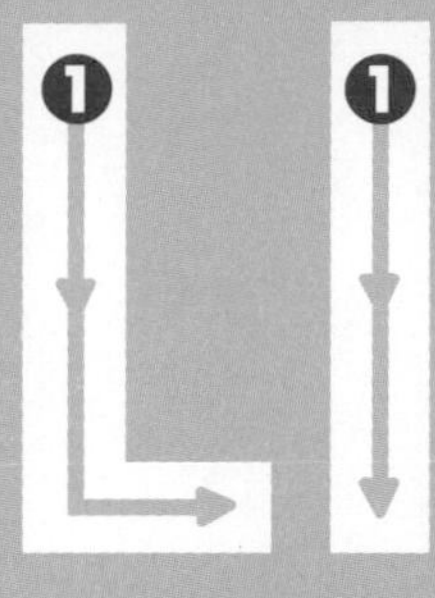

lollipop

Trace and write **l**'s.

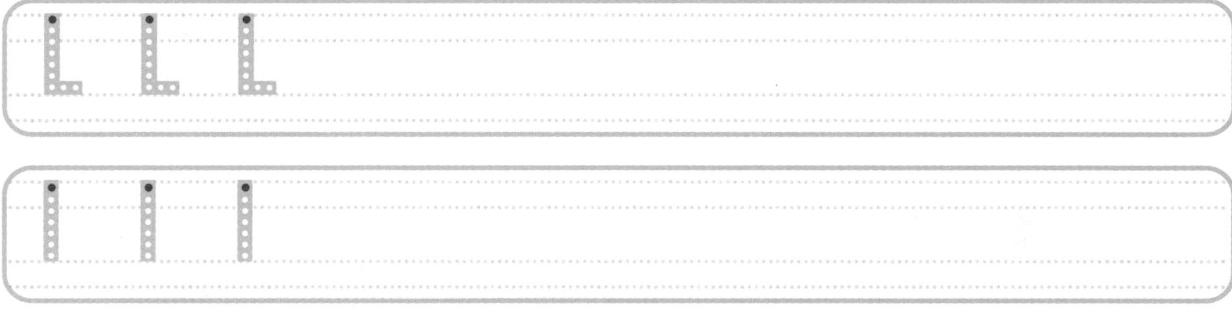

Write these words in alphabetical order.

lunch **likely** **lion** **London**

Write this sentence.

Layla learns a lovely lullaby.

Trace and write **m**'s.

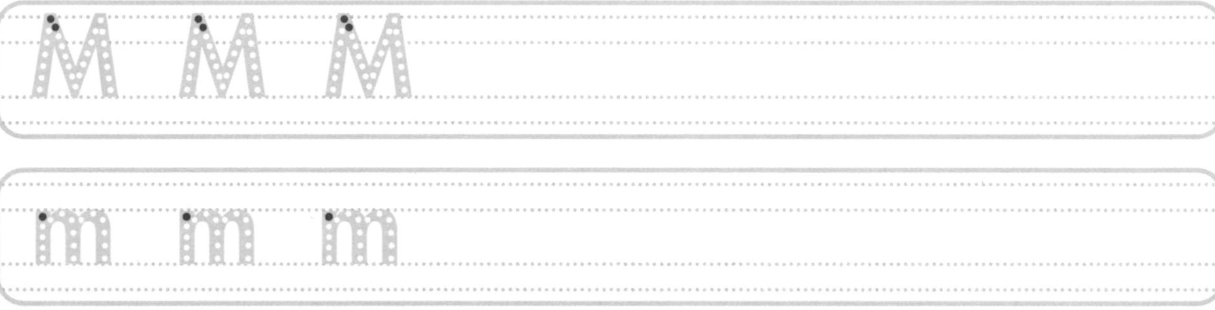

Write these words in alphabetical order.

mother **museum** **Mars** **mammal**

Write this sentence.

Mason makes modern music.

neon

ninja

Trace and write **n**'s.

N N N

n n n

Write these words in alphabetical order.

number **Norway** **none** **nest**

Write this sentence.

Nancy nibbled some nice nachos.

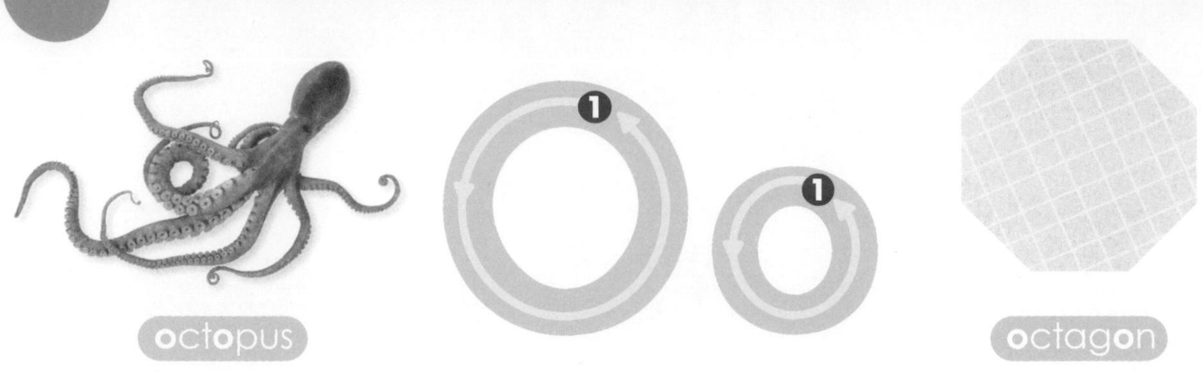

Trace and write **o**'s.

Write these words in alphabetical order.

onion **October** **owl** **ooze**

Write this sentence.

Ollie often orders orange juice.

puppy

popcorn

Trace and write **p**'s.

Write these words in alphabetical order.

Paris parrot paper people

Write this sentence.

Pippa puts pepper on her pasta.

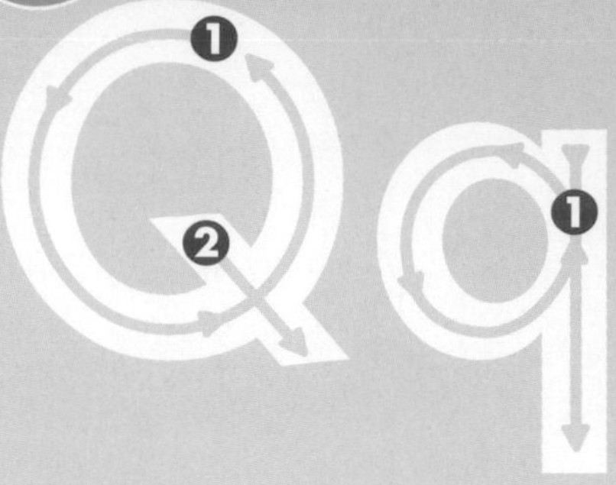

Trace and write **q**'s.

Q Q Q

q q q

Write this sentence.

Quinn quit the quirky quest.

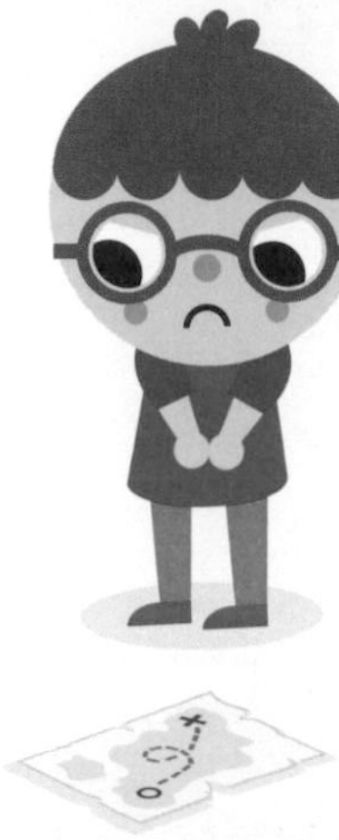

Trace and write **r**'s.

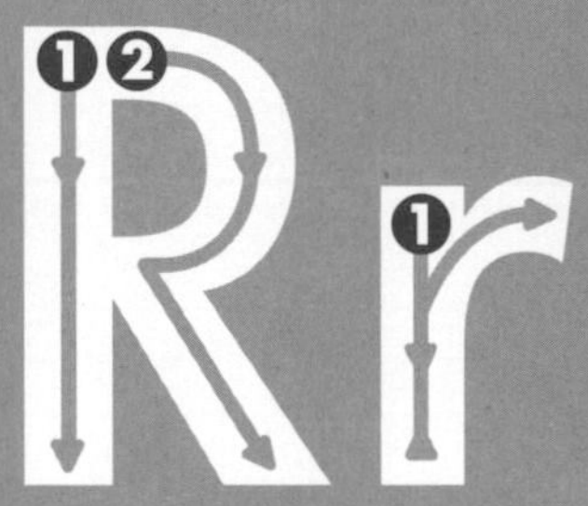

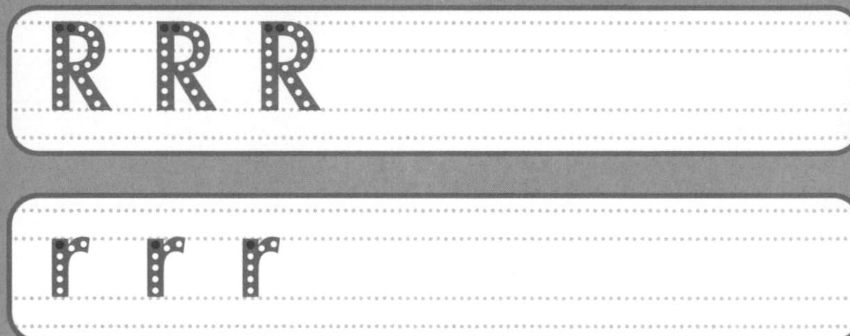

R R R

r r r

Write this sentence.

Rob rushed around the roller rink.

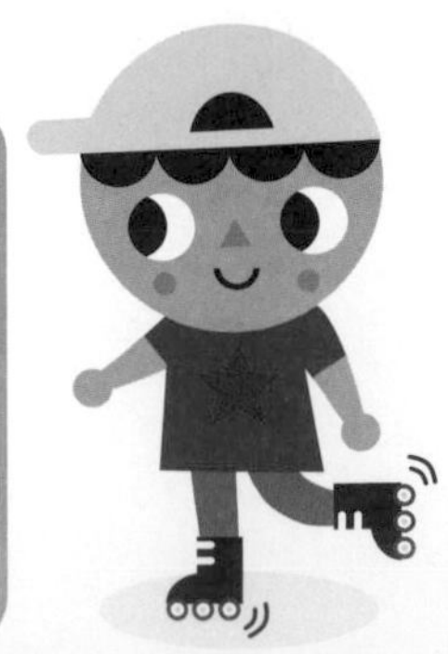

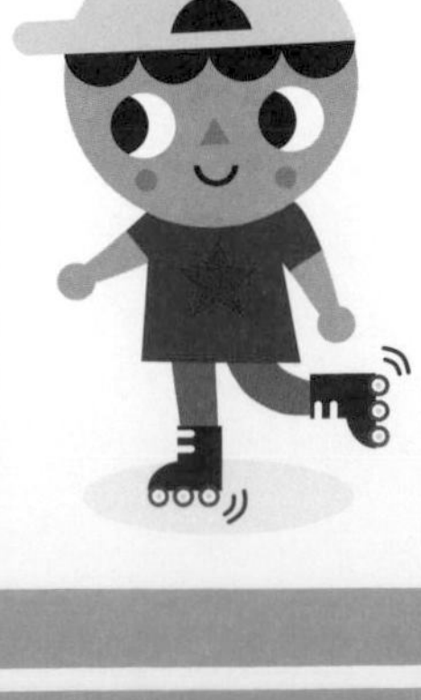

scissors

seesaw

Trace and write **s**'s.

Write these words in alphabetical order.

shark **sports** **Saturday** **shorts**

Write this sentence.

Sam swiftly swims to shore.

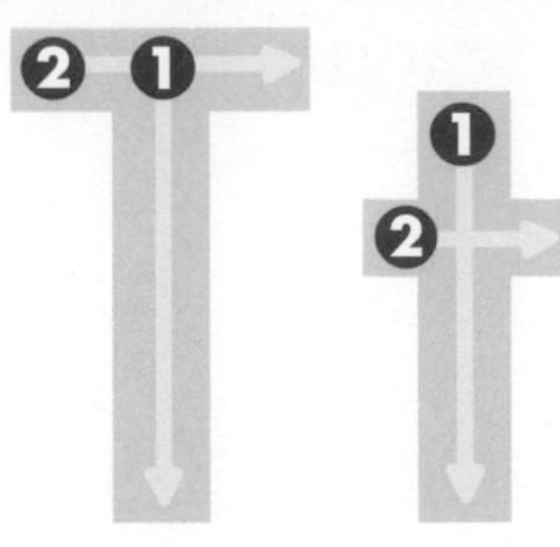

Trace and write **t**'s.

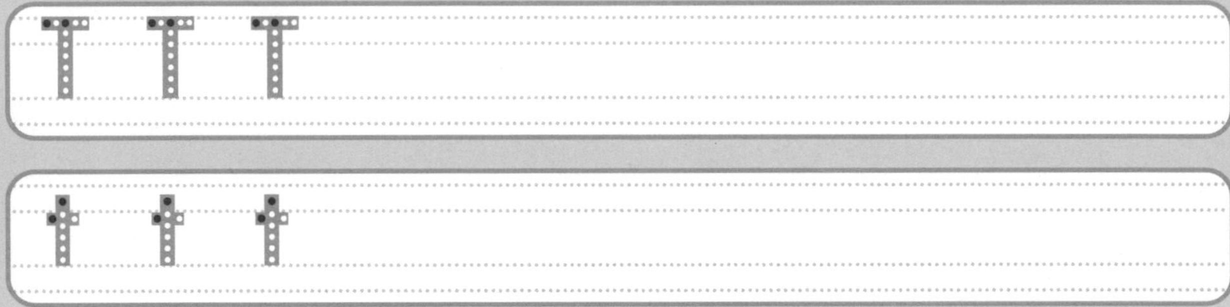

Write these words in alphabetical order.

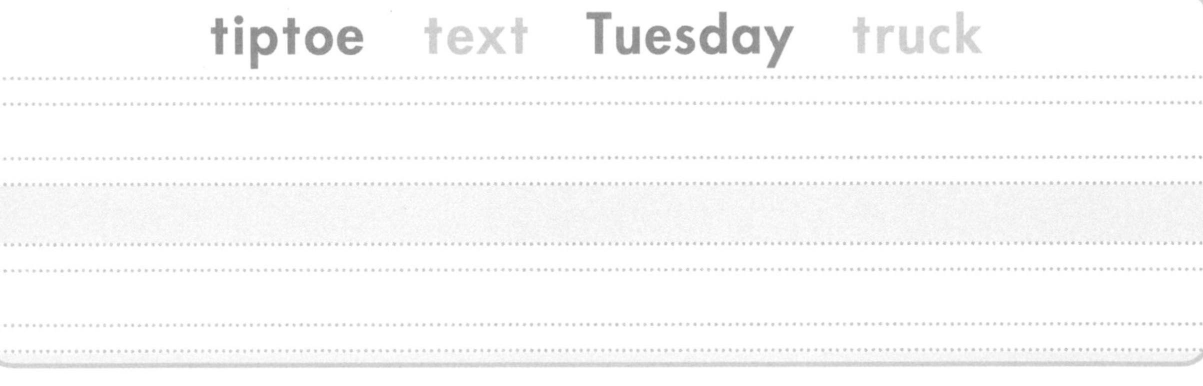

Write this sentence.

Toby talks to two tiny turtles.

ukulele

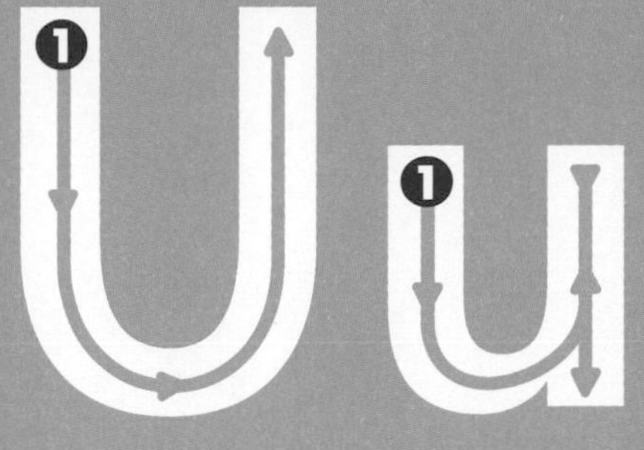

unicorn

Trace and write **u**'s.

Write these words in alphabetical order.

uncle under Uranus useful

Write this sentence.

Una uses an unusual umbrella.

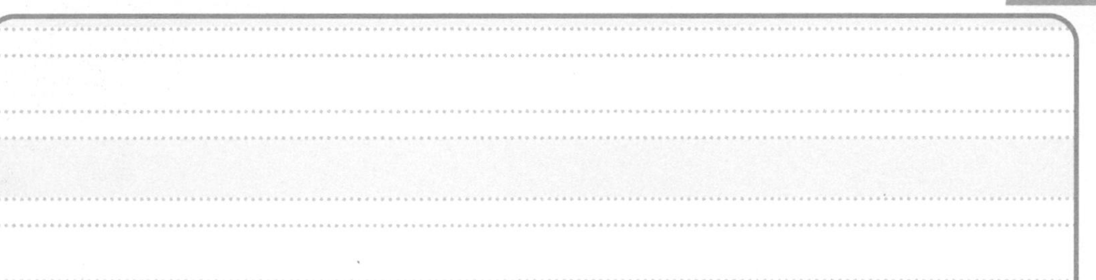

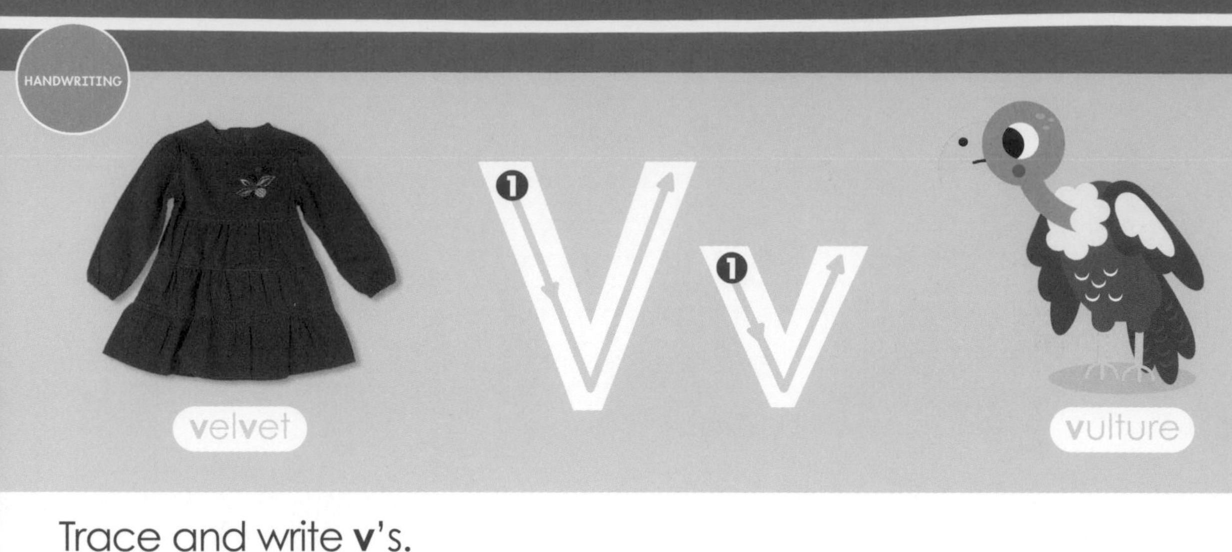

Trace and write **v**'s.

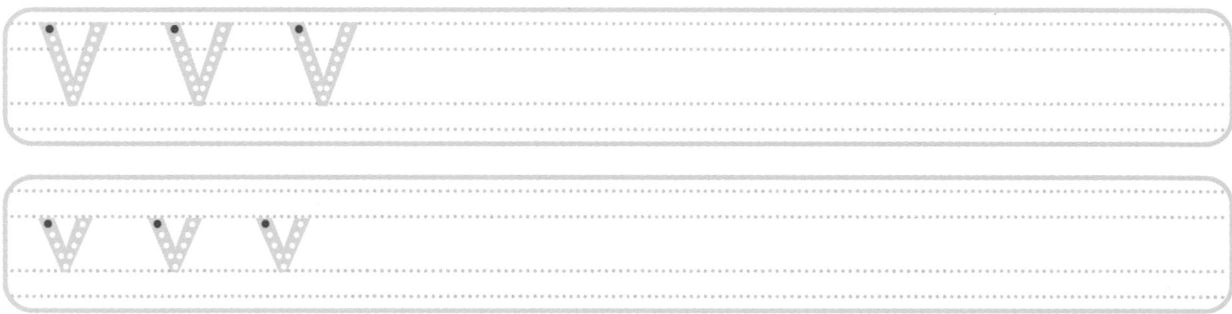

Write these words in alphabetical order.

Viking vivid video vanilla

Write this sentence.

Vivian viewed a vast volcano.

wheelbarrow

window

Trace and write **w**'s.

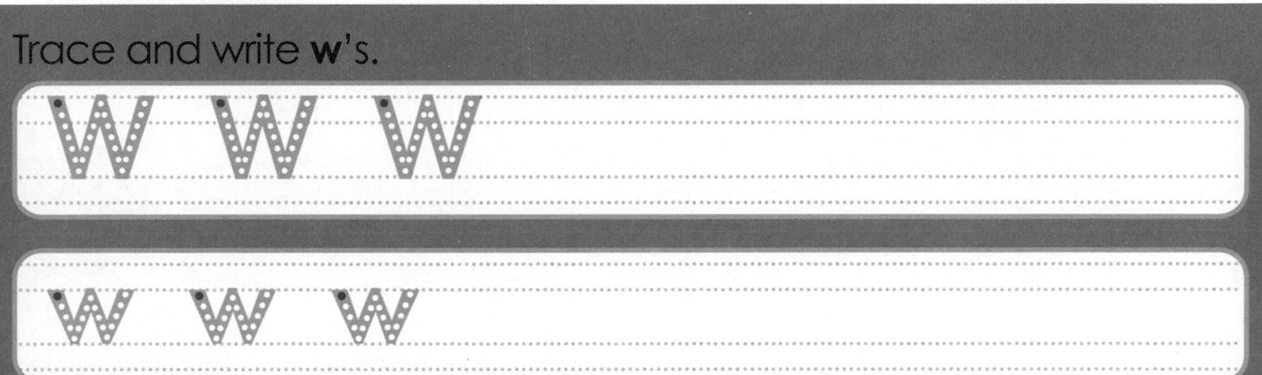

Write these words in alphabetical order.

willow **Wednesday** **walk** **walrus**

Write this sentence.

Which whale went westward?

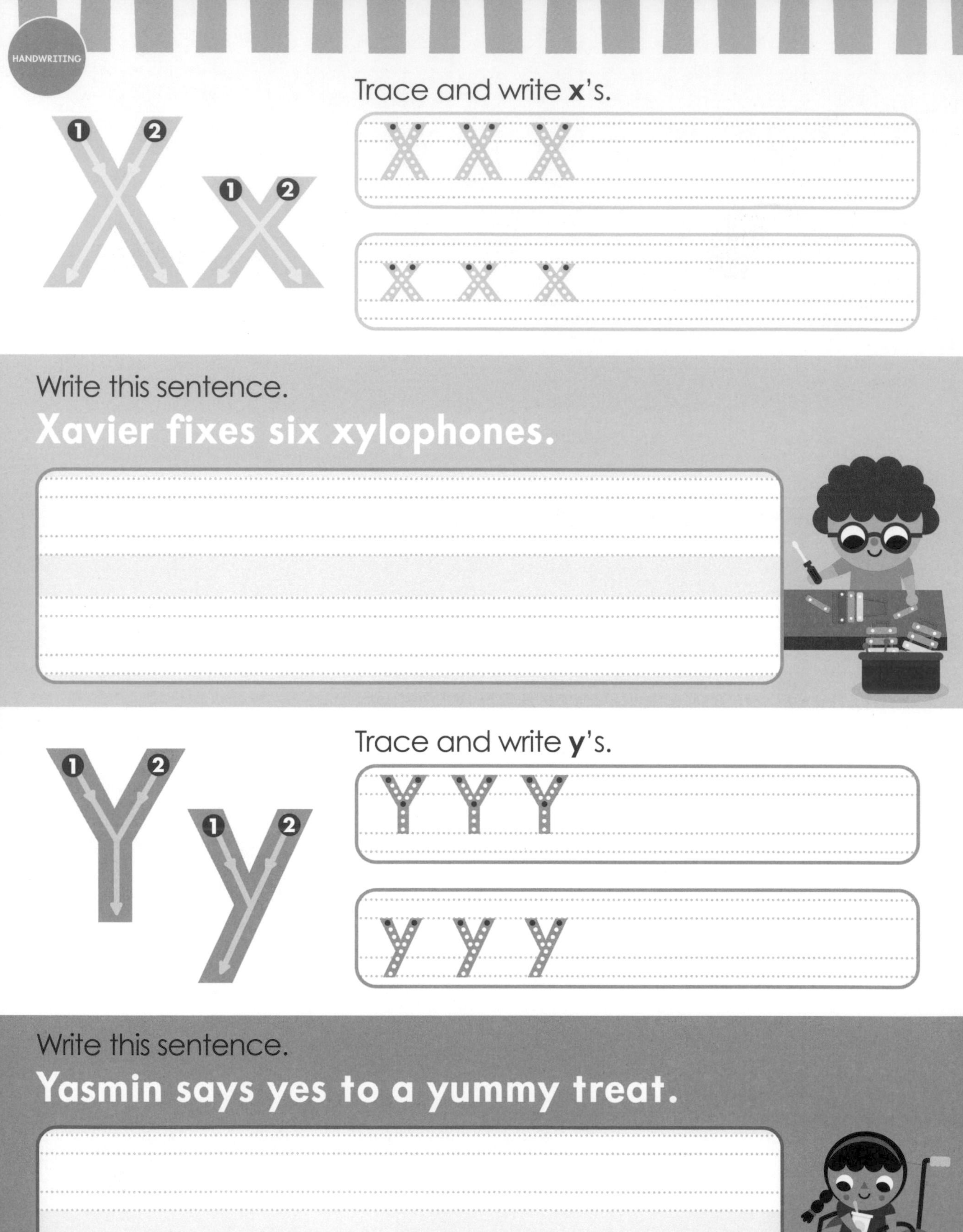

Trace and write **x**'s.

Write this sentence.

Xavier fixes six xylophones.

Trace and write **y**'s.

Write this sentence.

Yasmin says yes to a yummy treat.

zinnia

Zz

zigzags

Trace and write **z**'s.

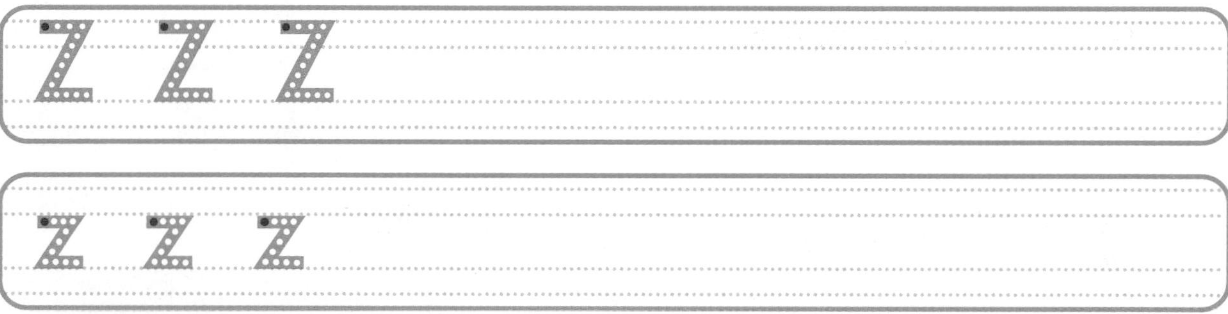

Write these words in alphabetical order.

zany **zilch** **Zanzibar** **zero**

Write this sentence.

Zach zooms by the zebras in the zoo.

Book Titles

The name of a book is called its **title**.

A book's title tells us about the book.
Draw lines to match the titles to the books.

Dinosaurs From Long Ago

How to Play the Drums

Let's Bake Cakes

Pete the Panda

Grade 1 Math

Tom Gets a Puppy

The title of my favorite book is ....

The Main Idea

The **main idea** is the point that covers the whole text.

Read the text below.

Sports for Children

Children play all sorts of sports. Many children like team sports, such as soccer and baseball. Other children enjoy sports they can do on their own, such as biking or skating. Some children take classes after school. They learn sports like dancing or karate. Those who live near the country often learn to ride horses.

1 Circle the word that describes what the whole text is about.

skating **sports** **team sports**

2 Underline the sentence in the text that tells you the main idea.

3 Circle the word below that tells you where the main idea is in this text.

start **middle** **end**

The Details

The **details** are the points that help explain the main idea.

Read the text below.

Komodo Dragons

Komodo dragons are real animals, but they are not real dragons. They are the biggest lizards in the world. The longest Komodo dragons reach 10 feet (3 meters). That's about as long as a tiger.

Baby Komodo dragons hatch from eggs. They live in trees when they are small. It takes about 8 years for them to grow to full size.

Komodo dragons have scales and a long tail. They also have a forked tongue, sharp teeth, and sharp claws. They hunt deer, pigs, and other big animals.

Circle the correct answers.

1 Komodo dragons are as long as

cats **deer** **tigers**

2 The skin of a Komodo dragon is

furry **scaly** **smooth**

3 Komodo dragons eat

plants **pigs** **potatoes**

4 Baby Komodo dragons live in

trees **caves** **houses**

Context Clues

Context clues are clues to a word's meaning in the nearby text and pictures.

Use the sentence to figure out the meaning of the word in bold. Circle the correct meaning.

1 The fire spread, and soon the whole forest was a blazing **inferno**.

a small child **a huge fire** **a flashlight**

2 The insect was **minuscule**, so it was difficult to see.

very small **very large** **very cute**

3 When the train crossed the **viaduct**, we saw the river below.

a railroad tunnel **a railroad bridge** **a train station**

4 The man looked up at the **colossal** statue high above him.

very large **very small** **very colorful**

5 After the **deluge**, rainwater flooded the fields.

light rain **fine weather** **heavy rain**

Choose two of the words below. Look them up in a dictionary, and then write sentences that would help others understand them.

elude **frond** **reveal** **thwart** **vex** **crucial** **feat** **contrive**

....

....

....

....

Fiction

Fiction texts are not true; they are made-up stories.

Things that cannot happen in real life often happen in fiction books. Check the sentence in each pair that is most likely to be fiction.

"Can I go to school, too?" asked Felix the fox. ✔
Foxes have red hair and thick bushy tails. ☐

Most birds use their wings to fly. ☐
James flapped his arms and flew up into the sky. ☐

Five fire trucks rushed to the fire. ☐
Freddie the fire truck was scared of fires. ☐

There was a dinosaur in Lucy's backyard. ☐
Dinosaurs lived long ago. ☐

Amy loves to read books about fairies. ☐
Fifi the fairy waved her magic wand. ☐

Story Structure

Stories have a **beginning**, a **middle**, and an **end**.

Read the story and draw lines to the correct parts of the story.

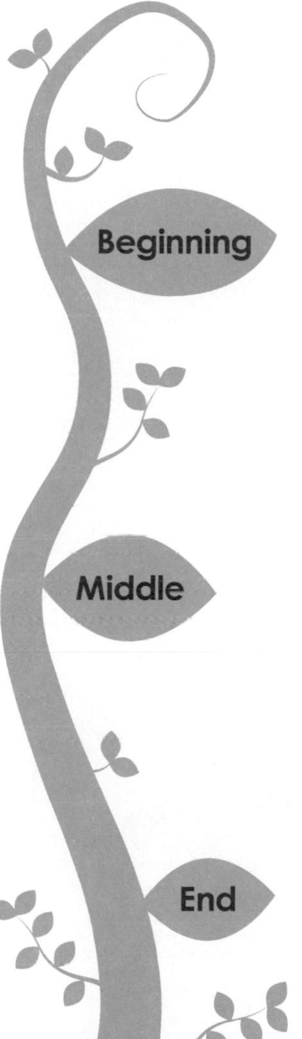

Jack and the Beanstalk

When Jack got to the bottom, his mother cut down the beanstalk. The giant fell and died.

After that, the goose lived with Jack and his mother. It laid golden eggs and they were soon rich. **They all lived happily ever after.**

Once upon a time, a boy called Jack lived with his mother. Jack spent all their money on three magic beans.

Jack's mother was angry. She threw the beans out the window.

One bean grew into a tall beanstalk. Jack climbed it and found a castle at the top. Inside, was a goose that laid golden eggs.

"**Fi, fi, foe, fum!**" shouted a giant. "**I smell the blood of an Englishman.**"

Jack picked up the goose and climbed down the beanstalk, but the giant followed him.

Fairy tales often start with these four words:

....

Fairy tales often end with these six words:

....

Non-Fiction

Non-fiction texts tell us about real things, people, and places.

Read the text and then follow the instructions below.

Reptile, Bird, or Mammal?

Scaly animals such as snakes, lizards, and turtles are called reptiles. Young reptiles hatch from eggs.

Birds have feathers covering their skin. Their babies also hatch from eggs. Many types of birds live on Earth, including owls, parrots, and eagles.

Mammals are animals with hair or fur to keep them warm. Most mammals do not lay eggs. Instead, they have live babies, which they feed milk. Rabbits, dogs, and tigers are all mammals.

1 Put a **blue R** in the box beside each reptile.

2 Put a **green B** in the box beside each bird.

3 Put a **red M** in the box beside each mammal.

4 Which groups of animals lay eggs? ....

Fables

A **fable** is a story with a moral, or a lesson.

Long ago, a Greek man known as Aesop wrote many fables. Read this one, and circle the correct answers.

The Fox and the Crow

A hungry fox saw a crow in a tree. The crow had cheese in its mouth. *I want that cheese,* thought the fox.

"Good morning, Crow," he said. "What pretty feathers you have."

The crow looked at the fox and nodded, but she kept her beak shut.

"I would love to hear your song," said the fox. "I bet it sounds beautiful."

The crow wanted to show off her voice. She opened her beak to sing, and the cheese fell out. The fox gobbled it up.

"Thank you," he said. "You have a lovely voice, but you are not very smart."

1 Why did the fox want the crow to sing?

to hear her voice **to make her drop the cheese**

2 Why did the crow drop the cheese?

it tasted bad **to give it to the fox** **to show off her voice**

3 Why did the fox think that the crow was not very smart?

She dropped the cheese. **She could not sing.**

4 Circle the moral below that goes with this story.

A kind deed is never wasted. **Do not trust people who flatter you.**

Legends

Legends are stories from long ago. Some started as true stories but changed over time.

Read this legend from ancient Greece.

King Midas and the Golden Touch

King Midas was a kind king, but he was also greedy. One day, a god granted him a wish.

"I wish for everything I touch to turn to gold," Midas said.

Soon after that, Midas touched a flower. It turned to gold. Midas danced with joy. Next, he touched a grape. It, too, turned to gold.

"Oh dear," said Midas. "How will I eat?" Tears fell from his eyes.

"What's wrong?" asked his daughter. She gave him a hug and then—ping—she turned into a golden statue. "My little girl," cried Midas, and he ran to the god.

"I was greedy," he said, "but I have learned my lesson. Please help me."

The god took away the wish and everything Midas had touched turned back to normal. King Midas was never greedy again.

King Midas was a real king, but the legend is not a true story. Check the sentences that might be true. Put an **X** by the sentences that are most likely not true.

A god granted Midas a wish. ☐

Midas was kind but greedy. ☐

Everything Midas touched turned to gold. ☐

Midas had a daughter. ☐

His daughter turned to gold. ☐

Poems

Poems are pieces of writing set out in lines.
Many have a regular rhythm, and some rhyme.

Read this poem aloud, and then circle the correct answers.

Caterpillar

by Christina Rossetti

Brown and furry,
Caterpillar in a hurry,
Take your walk,
To the shady leaf, or stalk,
Or what not,
Which may be the chosen spot.
No toad spy you,
Hovering bird of prey pass by you;
Spin and die,
To live again a butterfly.

1 Each line in this poem starts with

a lowercase letter **a capital letter** **a period**

2 The word in this poem that rhymes with *walk* is

leaf **toad** **stalk**

3 What does the writer mean by *spin and die*?

The caterpillar spins some wool and then dies.

The caterpillar spins a cocoon around itself.

4 How might we say *No toad spy you* in everyday words?

I hope no toads see you. **Do not spy on toads.**

READING

Comparing

When we **compare and contrast**, we look for things that are the same and things that are different.

Read the text and then check the boxes in the chart below to compare and contrast Sophy and Aria.

Sophy and Aria

Sophy and Aria are best friends. Sophy has two older brothers, and Aria has two younger brothers.

Both girls wish they had a sister to play with. Instead they play with each other.

Sophy likes to ride bikes. Aria likes riding bikes, too. She also likes playing with dolls, but Sophy doesn't.

	Sophy	Aria	Neither girl
Has older brothers			
Has younger brothers			
Has brothers			
Has sisters			
Likes to ride bikes			
Likes to play with dolls			
Has a best friend			

Question Words

Stories often answer these questions: who, what, when, where, why, and how.

Read the story and answer the questions below.

The Space Poster

It was Zoe's birthday. Her father gave her some glow-in-the-dark paints.

"I know what I'll do," Zoe said. "I'll paint a poster."

Zoe put a sheet of black paper on a table. She painted the moon and lots of stars and planets on the paper. When the paint was dry, she hung the poster on her bedroom wall with sticky tack.

That night, the stars and planets glowed. "Wow!" Zoe said. "I love it!"

Who is the main character in this story? ....

What did she make? ....

When did she get the paints? ....

Where did she hang her poster? ....

How did she stick the poster to the wall? ....

Why did the stars and planets glow? ....

What Next?

When reading, stop and ask yourself what will happen next. **Predicting** what might happen next can help you read better.

Read the story. Then circle the picture that shows what Lily and Liam will most likely do next.

Lost!

Lily and Liam went to a museum with their mom.

"Look!" said Lily. "There's Jack from school."

The children ran over to say hello, but it wasn't Jack. It was a boy they did not know. They went back to find their mom. They looked all around, but they could not see her.

"We are lost!" said Lily.

"What should we do?" asked Liam.

Just then a museum guard came around the corner.

Who do you think will help the children?

....

The Five Senses

Good writers tell us what things look, taste, smell, sound, and feel like.

Read the story and finish the sentences below.

Baking Bread

Tom helped Grandma bake some bread. He pushed and pulled at the dough. It **felt** sticky on his hands.

Grandma put the dough in the oven. Soon the lovely **smell** of warm bread filled the kitchen.

When they **heard** the timer beep, they knew the bread was ready. It **looked** golden brown, and it **tasted** fresh.

1 The dough **felt**

....

2 The kitchen **smelled** of

....

3 They **heard**

....

4 The bread **looked**

....

5 The bread **tasted**

....

Characters

The **characters** are the people or talking creatures in a story.

Draw lines to link the characters with their stories.

One of my favorite books is ....

In this book, the main characters are ....

Picture This!

It can help your reading if you picture, or imagine, the scene in your mind.

Read the text. Then read it again slowly while you color the picture and draw in the missing items.

Max and Mia

Max is Mia's puppy. He is brown with black spots. His collar is red, the same color as Mia's T-shirt. Max has a doghouse with his name on it. Inside the doghouse is a green blanket. In front of his doghouse, he has a yellow bowl, a pink ball, and an orange teddy bear.

Inferencing

Inferencing is using the clues in a text to figure out something the writer does not tell you.

Read the text and use the clues to circle the correct answer.

1 Mr. Green stopped the bus to let on more children.

What is Mr. Green's job?

office worker **bus driver** **teacher**

2 It was the end of a long day, and Ava was hungry.

What meal would Ava eat next?

breakfast **lunch** **dinner**

3 Leo raked up a pile of red and orange leaves.

What season was it?

fall **spring** **summer**

4 When Sarah got home, her legs were tired and her feet were sore.

How did Sarah get home?

she flew **she drove** **she walked**

5 Luke turned the page to find out what happened next.

What was Luke doing?

riding his bike **reading a book** **eating dinner**

6 "Get down from there, you bad cat," said Leah.

Where was the cat?

on the table **in its bed** **on the floor**

Inferencing

Read the text and use the clues to circle the correct answer.

1 Tom slammed the door and stamped his feet.

How is Tom feeling?

happy **angry** **surprised**

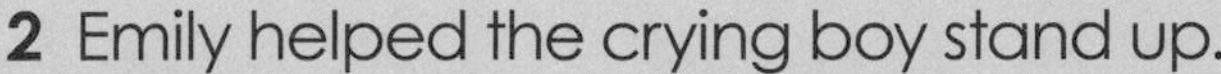

2 Emily helped the crying boy stand up.

What had happened to the boy?

He had fallen down. **He had won a race.** **He had seen a bird.**

3 Eve whispered the secret in her friend's ear.

Who did Eve want to know the secret?

everyone in the room **no one** **just her friend**

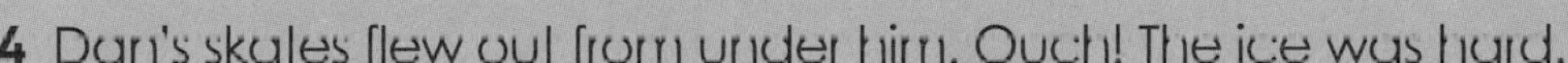

4 Dan's skates flew out from under him. Ouch! The ice was hard.

What had happened to Dan?

He had slipped on the ice. **He had turned his skates into wings.**

5 The dog grabbed Mike's cookie and quickly gobbled it up.

Was the dog allowed to eat the cookie?

no **yes**

6 Connor looked out the window at the passing fields.
"Are we almost there yet?" he asked his mom.

Where is Connor?

in bed **in a car** **in school**

Book Titles

The main words in a **title** begin with capital letters.

Write the correct title on each book.

How to Bake Cakes **Poems About Pets** **Mia the Mountain Climber**

Write a title for this book.

Beginnings

The **beginning** of a story often tells us who we're going to read about and where the story takes place.

Write names and places to complete these beginnings.

1 My name is .... On Saturday, I went to the ....

2 .... was in a rocket, flying to the ....

3 Once upon a time, there was a princess called ....

She lived in a ....

4 .... was a bee, who could not find his ....

Write a beginning for a story about an explorer.
Name the explorer and say where he or she is going.

....

....

Endings

The **ending** of a story brings it to a close. It should feel like a good place to stop.

Check ✔ the best ending for each story plan.

1

Sam is lost. Then he sees his teacher.

A Sam walks away from his teacher and stays lost. ☐

B Sam asks his teacher for help. She finds his family. ☐

2

Lily is a slow runner. This makes her sad.

A Lily trains hard. She learns to run faster and wins a race. ☐

B Lily gives up. She always runs slowly. ☐

3

Grace is scared about starting first grade.

A Grace stays in kindergarten forever. She is bored. ☐

B Grace is brave and goes into first grade. She likes it. ☐

4

Gerry is the only goat on the farm. He is lonely.

A The farmer lets Gerry live with the sheep. Now he has lots of friends. ☐

B The farmer lets Gerry eat lots of grass. He is still lonely. ☐

Plan an ending for this story idea.

Noah is mean to the other children. They do not like him. He is lonely.

....

....

....

Recall

Recall writing tells readers about things that happened to us.

Read Tom's recall writing. It has a beginning, a middle, and an end.

The beginning (who, when, where)
On Saturday, my friend Sophy came to my house.

The middle (what happened)
We rode bikes and jumped on the trampoline. Dad helped us build a treehouse. We ate lunch in the treehouse.

The ending (closing the story)
It was a fun day. I hope she comes to play again.

Now write about something that happened to you.
Write a beginning, a middle, and an end.

The beginning (who, when, where)

....

....

The middle (what happened)

....

....

....

The ending (closing the story)

....

....

WRITING

Create Characters

The **characters** are the people or animals in a story.
Often **characters** are either heroes or villains.

Write notes about a hero and a villain for a story.

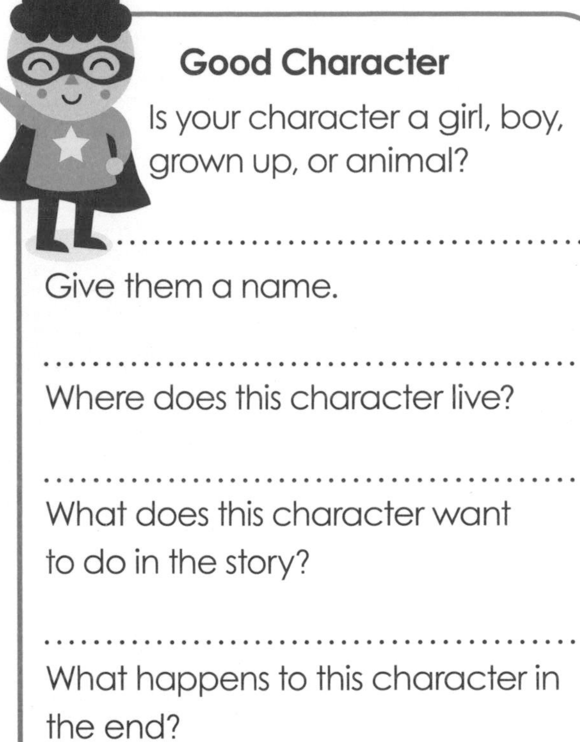

Good Character

Is your character a girl, boy, grown up, or animal?

....

Give them a name.

....

Where does this character live?

....

What does this character want to do in the story?

....

What happens to this character in the end?

....

Bad Character

Is your character a girl, boy, grown up, or animal?

....

Give them a name.

....

Where does this character live?

....

What does this character want to do in the story?

....

What happens to this character in the end?

....

Draw your characters in this box.
You could show a scene from your story idea.

Compare and Contrast

Some texts **compare and contrast** two people or things.
They tell us what things are the same and what are different.

Write words in the spaces to compare and contrast the children in the picture. Color the picture to match your writing.

Eve and Liam are twins. They are both .... years old. Both children have .... colored hair, but Eve's hair is .... and Liam's is ....

Today, they are both wearing shorts, but their shorts are not the same color. Eve's shorts are ...., and Liam's shorts are ....

Both children like to play outside. Eve likes to ride her ...., and Liam likes to ride his ....

Opinion Texts

We write **opinion texts** to try to make others agree with us.
An opinion text needs two or three good reasons.

Lucy is writing an opinion text. Help her finish it by writing her reasons.

Why I Should Get a Dog

I think my mom should let me get a dog.

Dogs need feeding, but Mom will not have to do it.

I will ....

Mom says dogs need lots of walks. This is okay because

....

....

Dogs can get muddy on walks. If my dog

gets muddy, I ....

....

I think I would make a great dog owner.

Do you agree?

Underline Lucy's beginning sentence in yellow. Underline her three reasons in orange, **red**, and green. Underline her conclusion in blue.

WRITING

Using Five Senses

Good texts often tell readers how things looked, smelled, tasted, felt, and sounded.

Write the correct sense word into the spaces in this story. Use the pictures to help.

 **felt**  **hear**  **look**  **smelled**  **tasted**

The Birthday Dinner

It was Grandpa's birthday. Grandma had put up balloons to make the room  .... pretty. We all sang *Happy Birthday* loudly so Grandpa could  .... it.

Grandma had baked an apple pie. My mouth watered when I  .... it. When I bit into my slice, it  .... great. Afterward, my stomach  .... full.

Write some notes about a family celebration you have been to.

I saw ....

I heard ....

I smelled ....

I tasted ....

I felt ....

Settings

Writers choose a **place** to **set** each story.
They tell readers what it is like to be in this place.

Imagine you are writing a story set in the place you are right now. Write notes about it here.

My place is ....

What would people see if they were there? ....

....

What sounds would they hear? ....

....

What smells might they smell? ....

What happens in this place? ....

Write some describing words about this place. ....

....

What and When

Transition words and phrases tell readers the order in which things happened. These words and phrases include: first, next, then, after that, when, at last.

Read the story and cross out the incorrect transition in each pair.

It was an exciting day. **Last / First** we climbed into our rocket. **Then / First** it blasted off and zoomed into space.

Once upon a time / When we reached Mars, the rocket landed. **After that / before that**, the door opened, and we stepped out. **First / At last**, we were on the red planet.

Now write a short story about something fun you have done. Use transition words or phrases. Underline them when you finish.

....

....

....

....

....

....

....

....

....

Fantasy Stories

Fantasy stories are about things that are not real or are unknown, such as dragons, fairies, or aliens.

Choose one of these fantasy ideas, and then write your own fantasy story.

1 You can make yourself invisible. You use this skill to escape danger.

2 You find a dragon baby and keep it as a pet. It helps save you.

3 A fairy lives in the tree outside your window. How can you stop your parents cutting down the tree?

4 One day you wake up in the world of your favorite book. What will you do?

5 Your rocket lands on a planet with huge aliens. How will you survive?

6 Choose your own fantasy story idea.

Biographies

Biographies tell the stories of real people's lives. They are true stories.

Biography writers look up, or research, facts. Pick one of these famous people or someone else. Use encyclopedias, library books, or the Internet to answer the questions.

Amelia Earhart **Barack Obama** **Abraham Lincoln**
Frida Kahlo **Serena Williams** **Helen Keller** **Bruce Lee**

1 I chose ....

2 This person was born in (when?) ....

3 They grew up in (where?) ....

4 This person is famous because (why?)

....

....

....

....

5 I like this person because (opinion)

....

....

....

....

Draw a picture of your person.

Interviews

Writers talk to other people, or **interview** them, to learn new things.

Find out what life was like before you were born. Interview a grandparent, parent, or other trusted adult. Here are some questions for you to ask.

1 In what year were you my age? ....

2 How was life different then? ....

....

3 What machines were different then? ....

....

4 How were clothes different then?

....

....

5 What do you think was better then?

....

....

6 What do you think is better now?

....

....

Step by Step

Step-by-step instructions tell people how to do or make something. Recipes are step-by-step instructions.

Read the recipe and use the pictures to fill in the missing words.

How to Make Mini Pizzas*

You will need:

- 1 pita bread per pizza
- .... sauce
- spinach leaves
- grated ....
- other toppings, such as sliced olives ,
- ham , or red onion

What to do:

1 Spread the tomato sauce over the ....

2 Wash the .... leaves. Then lay them on top.

3 Sprinkle the cheese over the spinach.

4 Add any other toppings.

5 Put the finished .... in the oven.

6 Cook them until the .... has melted.

* If you make this recipe, ask an adult to help you use a knife and the oven.

WRITING

Write Instructions

Step-by-step instructions often start with a list of things you need. After this comes the numbered steps.

Watch someone prepare food. It could be pancakes, a sandwich, or part of a meal. List the ingredients and write the steps.

How to make ....

You will need:

- ....
- ....
- ....
- ....
- ....

What to do:

1 ....

2 ....

3 ....

4 ....

5 ....

6 ....

Retell a Story

Retell a story in order. Introduce the characters and where they live. Explain the problem in the middle. Show the solution in the ending.

Choose a story you like. It might be from a book, a fairy tale, or a legend. Rewrite the story here.

The title of the story is: ....

....

The beginning: ....

....

....

....

The middle: ....

....

....

....

The end: ....

....

....

....

....

WRITING

Write a Letter

A **letter** is a formal way of writing a message.

Imagine you have a won an exciting birthday party.
Write a letter to a friend inviting them to come along.

(Write your address here.)

....

....

....

(Write the date here.)

....

Dear .... , (Write your friend's name here.)

I have won a prize! It is a birthday party at ....

I hope you can come.

It's on my birthday, which is .... Guess what!

A famous person is coming to my party. It is ....

The party starts at .... o'clock. Some fun things will happen.

First .... Then ....

Please write back to let me know if you can come.

Yours truly,

.... (Sign your name here.)

Shape Poems

A **shape poem** is both a poem and a picture made with words.

Read this shape poem.

Write your own shape poem. Use one of these ideas or choose one of your own.

 **a ball**

 **an ice-cream cone**

 **a boot**

 **a flower**

 **a face**

 **raindrops**

WRITING

Rhyming Poems

Some **poems** have lines that **rhyme** with other lines.

Read the first three stanzas of a poem by Edward Lear. Then underline the rhyming words at the ends of the lines.

Nonsense Alphabet

A

A was an ant
Who seldom stood still,
And who made a nice house
In the side of a hill.

a

Nice little ant!

B

B was a book
With a binding of blue,
And pictures and stories
For me and for you.

b

Nice little book!

C

C was a cat
Who ran after a rat;
But his courage did fail
When she seized on his tail.

c

Crafty old cat!

Now write a stanza for the letter D. Make it **rhyme** if you can.

D

D was a ....

....

....

....

d

..................................!

Plan a Story

Good writers often make **notes** to **plan** their stories before they start.

Read these notes by a writer planning a children's story.

Story Plan

Topic ideas: playing with other children, sports, maybe baseball or basketball.

Main character: a boy called Liam.

Setting: a neighborhood in a small town.

Problem: Liam is new to the neighborhood. He has no friends and is lonely.

Ending: Liam is brave and asks to join some other children playing basketball. He has a fun time and makes new friends.

Now plan your own story. You don't have to write full sentences. Choose a topic that interests you. It could be about people, school, sport, space, animals, or anything else.

My Story Plan

Topic ideas:..

Main character:..

Setting:...

Problem:..

....

Ending:..

....

Draft a Story

For important pieces of writing, writers often make a **rough draft** first.

Write the first draft of your story from page 63. Remember to have a beginning, a middle, and an ending.

Read your draft aloud. Then make these checks:

1 Circle any spellings you need to check in a dictionary.
2 Check your sentences start with a capital letter and end with a period.
3 Make sure your sentences make sense.
4 Decide which parts you want to change or improve.

Write a Story

Writers write a **final version** of a story using their draft and making changes to improve it.

Write the final version of your story here.

Draw a picture to go with it.

WORD STUDY

Beginning Letters

Trace the first letter and say the sound. Then say the whole word.

Fill in the missing letter. Then say the word aloud.

_ock _ump _ug

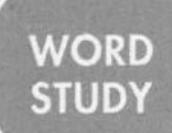

Middle Letters

The letters **a, e, i, o, u** are called **vowels.**

Circle the vowel in each word. Then say the word aloud.

stand hen mix

map best slug

drip jog frost fun

Use a sticker to fill in each missing letter.
Say the word when you've placed the sticker.

WORD STUDY

End Letters

Fill in the missing letter. Then say the word aloud.

ten_ **dru_** **cra_**

boo_ **mu_**

Find and circle the words in the word search. Then color the last letter of each word in green to reveal a hidden word.

bee
owl
snake
sheep
fish
zebra
lion
rabbit

r	a	b	l	y	a	l	w	d	k
a	i	e	o	w	r	n	x	a	u
b	v	e	w	j	k	c	s	t	w
e	n	m	l	f	j	f	u	d	z
s	n	a	k	e	h	i	v	d	f
b	s	h	e	e	p	s	o	l	d
t	e	s	n	q	g	h	b	i	l
s	m	r	z	e	b	r	a	o	i
a	o	s	x	r	t	f	k	n	s
b	d	k	y	r	a	b	b	i	t

Write the hidden word here:

e _ _ _ _ _ _ _

Word Maker

Use the clues to fill in the boxes. Then draw the missing pictures.

b e a r

Something you can use to clean floors.

___ ___ ___

___ ___ ___

Something you wear on your head.

___ ___ ___

___ ___ ___

A living thing with a stem and leaves.

___ ___ ___ ___ ___

___ ___ ___ ___

The place where you live.

___ ___ ___ ___

A place for putting books in your home.

___ ___ ___ ___ ___

WORD STUDY

Count Syllables

Words are made up of units of sound called **syllables**.
We break words into their **syllables** like this: **cat; fun/ny; el/e/phant.**

Read each word slowly and clap once for each syllable.
Then count the syllables in each word and write the number.

square = [1] syllable

circle = [ ] syllables

rectangle = [ ] syllables

triangle = [ ] syllables

Words break into **syllables** between different sounds. If a word has double letters, the break comes between the two letters. For example: **but/ter.**

Read each word slowly and clap once for each syllable.
Then draw a line between the syllables.

win|dow	**bubble**
letter	**potato**
puddle	**dinosaur**
apple	**kangaroo**
robot	**hippopotamus**

Count Syllables

Follow the words that have two syllables to guide the baker to the cupcakes.

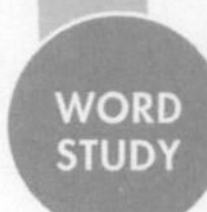

Prefixes

A **prefix** is a group of letters added to the start of a word to change its meaning.
For example, the prefix **un-** changes the word **happy** to **unhappy**.

Circle all the words that start with the **un-** prefix in **blue**.
Circle all the words that start with the **dis-** prefix in **red**.

unwell

dishonest

unfair

dislike

disappear

unlock

disconnect

disappoint

untrue

unclean

Underline the prefixes in these words.

untie	unlucky
disbelieve	unfold
disobey	dispose
unkind	uneven

Prefixes

Circle all the words that start with the re- prefix in green.
Circle all the words that start with the in- prefix in yellow.

redo
incorrect
replay
incomplete
inspect
reappear
remove
incredible
inside
refill

Underline the prefixes in these words.

invisible	react
rewind	include
invent	reopen
reread	inform

WORD STUDY

Suffixes

A **suffix** is a group of letters added to the end of a word to change its meaning. For example, the suffix **-ful** changes the word **help** to **helpful**.

Trace the suffixes in these words.

lucky thankful painting

heavy breakable slowly

singing quickly helpful

Draw lines to join the words with the same suffixes.

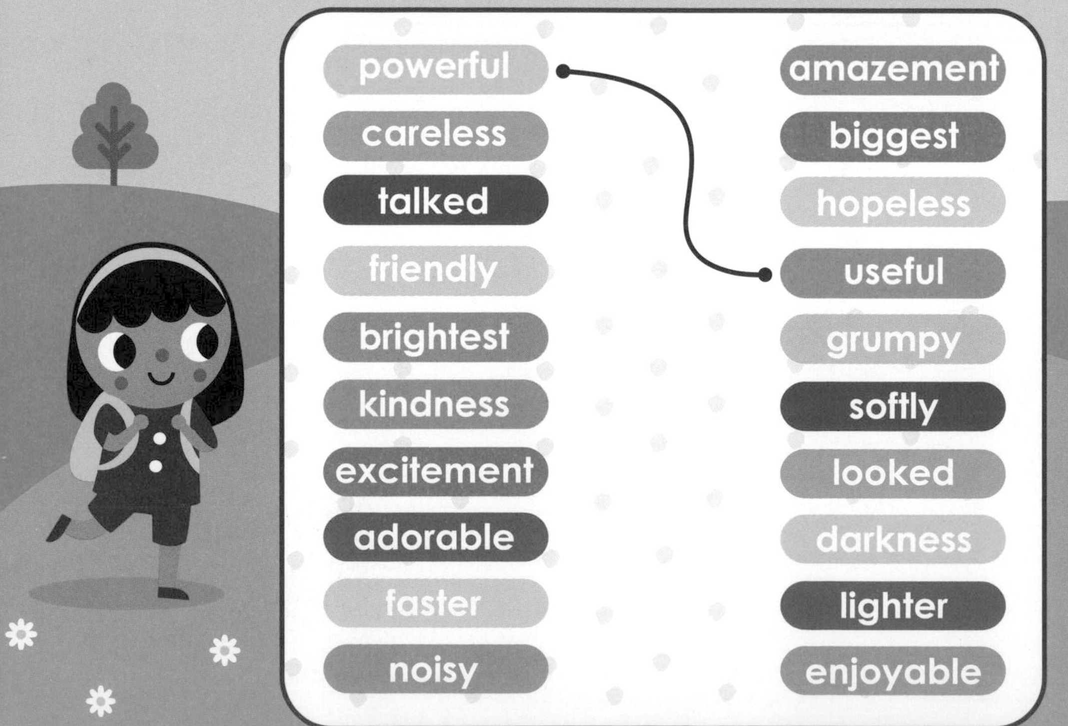

WORD STUDY

Suffixes

Sort the words. Draw lines from the words to the suffixes.

hopeful

piglet

powerless

cheerful

booklet

helpless

truthful

-let
Meaning: to be small

-ful
Meaning: to be full of something

-less
Meaning: to not have something

hopeless

playful

droplet

powerful

owlet

wonderful

bracelet

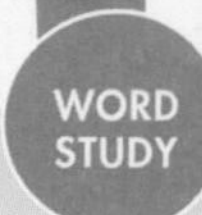

Root Words

The part of a word to which we add prefixes and suffixes is called the **root word**. For example, **play** is the root word of **playful** and **playing**.

Draw a line from each word to its root word.

In each row, circle the words that have the same root word.

Root Word			
care	careful	cat	caring
hope	chop	hopefully	hopeless
friend	friendship	fries	friendly
joy	enjoy	joke	joyful

WORD STUDY

Alphabetical Lists

When words are sorted in **alphabetical order**, the first word begins with the letter closest to A, and the last word begins with the letter closest to Z. Any words in between follow the order of the alphabet from A to Z.

Rewrite each list in alphabetical order.

top, bottom: ...bottom... , ...top...

leg, hand: .... , ...

jeans, socks, coat: .... , ... , ...

doll, book, kite: .... , ... , ...

blue, yellow, red, green: .... , ... , ... , ...

If two words begin with the same letter, then look at their second letters to see which comes first in the alphabet. The word with the second letter that is closest to A comes first.

Rewrite each list in alphabetical order.

run, ride, skip: .... , ... , ...

sleepy, shocked, sad: .... , ... , ...

plum, pineapple, pear: .... , ... , ...

WORD STUDY

Compound Words

A **compound word** is two words joined together to make a new word. For example, **rain** and **bow** make **rainbow**.

Trace the words and say them aloud. Then write each compound word and say it aloud.

under	stand	
super	hero	
after	noon	
book	case	
flower	pot	
pan	cake	
rain	coat	
sun	shine	
wheel	chair	

WORD STUDY

Compound Words

Write the compound words. Use the pictures to help you.

basketball butterfly sunglasses
paintbrush strawberry cupcake

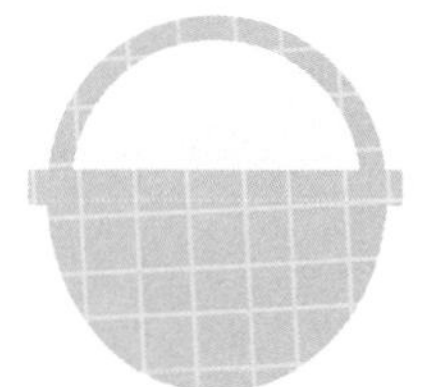 +  = ... 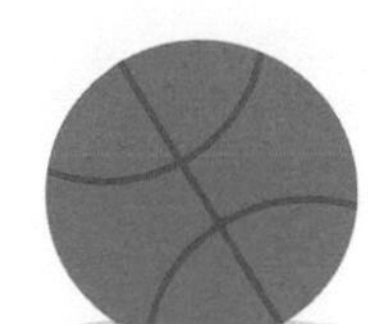

 +  = ... 

 + = ... 

 +  = ... 

 +  = ... 

 + 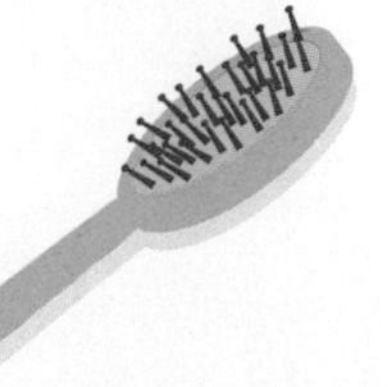 = ... 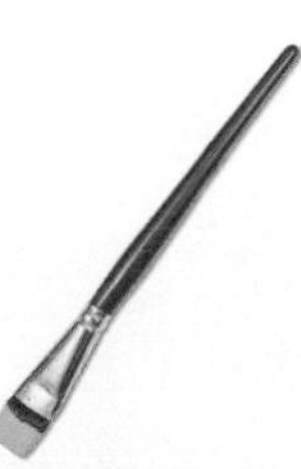

Synonyms

A **synonym** is a word that has the same meaning as another word.
For example, a synonym of **happy** is **cheerful**.

Draw lines to match each word with a synonym.

Replace each crossed-out word with a synonym.

~~tired~~

I feel .... at night.

~~fast~~

The race car is very ....

~~small~~

My puppy is .... and cute.

Antonyms

An **antonym** is a word that has the opposite meaning to another word. For example, an antonym of **big** is **little**.

Check the antonym of each word.

big	little ☑	huge ☐	large ☐
hard	solid ☐	soft ☐	spiky ☐
empty	full ☐	clear ☐	pink ☐
light	bright ☐	day ☐	dark ☐
hot	boiling ☐	cold ☐	warm ☐

Replace each crossed-out word with an antonym.

~~light~~
It is .... at night.

~~small~~
The truck is very ....

~~cold~~
The sun is ....

WORD STUDY

Using Words

Read the sentences. Then use one of the words to fill in the blank.

1 Limes are ....
Trees are this color, too.

blue

green

2 When the weather is ....,
I wear a coat to keep me warm.

hot

cold

3 On the farm, soft, woolly
.... eat grass.

sheep

hens

4 I use my legs to ....
really fast.

run

sleep

5 I use my nose to ....
sweet, chocolate cupcakes.

hear

smell

6 Some .... meow
when they are hungry.

dogs

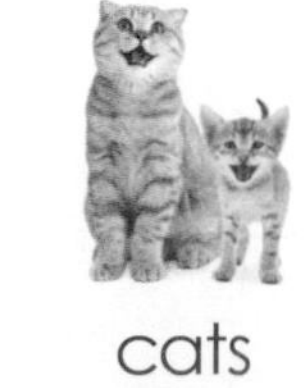
cats

WORD STUDY

Dictionary Practice

We use a **dictionary** to find the meaning and spelling of a word. Dictionaries list words in alphabetical order.

Use a dictionary to find the meaning for each word. Then use each word in a sentence.

Word	Meaning	Sentence
enormous	....	....
hibernate	....	....

Use a dictionary to find two new words. Then write them in a sentence.

Word	Sentence
....	....
....	....

Adjectives

A describing word is also called an adjective. Big and hot are adjectives.

Circle each adjective.

happy baby fast car
small mouse slow snail
sweet apple
big truck tall giraffe
soft kitten noisy fireworks
sleepy zebra hot sun kind sister

Choose an adjective to write in each sentence.

pink big fluffy

The .... elephant stomps around.

naughty green tall

My .... dog chews my shoes.

blue sparkly loud

The .... lion gives a roar.

Using Adjectives

Underline the adjectives. Some sentences have two.

The brave woman climbed the mountain.

The speedy shark went for a swim.

The lazy bear went to sleep.

The fluffy bunny hopped across the field.

The clumsy teacher dropped his new book.

The clever astronaut built a huge spaceship.

The hungry horse ate some green grass.

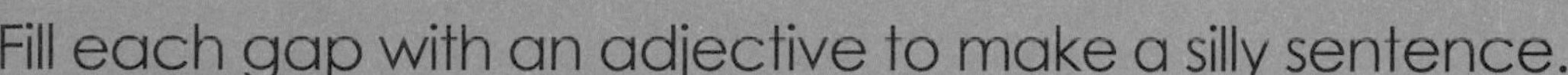

Fill each gap with an adjective to make a silly sentence.

silly
happy
smelly
tiny
giant
fluffy
friendly
tasty
brave
magical
red

The .... dinosaur ate some .... leaves.

A .... unicorn flew over a .... house.

A .... sailor sailed his .... boat to a .... island.

GRAMMAR AND PUNCTUATION

Verbs

A **doing word** is also called a **verb**. **Dance** and **fly** are **verbs**.

Circle the correct verb.

run
swim

sleep
eat

swing
slide

read
play

paint
bake

Underline the verbs.

The frog hops across the pond.

I ride my bike to school.

Puppies like to play and sleep.

That man dances and sings.

Tenses

To write about things that have already happened, we use the **past tense**. Sometimes we add **-ed** to a **verb** to make it **past tense**.

Say each word aloud. Then add -ed to the word, and say the new word aloud.

walk<u>ed</u> kick_ laugh_

jump_ plant_ talk_

look_ play_ watch_

paint_ wash_ cook_

Circle the past-tense verbs.

The family walked to the park.

Some people played soccer.

A small dog chased a cat.

The children wanted ice cream.

They watched the birds in the sky.

They cooked pizza for dinner.

They listened to the radio.

At bedtime, they closed their eyes to sleep.

Nouns

A **naming word** is also called a **noun**. **Cat**, **school**, and **table** are **nouns**.

Trace each noun.

I like bananas.

That is a pretty flower.

The farmer drives a tractor.

My dog is called Thomas.

Check the naming word in each sentence.

The teacher looks happy.

a teacher  ✔ b happy  c looks 

Rockets fly very fast.

a fly  b rockets  c fast

I have a new book to read.

a new  b have  c book

The pizza was tasty.

a pizza  b was  c tasty

Whose is it?

A **possessive noun** is a **naming word** that owns something.
We often add **-'s** to a **noun** to make it **possessive**.

Circle the possessive nouns.

It is Grandma's house.

The lamb's wool is soft.

This is the cat's dinner.

Where is the boy's coat?

The shark's teeth are sharp.

The bird's feathers are blue.

Add -**'s** to each noun to make it possessive.

The lion's roar was very loud.

The child...... room was full of toys.

The boy...... socks were smelly.

Kate...... friends made her a cake.

There was a monkey on Leo...... backpack.

GRAMMAR AND PUNCTUATION

Personal Pronouns

Personal pronouns can replace **nouns**. These words are **personal pronouns**:
I, you, he, she, it, we, they, me, us, him, her, them.

Circle the personal pronouns and say them aloud.

We went to the zoo.

They ate pasta for lunch.

I love apples. They make tasty snacks.

It is a big box.

He shared a cookie with me.

I like playing tag. It is a fun game.

She asked me to help her.

She played soccer with them.

Read each sentence and write the personal pronoun.

Give the ball to her.	.....her.....
Where is he going?	....
Look at me!	....
They ran up the hill.	....
I have a pet rabbit.	....
She watched a movie.	....
Max asked them a question.	....

Possessive Pronouns

Possessive pronouns tell us who something belongs to.
Mine, **yours**, **his**, **hers**, **its**, **ours**, and **theirs** are **possessive pronouns**.

Trace it.	Write it.	Use it in a sentence.
his		The dog loves .... toy bone.
hers		This umbrella is ....
mine		That sandwich is ....
yours		Is this hat .... ?
theirs		Our car looks the same as ....

Write the correct possessive pronoun in each sentence.

My family lives here. This house is ....

I ate all my dinner, but Lucy did not eat ....

He bought new gloves. They keep .... hands warm.

My shoes are too tight. Do .... fit you?

That tree has a nest in .... branches.

The glasses belong to me. They are ....

mine
yours
his
hers
its
ours

Contractions

A **contraction** is two words joined together. We use an **apostrophe** to replace missing letters. **I'm** is a **contraction** of **I** and **am**.

Trace the contractions.

I'm = I am

aren't = are not

I've = I have

we're = we are

I'll = I will

it's = it is

we'll = we will

isn't = is not

Draw lines to link each pair of words and its contraction.

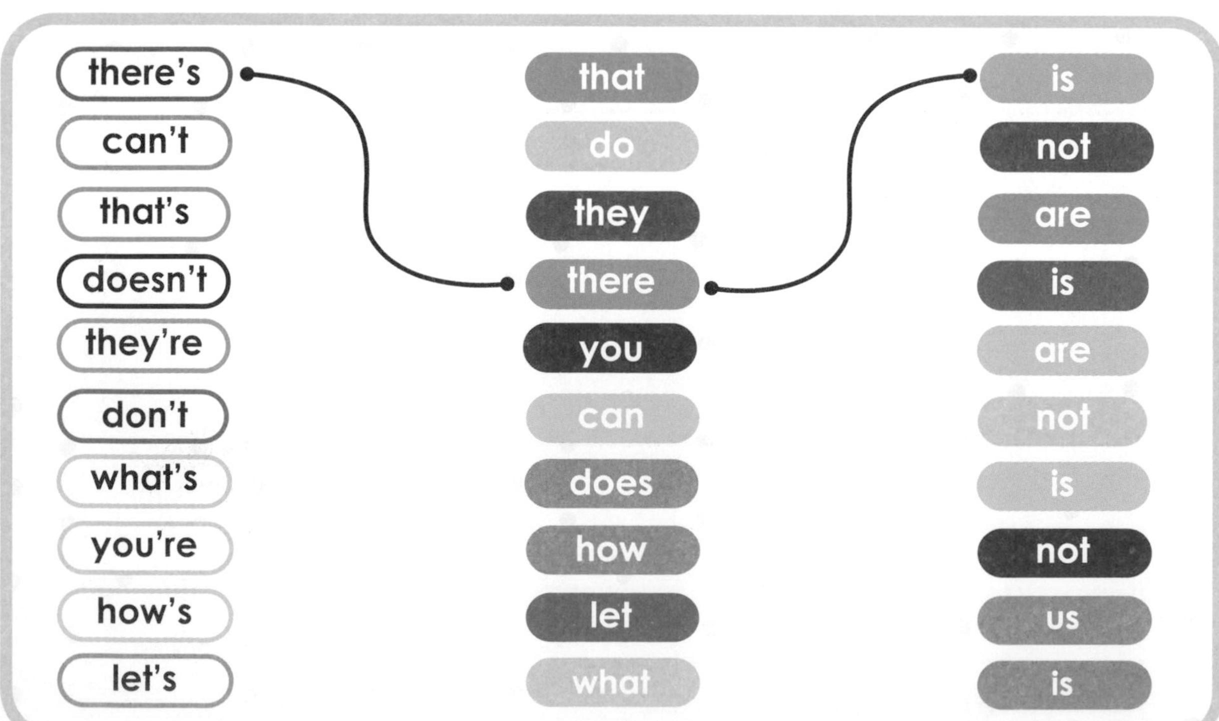

Singular and Plural

Adding **-s** to a **noun** makes it **plural**. **Eggs** is the **plural** of egg.
Some words that end in **-y** use **-ies** to form the **plural**. **Bunnies** is the plural of bunny.

Draw lines to match the words to the plurals.

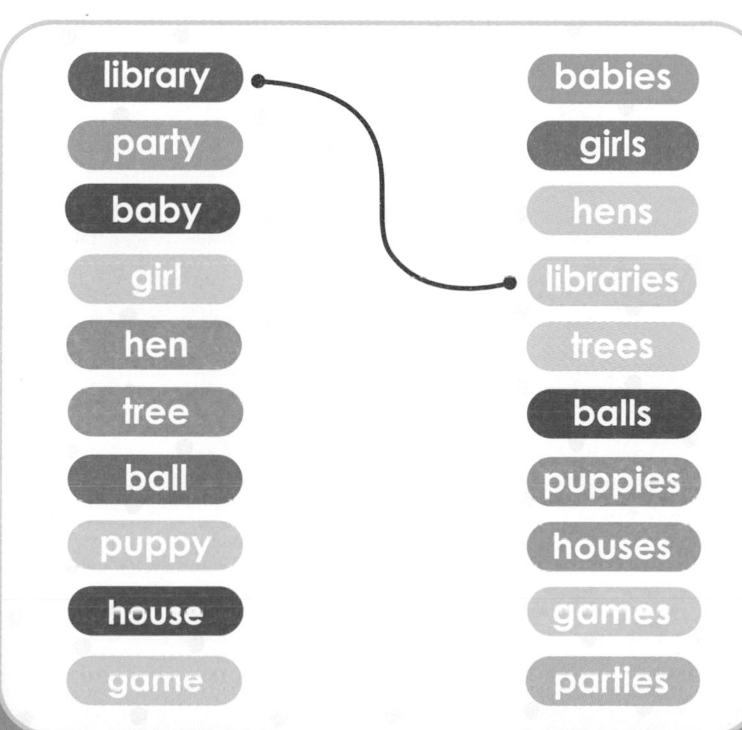

Circle the singular words in green.
Circle the **plural** words in **red.**

apples strawberry flowers

crayons

flower

strawberries apple crayon

Capital Letters

The names of people, places, events, days, and months are **proper nouns**. They start with a capital letter. **Tom**, **New York**, and **New Year's Eve** are **proper nouns**.

Draw lines from the words to the categories they belong to.

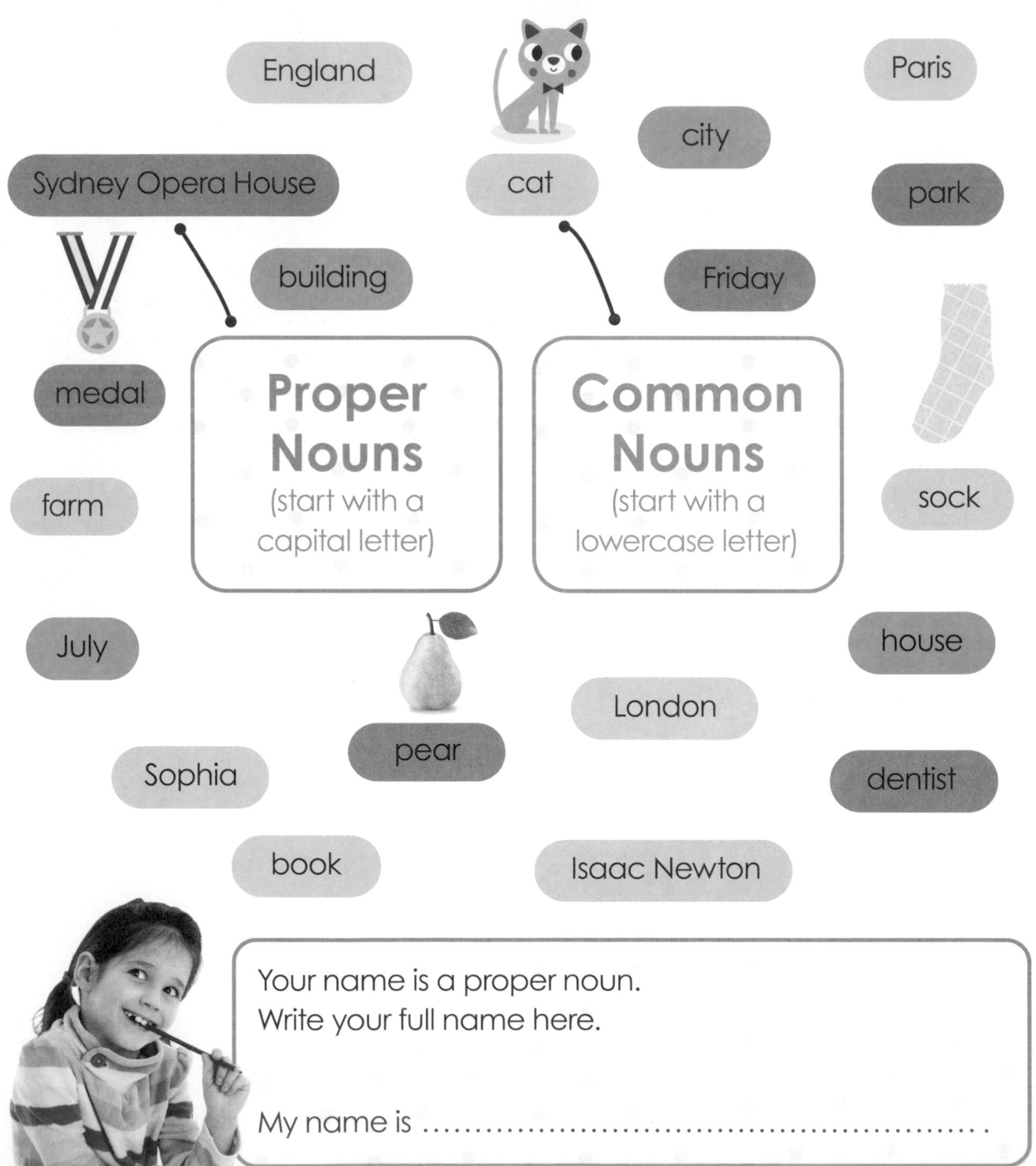

Your name is a proper noun.
Write your full name here.

My name is ....

Articles

The words **the**, **a**, and **an** are called **articles**.
Use **a** before a **consonant**, and use **an** before a **vowel**.

Sticker the articles into the sentences.

What is ____ time?

____ mouse ate some cheese.

I would like ____ orange.

____ helicopter flies up high.

Can I have ____ pencil, please?

____ alligator has sharp teeth.

Find five of each article: **an**, **a**, and **the**. Find each **an** first.

a	k	d	a	u	v	t	h	e	b
c	j	w	i	m	a	r	o	d	a
t	z	g	a	l	n	f	x	p	n
h	l	m	s	t	g	i	m	a	i
e	v	a	o	h	x	a	o	z	c
o	d	n	d	e	c	n	l	g	o
r	z	r	p	r	j	w	t	h	e
w	f	z	p	a	o	s	q	f	p
a	o	d	f	p	g	m	d	j	f
n	g	t	r	o	m	t	h	e	b

GRAMMAR AND PUNCTUATION

Prepositions

Some **prepositions** tell us the position of the noun.
On, **in**, and **under** are **prepositions**.

on	under	beside	between	in	behind	in front of

Write the correct preposition in each sentence.

The frog is
.... the log.

The horse is
.... the barn.

The kitten is hiding
.... the bed.

The boy is
.... the pool.

The bird is sitting
.... the branch.

The sun is
.... a cloud.

The girl's hands are
.... her eyes.

The rug is ....
the chairs.

The tree is
.... the tent.

The cup is ....
the table.

Sentences

Sentences start with a capital letter. Most sentences end with a period. Circle the capital letters and periods.

This is my room.

Look at my toys.

We like to read.

Have a great day.

It's my birthday.

Rewrite the sentences. Use capital letters at the start and periods at the end.

let's go swimming	....
i can sing	....
my dog barks	....
here are my shoes	....
the lion roars	....

GRAMMAR AND PUNCTUATION

Commas

We use **commas** to separate items in a list.

Trace the commas.

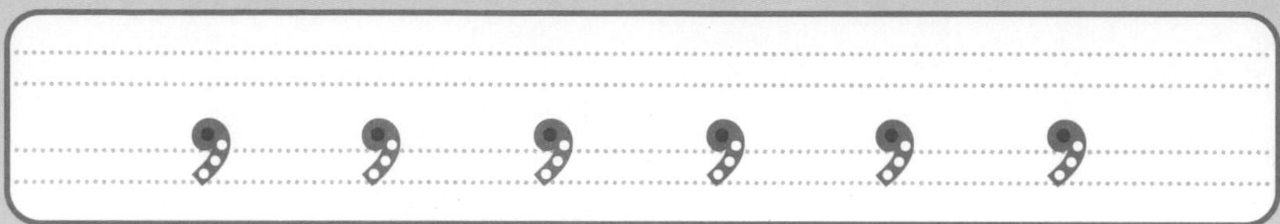

Add commas to the lists.

My favorite colors are green, orange, yellow, and blue.

My friends are Kim Pedro and Mia.

We eat red green and purple grapes.

I play hockey tennis and basketball.

I have a pen a pencil and some paper.

I like strawberry chocolate and vanilla ice cream.

Rewrite the lists, adding commas and removing all but the final **and**.

I have a dog and a cat and a fish.

I have a dog, a cat, and a fish.

Let's buy bread and milk and eggs.

....

The farm has sheep and cows and pigs.

....

My T-shirt is blue and white and yellow.

....

Linking Sentences

Read the paragraphs. Then underline each sentence in a different color, and count how many there are.

One day, four children went to the park for a picnic. They went on the swings, and then they ate their lunch. After that, they played catch until it was time to go home. ☐

Alice likes to read books. She has more than 100 books in her bookcase. Her favorite book is about a bear who lives in the jungle and is friends with a lion.

Write two sentences about each picture.
Use capital letters and periods.

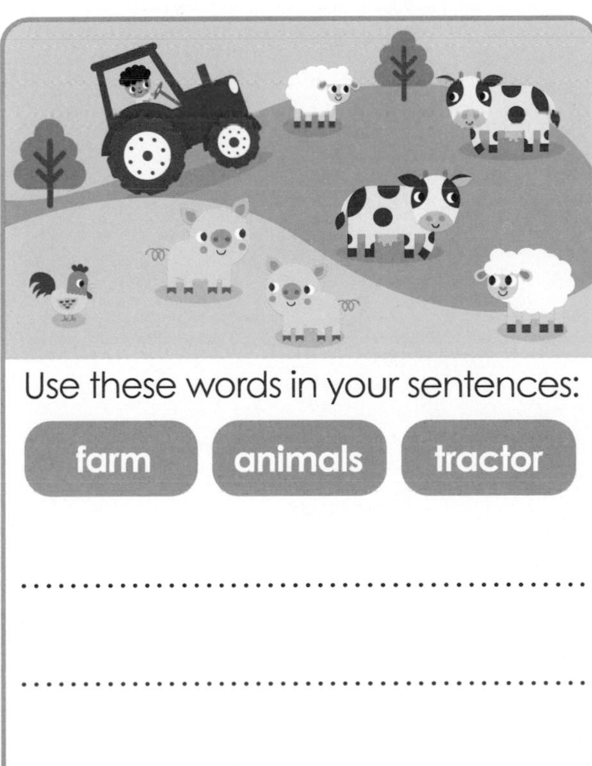

Use these words in your sentences:

farm | animals | tractor

....

....

....

Use these words in your sentences:

snowman | children | play

....

....

....

GRAMMAR AND PUNCTUATION

Question Marks

We use a **question mark** at the end of a sentence that asks a question.

Trace the question marks.

Who? What?

When? Where?

Why? How? Which?

Write a period or question mark at the end of each sentence.

What is your name

How old are you

I have a pet kitten

The baby is crying

Where do you live

I saw an alien

Which animal do you like best

GRAMMAR AND PUNCTUATION

Question Words

A question often starts with a **question word**.
Who, **what**, and **when** are **question words**.

Add a question mark to each question.

What is the time

How many apples are in the bowl

Do you like cupcakes

Would you like a strawberry

Write a question word in each sentence.

Why **What** **When** **Who**

.... are we eating for lunch?

.... wants to play outside?

.... is the dog barking?

.... is your birthday?

Look at the pictures. Write a question for each picture.

....

....

....

....

Exclamations

We use an **exclamation mark** after a word or short phrase to show shock or surprise.

Trace the exclamation marks.

Write an exclamation in each speech bubble.

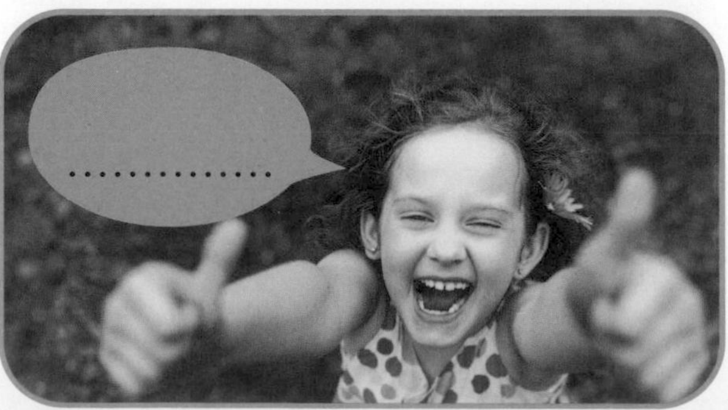

Exclamations

Add exclamation marks to these exclamations.

Shall we go to the park? Yes

Wow The fireworks look magical.

You did a great job on your homework. Good job

I heard you passed your test. Congratulations

Sort and write the phrases in the correct categories.

Oh, no! | Why not? | Who is it? | Phew!

How are you? | Hi! | Yippee! | Where is it?

Exclamation!	Question?
....	....
....	....
....	....
....	....

Short a and i

Trace each word. Then write it, cover it, and write it again.

Spell it aloud.	Trace it.	Write it.	Practice it.
j a m	jam	jam	
m a p	map		
s i t	sit		
d i d	did		

Circle the letters to spell the word. Then write the word, cover it with your hand, and write it again.

		Write it.	Practice it.
cat	l o c e r a t s		
mat	n m e a g t p		
pig	p o e i y g d		
pin	r f p i v u l n		

Short o and e

Trace each word. Then write it, cover it, and write it again.

Spell it aloud.	Trace it.	Write it.	Practice it.
b e d	bed		
p e n	pen		
d o g	dog		
h o t	hot		

Trace each word, fill in the missing vowel, and then cover the word and write it again.

	Trace it.	Fill in the blanks.	Write it.
	fox	f_x	
	log	l_g	
	net	n_t	
	web	w_b	

Short u

Trace each word. Then write it, cover it, and write it again.

Spell it aloud.	Trace it.	Write it.	Practice it.
b u g	bug		
s u n	sun		
n u t	nut		
b u t	but		

Circle the letters to spell the word. Then write the word, cover it with your hand, and write it again.

		Write it.	Practice it.
hut	j a e h u m t		
bus	b f a u o k s		
hug	f h e a u g r		
cub	c r u a w e b		

Word Search

Trace each word, fill in the missing vowel, and then cover the word and write it again.

	Trace it.	Fill in the blanks.	Write it.
	sun	s _ n	
	bed	b _ d	
	dog	d _ g	
	cat	c _ t	
	pig	p _ g	

Find the words in the word search.

d	c	i	e	a	p	o	h
z	s	u	n	y	i	x	p
d	v	f	o	h	g	l	e
o	e	c	a	t	m	r	i
g	k	j	w	u	b	e	d

sn, st, and sh

Fill in the blanks with **sn** to complete each word. Then write the word, cover it, and write it again.

	Finish it.	Write it.	Practice it.
	__ail		
	__ow		

Fill in the blanks with **st** to complete each word. Then write the word, cover it, and write it again.

	Finish it.	Write it.	Practice it.
	__ar		
	__one		

Fill in the blanks with **sh** to complete each word. Then write the word, cover it, and write it again.

	Finish it.	Write it.	Practice it.
	__ip		
	__ell		

cl and fl

Read the words in the box aloud.

club flop flip

clock flat

flap

clip clap

Write the words under the correct headings.

cl	fl

Cover each word and write it again.

cl	fl

ch, th, and wh

Circle a **ch**, **th**, and **wh** word in each sentence.

1 That whale sings too much.

2 Where is the cheese?

3 Why did they get one each?

Write the words that contain each sound in separate lists.

ch	th	wh
much		

Spell each word aloud. Then cover it and write it below.

ch	th	wh

ng, gh, and ph

Fill in the blanks with **ng** to complete each word. Then write the word, cover it, and write it again.

	Finish it.	Write it.	Practice it.
	ki__		
	ri__		

Fill in the blanks with **gh** to complete each word. Then write the word, cover it, and write it again.

	Finish it.	Write it.	Practice it.
	cou__		
	lau__		

Fill in the blanks with **ph** to complete each word. Then write the word, cover it, and write it again.

	Finish it.	Write it.	Practice it.
	__one		
	tro__y		

Final e

A silent **e** makes the other vowel say its name. The other vowel changes from **short** to **long**. For example, adding **e** to **cut** changes it to **cute**.

Trace the vowels. Next circle the letters to spell the words. Then write them.

gate

u g s a t e

cake

l c a k r e

chase

c h f a s e

tube

t r u v b e

kite

y k i t e h

cone

c p o i n e

Long a and e

Trace the long-a sound in each word.

Write the words under the correct headings. Then write them again.

ay	ai	a_e

Trace the long-e sound in each word. Then write the word under the correct heading, cover it, and write it again.

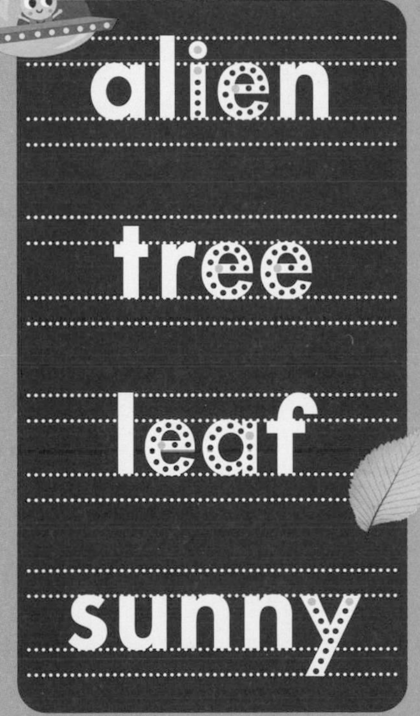

ee	y
ea	**ie**

Long i and o

Trace the long-i sound in each word. Then write the word under the correct heading, cover it, and write it again.

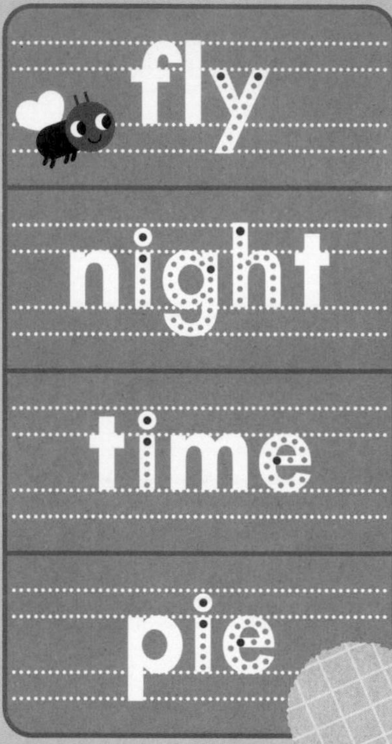

i_e	igh
ie	**y**

Trace the long-o sound in each word. Then write the word under the correct heading, cover it, and write it again.

road mow

ow	oa

Long u

Trace the long-u sound in each word.

menu use value

Write each word under the correct heading, cover it, and write it again.

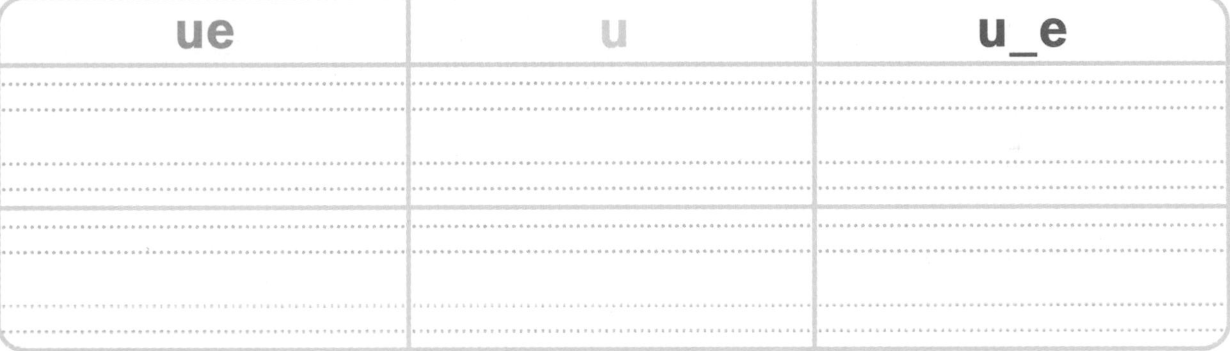

ue	u	u_e

Write the word, cover it, and write it again.

cube		
music		
huge		
human		
rescue		

s, ed, and ing

Trace the endings of the words in the list.

Root word	s	ed	ing
look	looks	looked	looking
play	plays	played	playing
walk	walks	walked	walking

Match each base word to its inflected endings.

s, ed, and ing

Write the base word with the correct endings in the table.

Root word	Add s	Add ed	Add ing
cook			
ask			

Some words drop the -e at the end before adding -ing.
Write each word, cover it, and write it again.

bake	bakes	baked	baking

use	uses	used	using

Word Maze

Some words double the last letter before adding -ed or -ing.
Color or trace the words to guide the frog to its friend.

Start

hop

hops

hopped

skips

skip

hopping

skipped

jump

jumps

skipping

jumped

jumping

Finish

Irregular Endings

Some words add an -e before adding -s.
Trace, write, and practice these words.

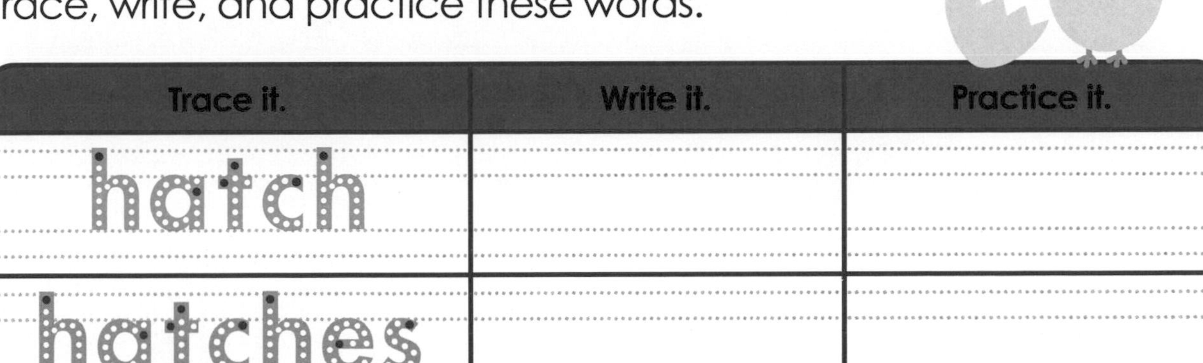

Trace it.	Write it.	Practice it.
hatch		
hatches		
hatched		
hatching		

Some words change the -y to -i before adding -es or -ed. Trace, write, and practice these words.

Trace it.	Write it.	Practice it.
cry		
cries		
cried		
crying		

Odd or Even?

Circle all the **odd** numbers with a **red** pencil.
Circle all the **even** numbers with a **blue** pencil.

20

nineteen

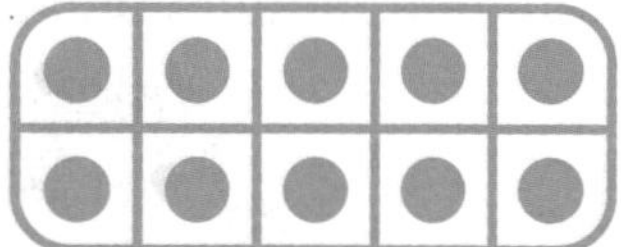

15

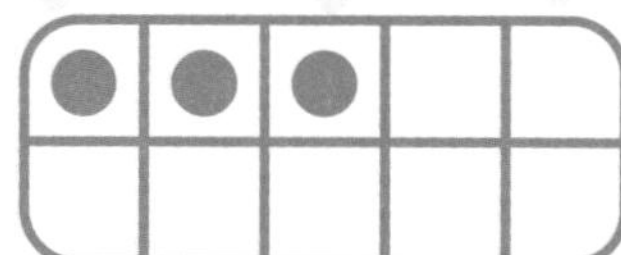

nine

6

eight

Left or Right?

Trace the words under the shoes.

Draw lines to show which direction each object is facing.

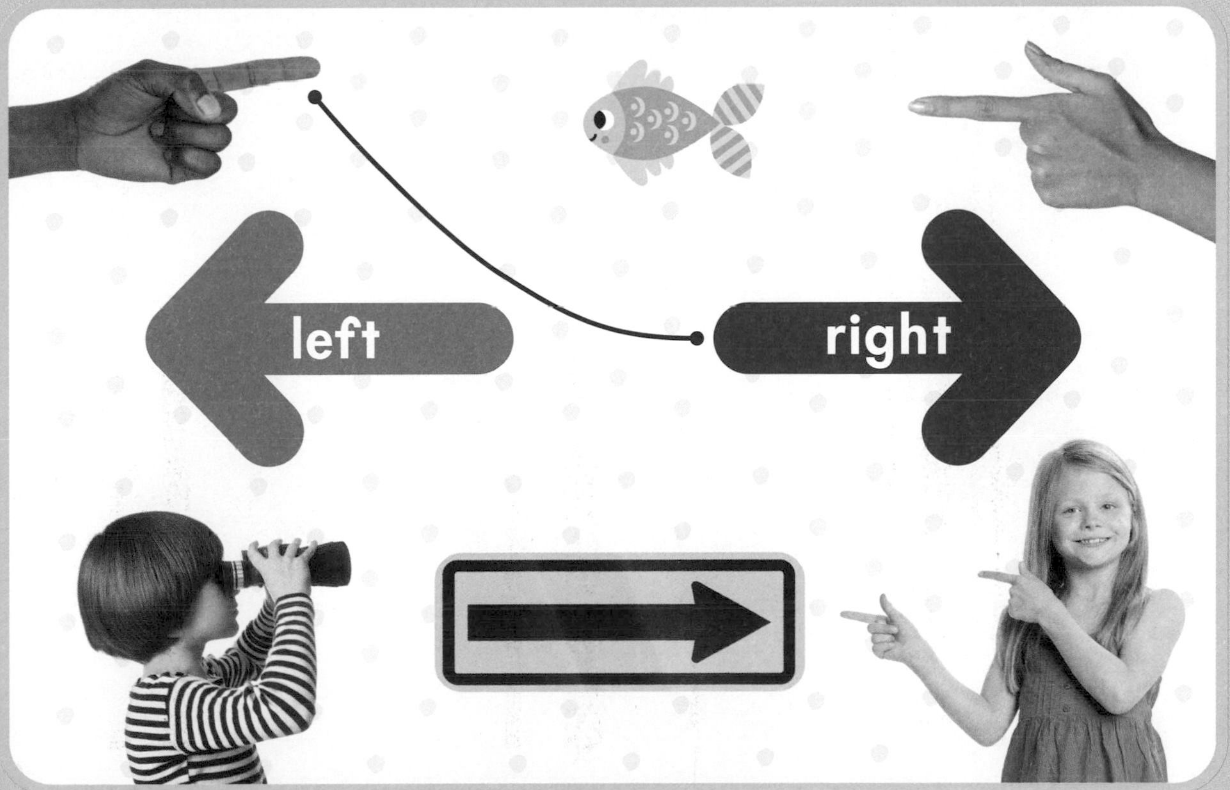

Sort 2D Shapes

Sticker the correct word below each picture.

Sort 3D Shapes

Sticker the correct word below each picture.

sphere

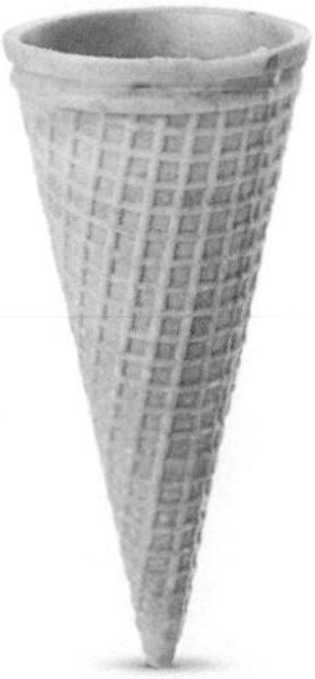

Sort Letters

Write each lowercase letter inside the boxes that it belongs in.
Some letters belong in more than one box.

abcdefghijklmnopqrstuvwxyz

Letters with curved lines

a

Letters with straight lines

a

Letters with dots above them

i

Letters with slanted straight lines

k

Group Cats

Give each group of cats a name that fits all the members of the group.

....

....

....

....

Sort Two Ways

Draw different lines to sort the objects.

Sort Three Ways

Draw different lines to sort the flowers.

An Ice-Cream Treat

Number the pictures from 1 to 6 in the order that they happened.

An Oak's Life

Number the pictures from 1 to 6 to show how the tree grew and changed over time.

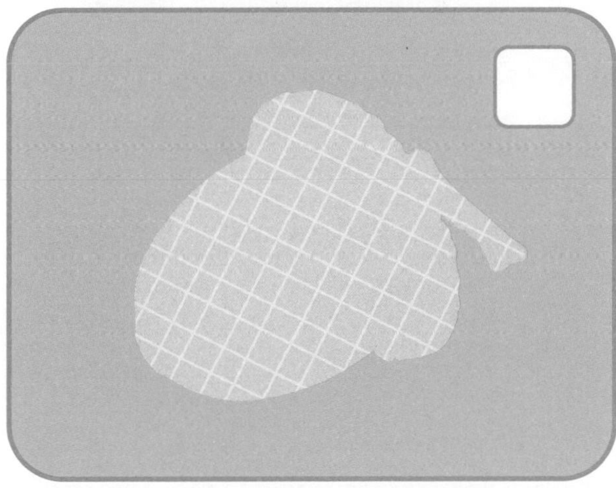

Naming Words

Naming words are called **nouns**. Sort the nouns into two groups. Write the words in the boxes and give each group a name.

apple
rabbit
banana
bird
orange
deer
squirrel
pear
fox
plum

Describing Words

Describing words are called **adjectives.** Sort the adjectives into two groups. Write the words in the boxes and give each group a name.

kind rude mean fun friendly

wise happy selfish brave bossy

....

....

What adjectives would you like people to use to describe you? Write some words in this box.

....

....

Necklace Patterns

Follow the patterns to finish coloring the beads on the necklaces.

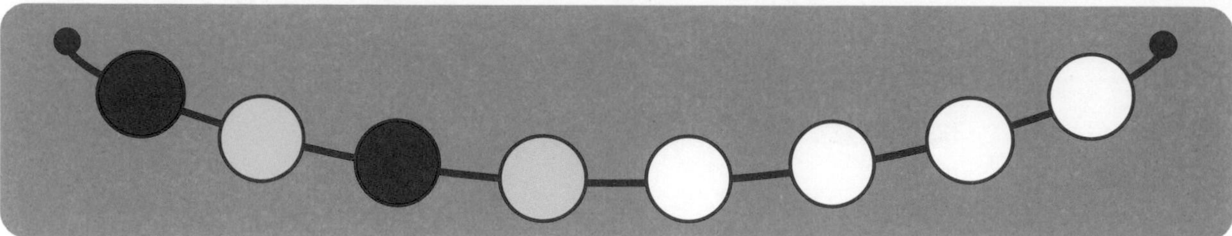

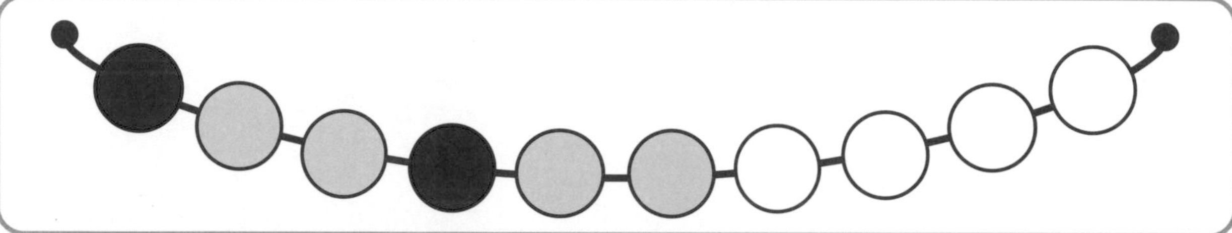

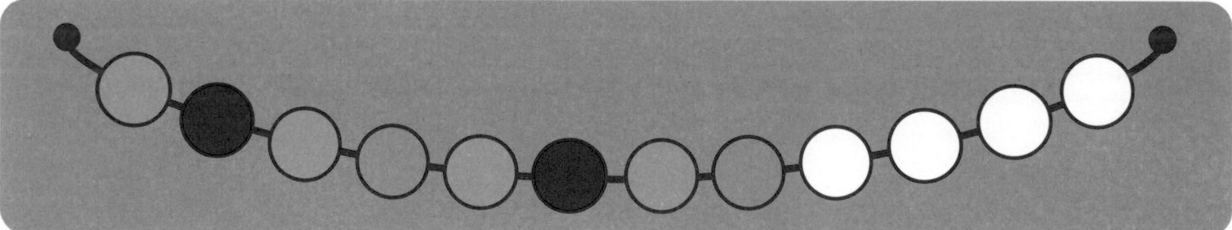

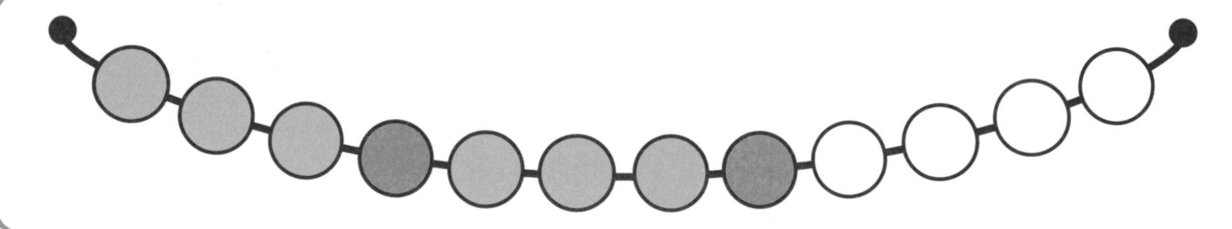

Create your own patterns on these necklaces.

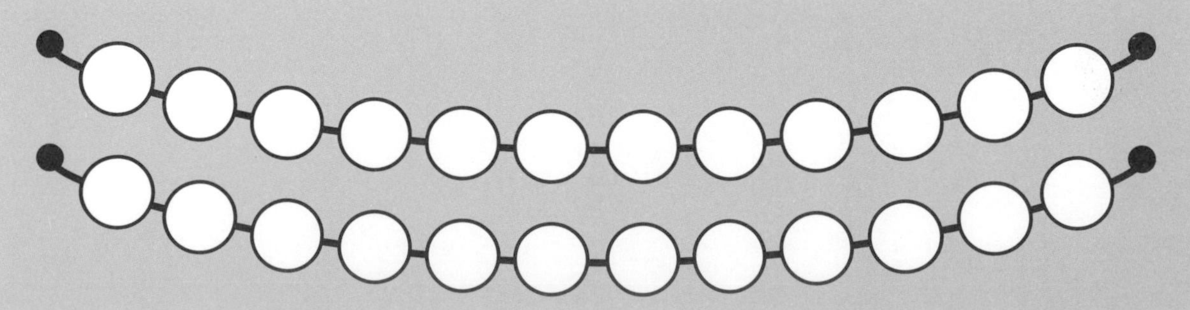

Beetle Count

Color and count the beetles in each group.

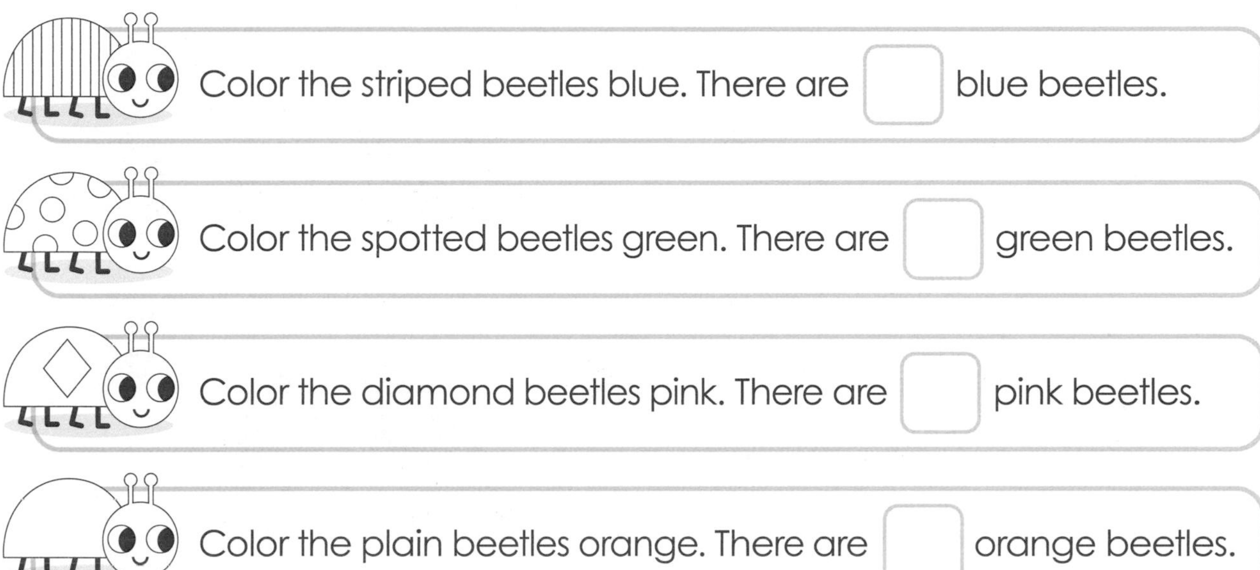

Color the striped beetles blue. There are ☐ blue beetles.

Color the spotted beetles green. There are ☐ green beetles.

Color the diamond beetles pink. There are ☐ pink beetles.

Color the plain beetles orange. There are ☐ orange beetles.

Bird Graph

Count how many birds of each type live at the bird park.
Color one square for each bird.

flamingo					
parrot					
owl					
duck					
pelican					

Which bird is most common?

....

Which bird is least common?

....

Venn Diagram

Trace the words. Then draw one more hat in each part of the diagram.

This circle has **orange** hats.

This circle has **blue** hats.

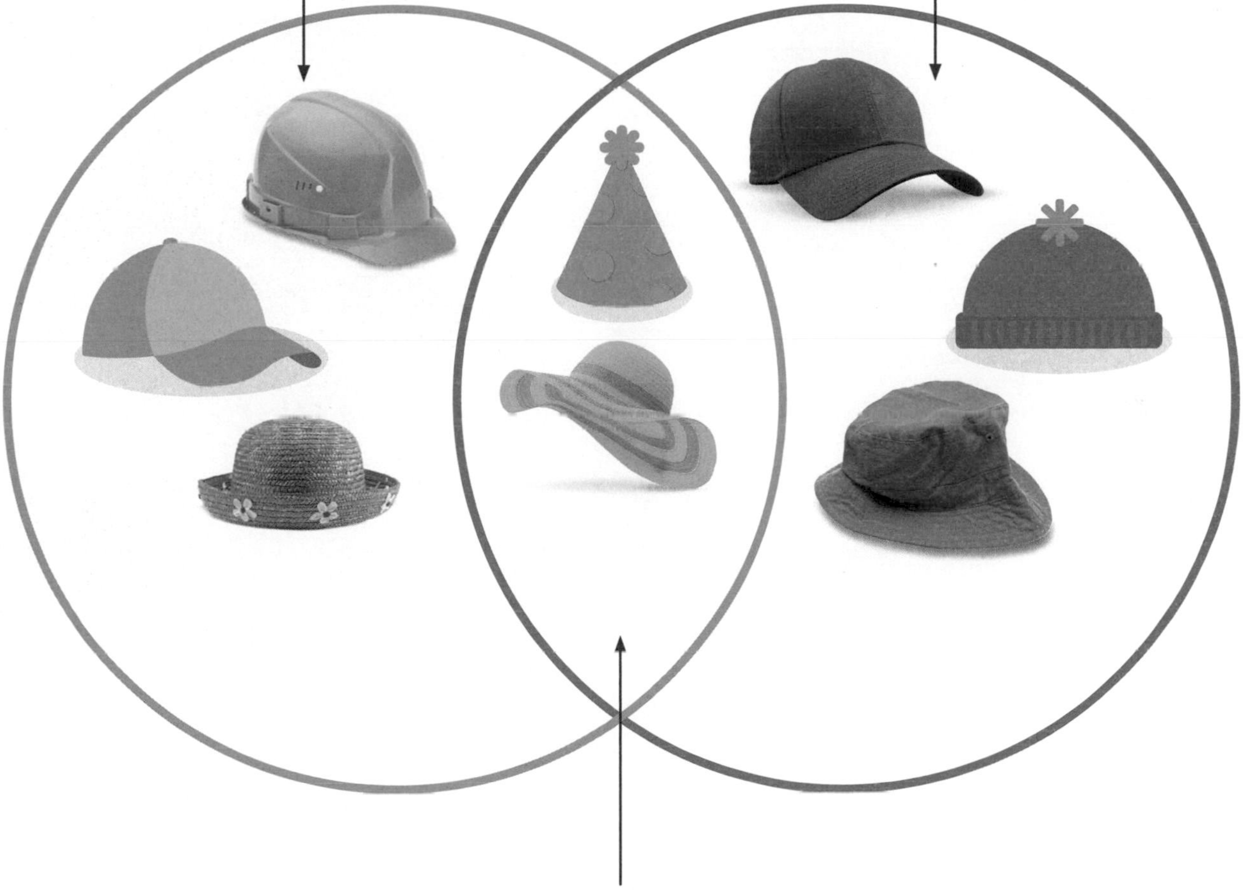

The overlap has **orange** and **blue** hats.

Tally Chart

Count the tally marks to complete the totals. Then answer the questions below.

Sea creatures seen	Tallies	Total
sharks	𝍸	5
turtles	||||	
small fish	𝍸 𝍸	
octopuses	||	

1 How many turtles did the diver see? ☐

2 Which creature did she see the most of? ....

3 Which creature did she see the fewest of? ....

4 How many sharks and turtles did she see altogether? ☐

5 How many more small fish did she see than sharks? ☐

Pie Chart

The children in Mr. Smith's class chose a Popsicle each. This pie chart shows how many children chose each flavor.

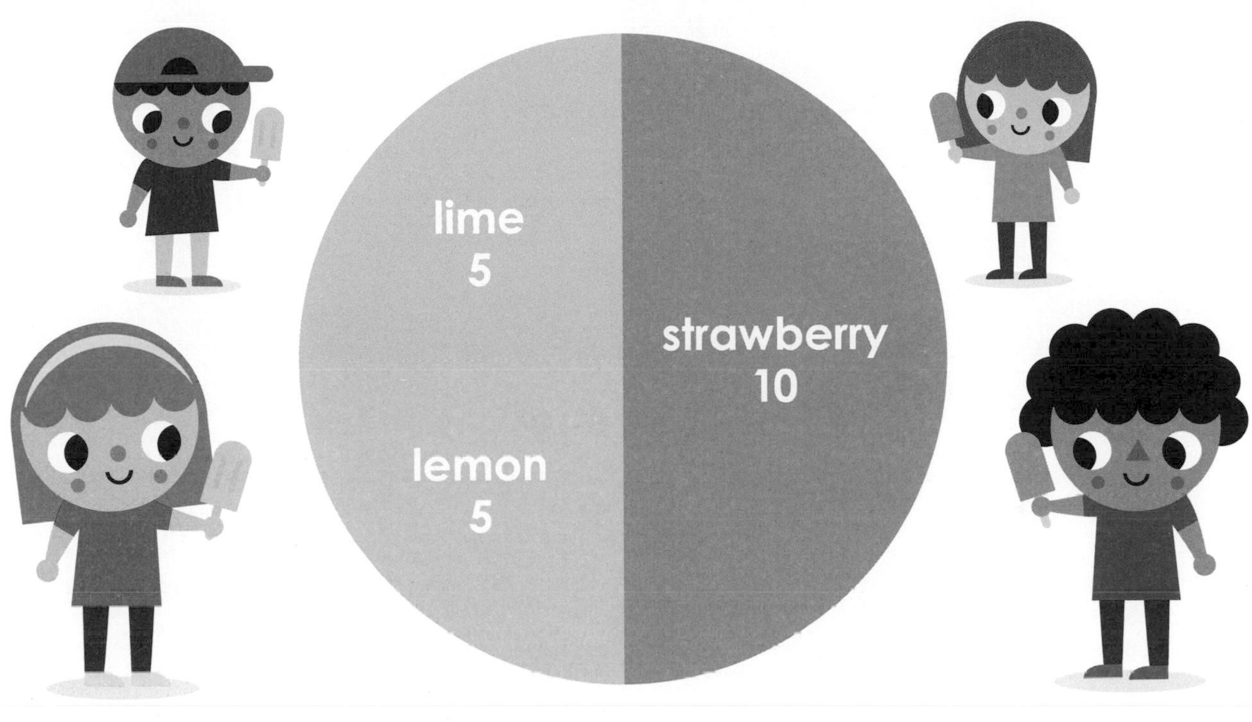

1 How many flavors of Popsicle were there? ☐

2 What was the most popular flavor? ....

3 Which two flavors were equally popular?

.... and ....

4 Half the children chose the same flavor.

What did they choose? ....

5 How many children chose either lemon or lime? ☐

6 How many children were in Mr. Smith's class? ☐

NUMBER SENSE

Revise 1 to 10

Trace the numbers. Then draw lines to match the numbers to the ten frames and the tally marks.

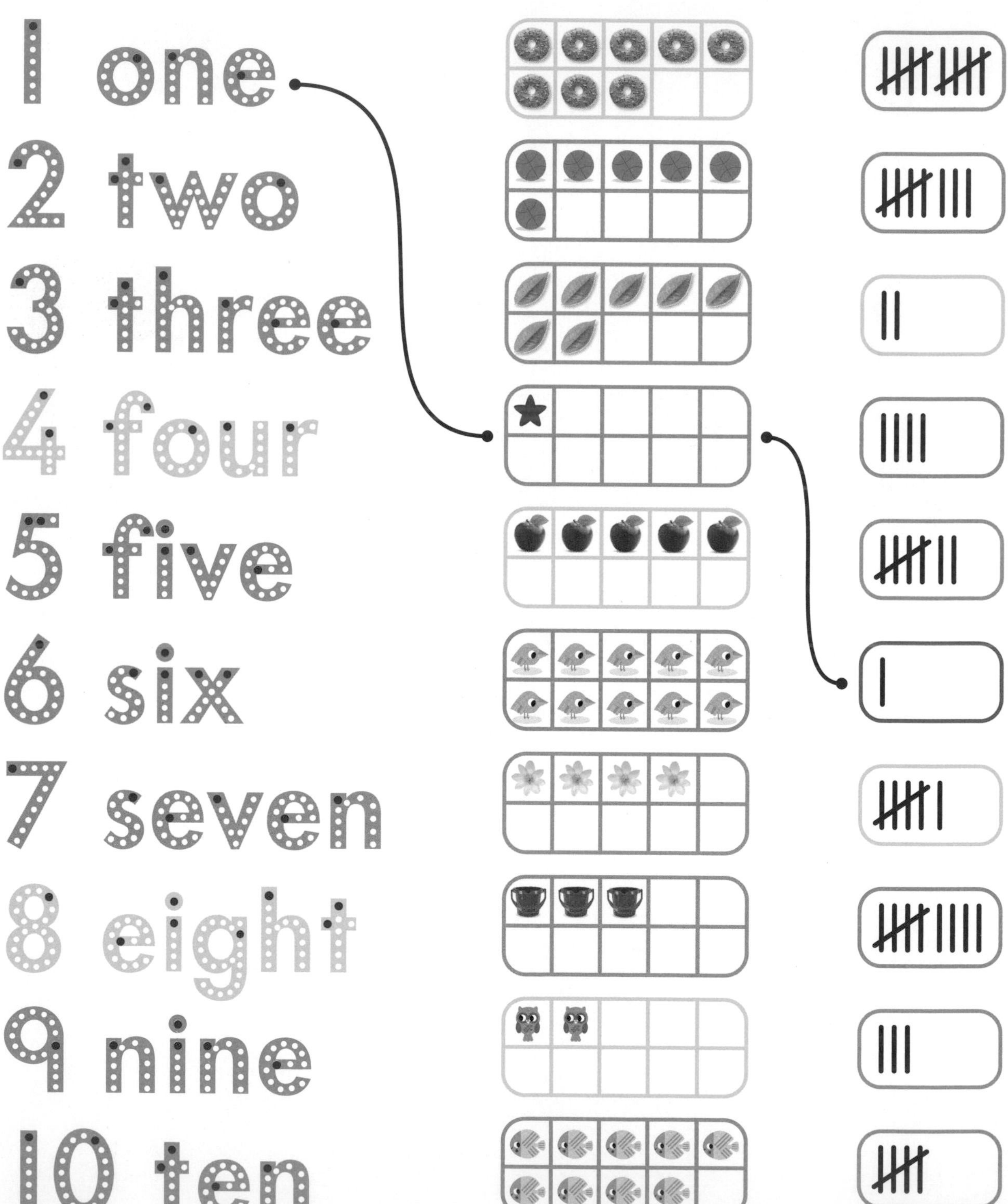

Revise 11 to 20

Trace the numbers. Then draw lines to match the numbers to the ten frames and the tally marks. Finish coloring the ten frames.

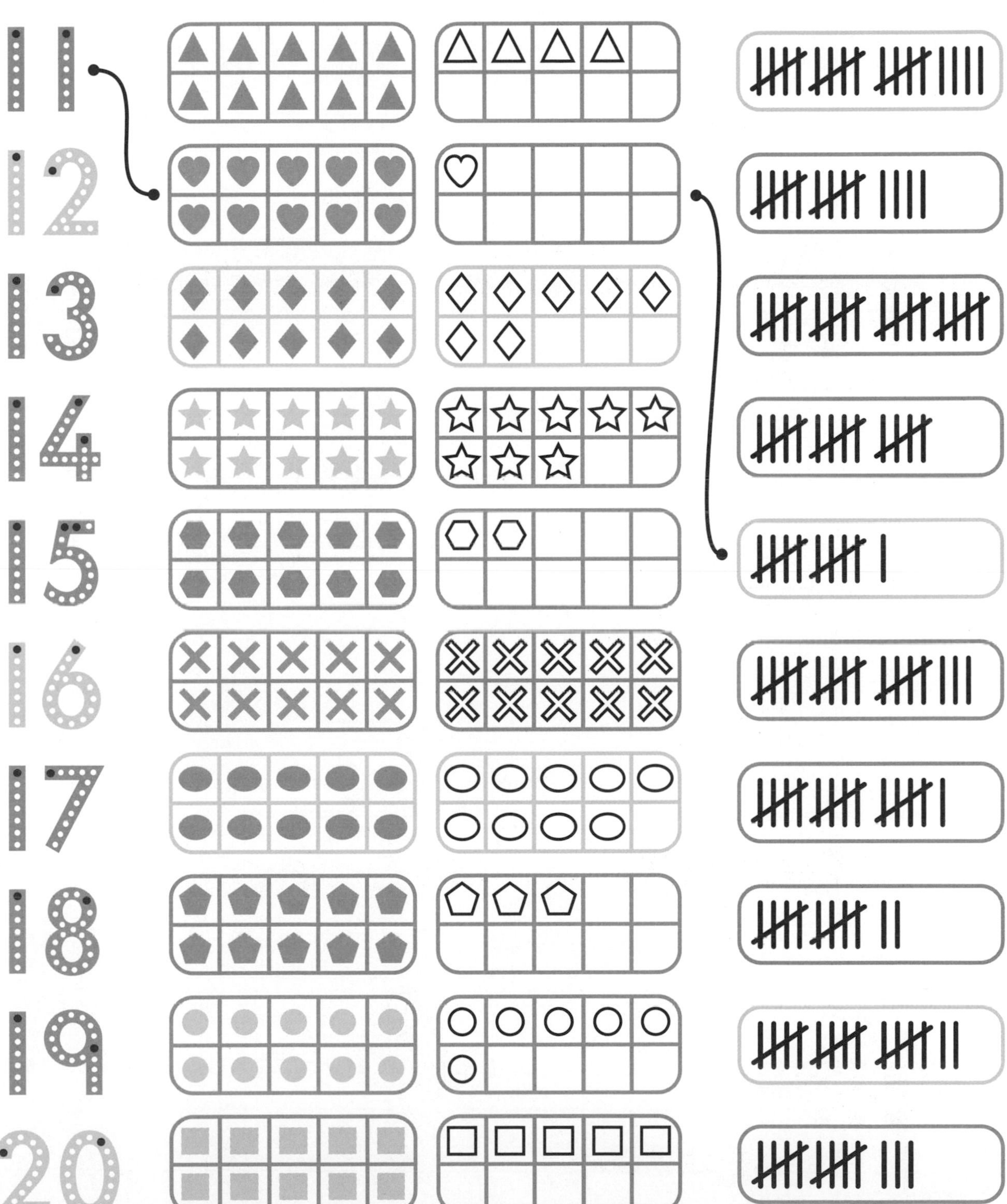

NUMBER SENSE

Ordinal Numbers

The race cars are reaching the finish line. Write the correct ordinal number above each car.

1st 2nd 3rd 4th 5th 6th 7th 8th 9th 10th

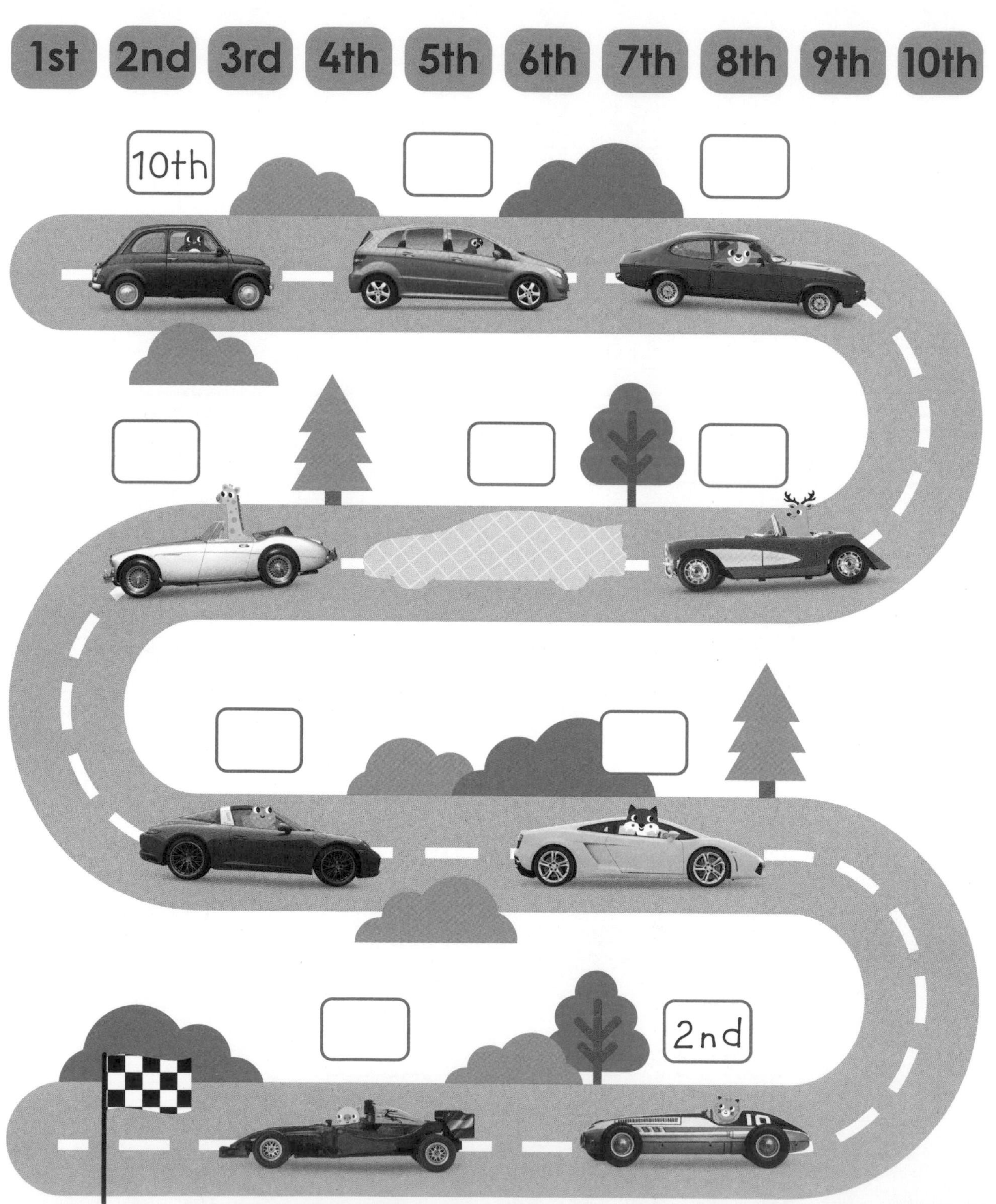

NUMBER SENSE

Equal Amounts

Circle the group that is the same size as the first group.

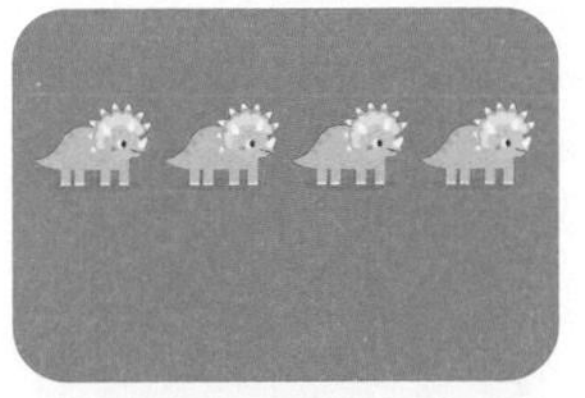

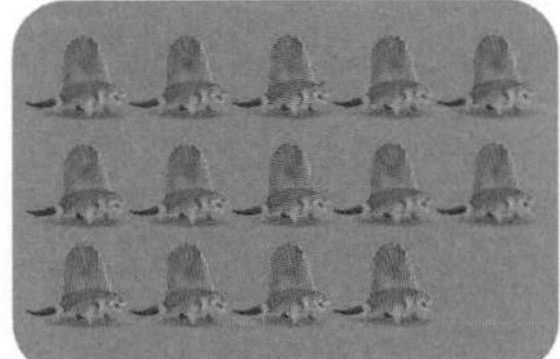

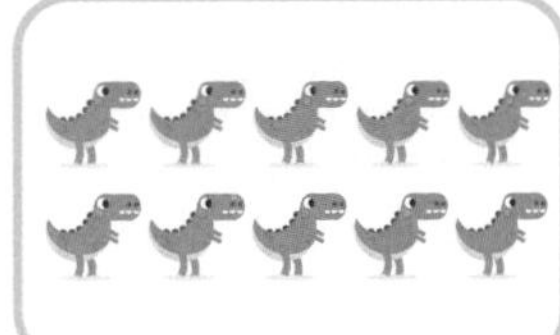

Draw the same number of objects in the second box as in the first box.

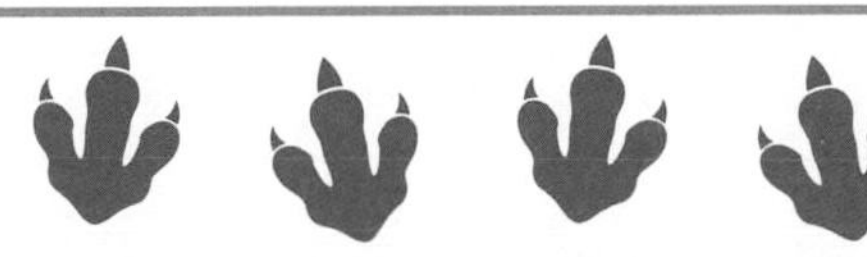

NUMBER SENSE

More or Less

1 Circle the drink in each pair with **more** liquid than the other.

2 Circle the serving in each pair that has **less** food than the other.

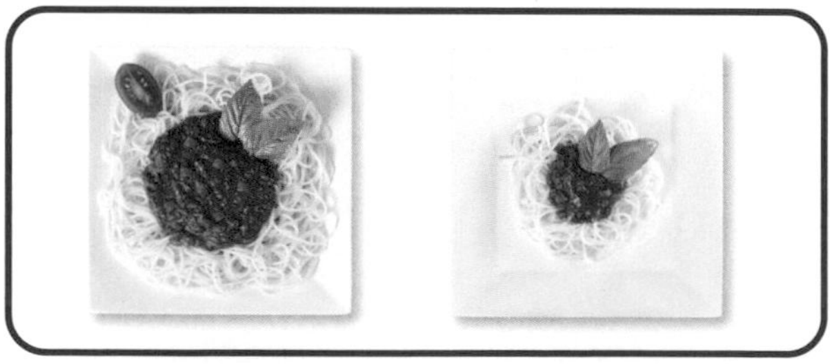

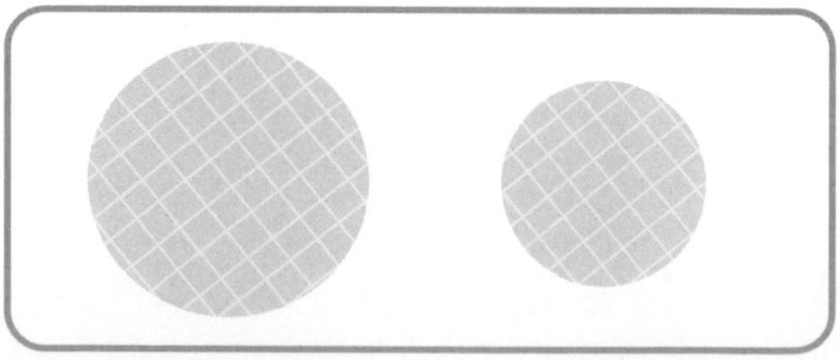

NUMBER SENSE

More or Fewer

1 Count the fruit and finish the sentences.

There are 3 more apples than bananas.

There are ☐ more pineapples than oranges.

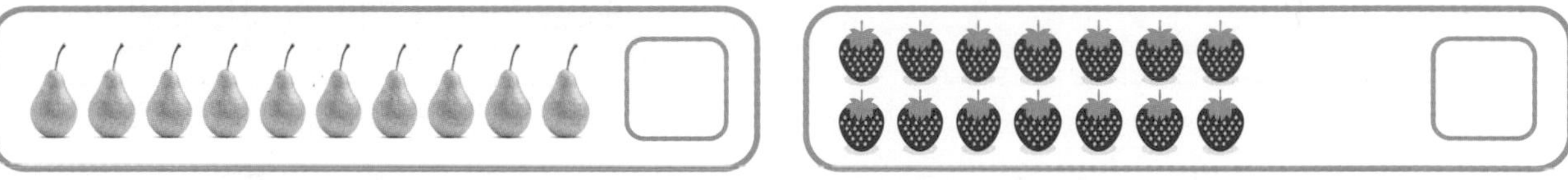

There are ☐ more strawberries than pears.

2 Count the sweet treats and finish the sentences.

There are ☐ fewer Popsicles than ice-cream cones.

There are ☐ fewer cupcakes than donuts.

There are ☐ fewer orange candies than green candies.

Using Symbols

Count the vehicles in each group. Then write **>** (more than), **<** (less than), or **=** (equal to) between the boxes.

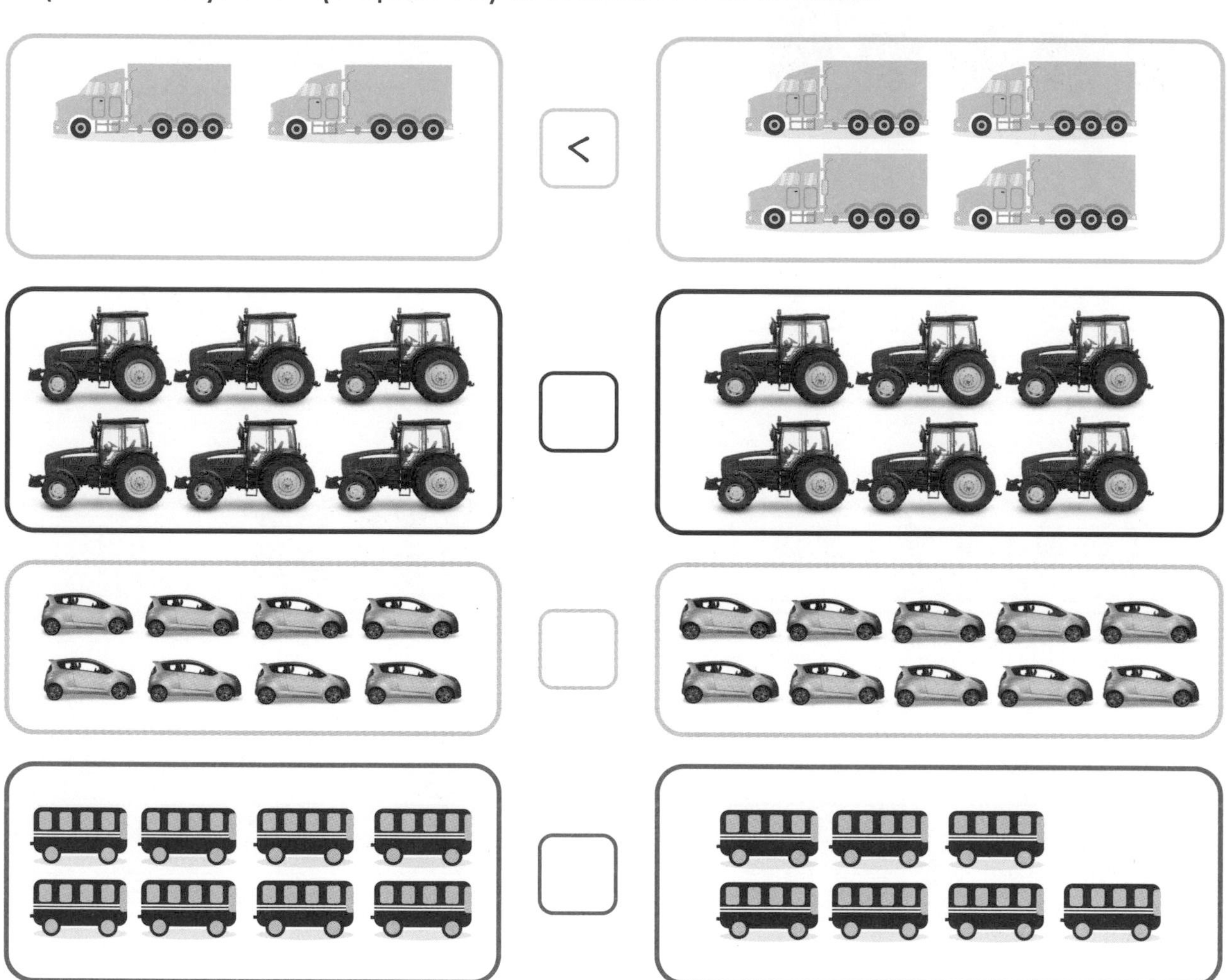

Write **>** (more than), **<** (less than), or **=** (equal to) between the numbers.

5		**1**
8		**8**
11		**10**

11		**15**
18		**8**
1		**4**

10		**8**
11		**11**
18		**20**

Revise 1 to 100

Write the last number in each row to complete the numbers to 100.

11 12 13 14 15 16 17 18 19

21 22 23 24 25 26 27 28 29

31 32 33 34 35 36 37 38 39

41 42 43 44 45 46 47 48 49

51 52 53 54 55 56 57 58 59

61 62 63 64 65 66 67 68 69

71 72 73 74 75 76 77 78 79

81 82 83 84 85 86 87 88 89

91 92 93 94 95 96 97 98 99

Revise 1 to 100

Fill in the missing numbers on the hundred chart.

1	2		4	5	6	7		9	10
11	12	13		15	16	17	18	19	
21		23		25	26	27		29	30
	32	33	34	35	36	37	38		40
41	42	43	44		46	47	48	49	50
51	52	53	54	55	56		58	59	
	62	63	64	65	66		68	69	70
71			74	75	76	77	78	79	80
81	82	83	84	85	86	87	88		
91	92	93	94	95		97	98	99	

Skip Count by 2

1 Follow the bee's path with your finger, counting by 2's as you go. Then trace the path and the numbers the bee lands on.

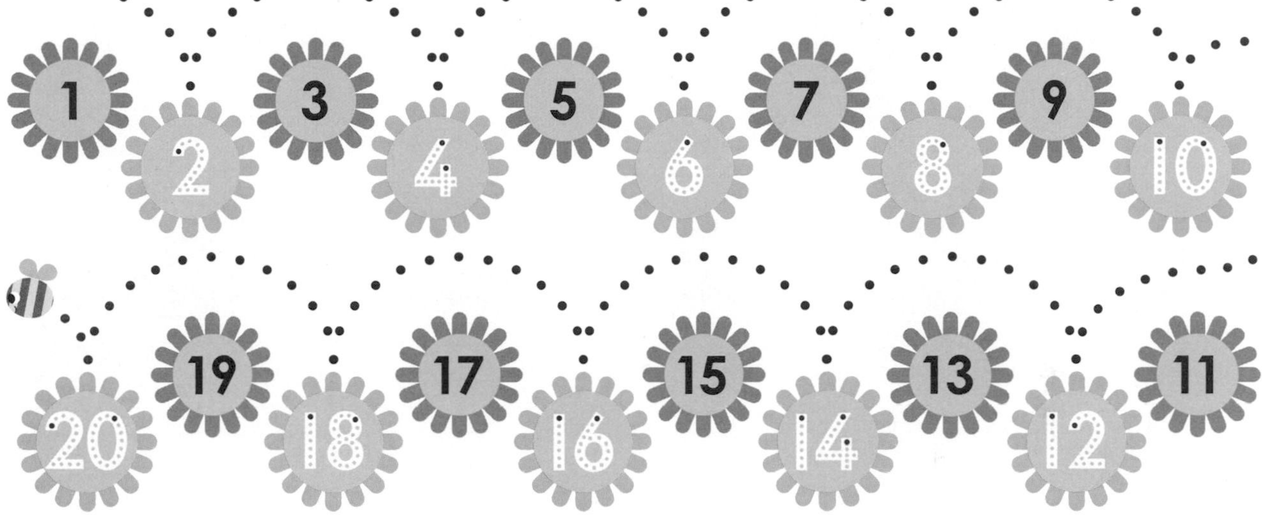

2 Count the socks by skip counting in 2's. Write the numbers in the boxes as you go.

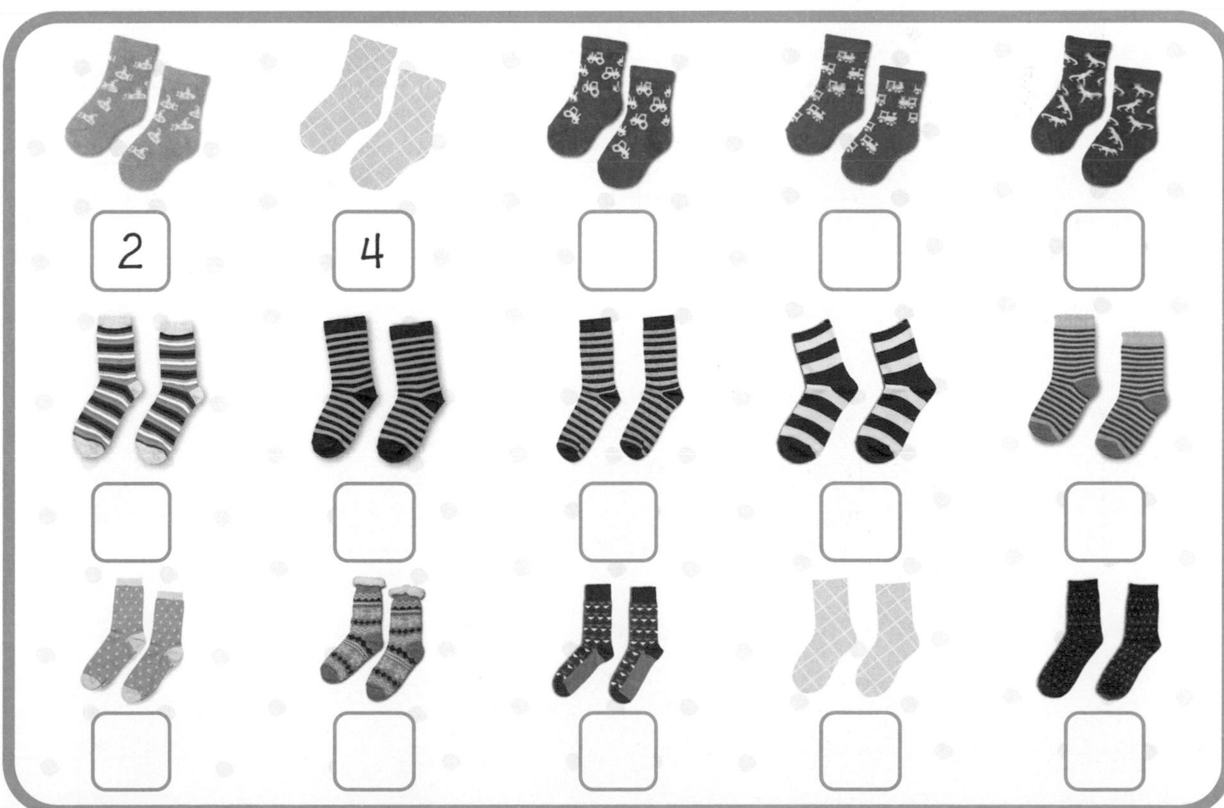

Skip Count by 5

1 Follow the spaceship's path with your finger, counting by 5's as you go. Then trace the path and the numbers of the planets the spaceship lands on.

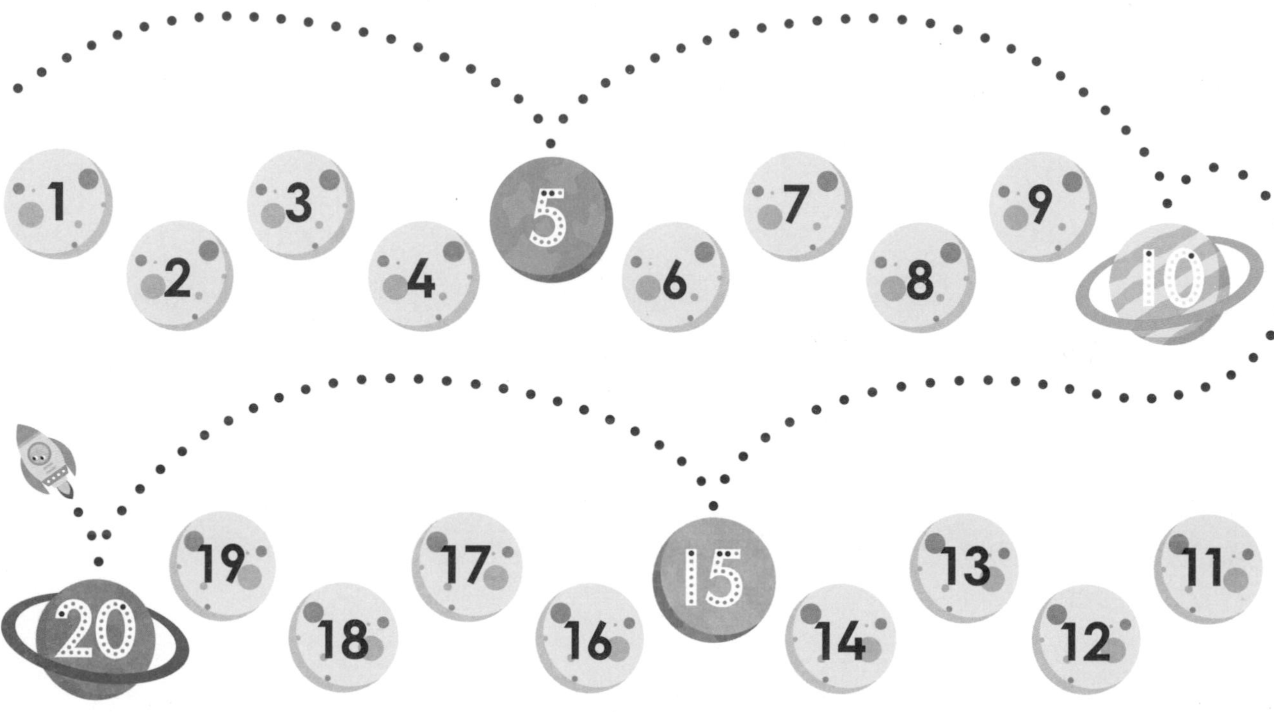

2 Count the fingers by skip counting in 5's. Write the numbers in the hands as you go.

NUMBER SENSE

Skip Count by 10

1 Count by 10's to fill in the missing numbers on the train.

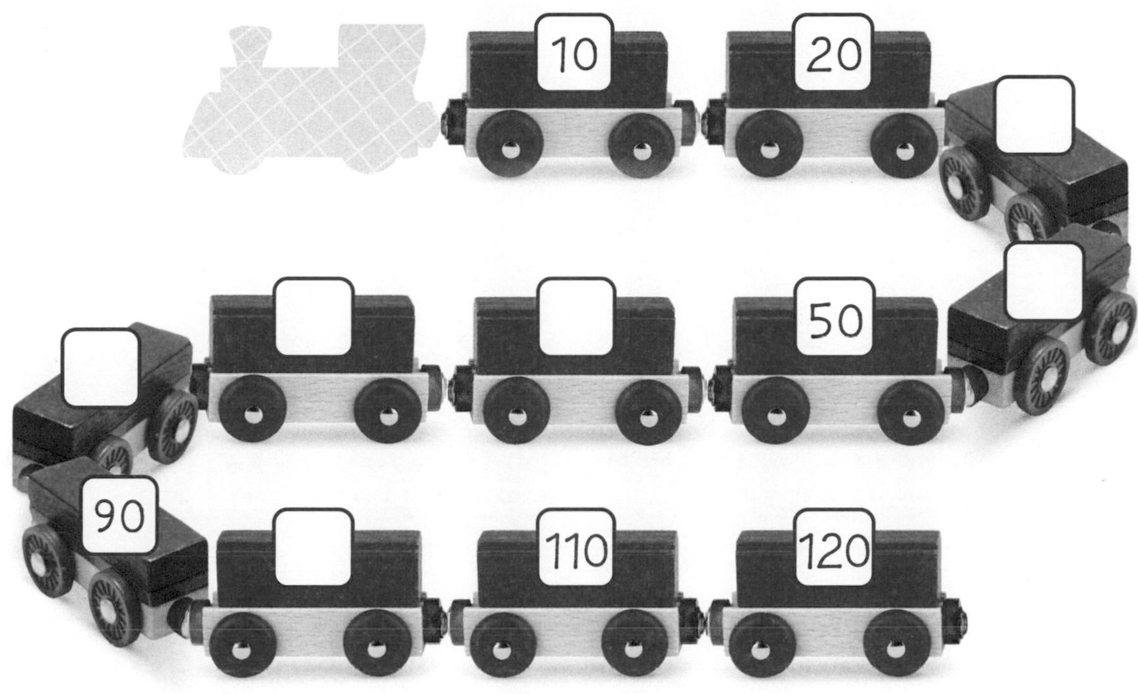

2 Count all the candles by skip counting in 10's.

Count Tens

1 The number ten is made of 10 ones. Trace the number sentence.

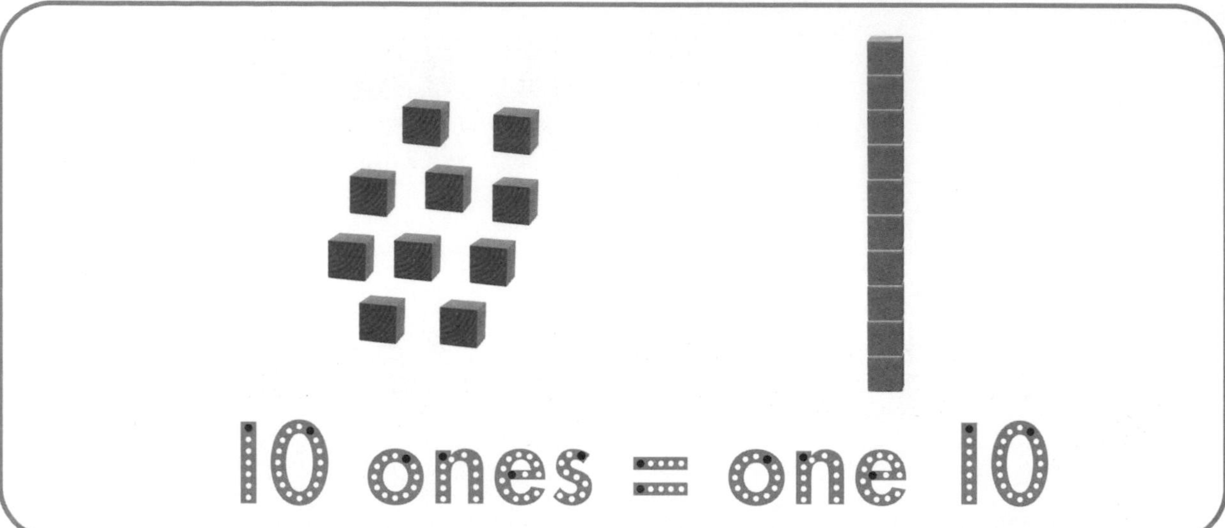

2 Trace the first two problems, and then complete the others.

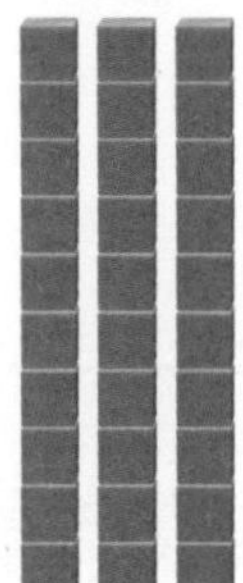

3 tens = 30 ones

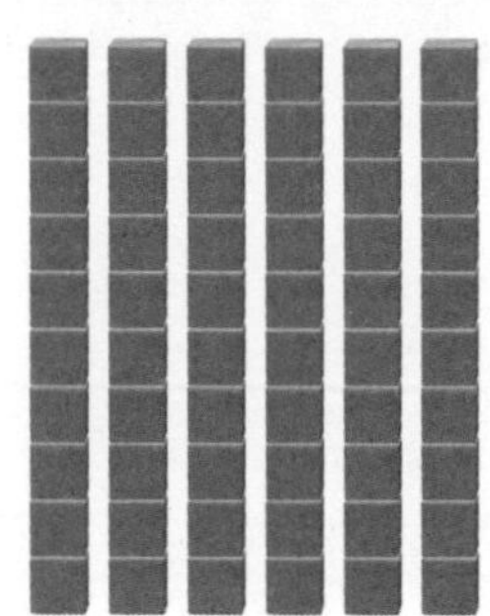

6 tens = 60 ones

4 tens = ☐ ones

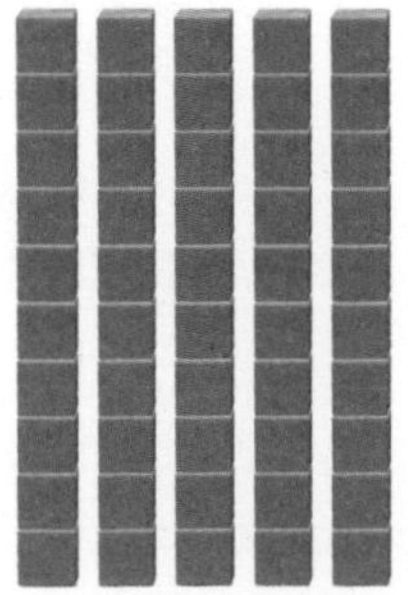

5 tens = ☐ ones

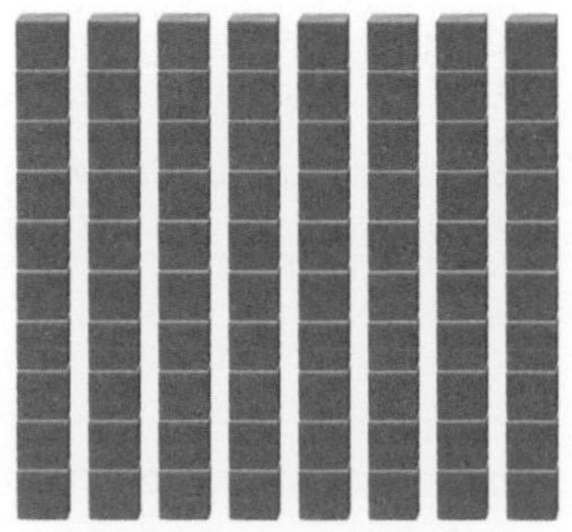

8 tens = ☐ ones

10 tens = ☐ ones

Ten and Ones

1 Color the rod and the 2 ones to show 12.

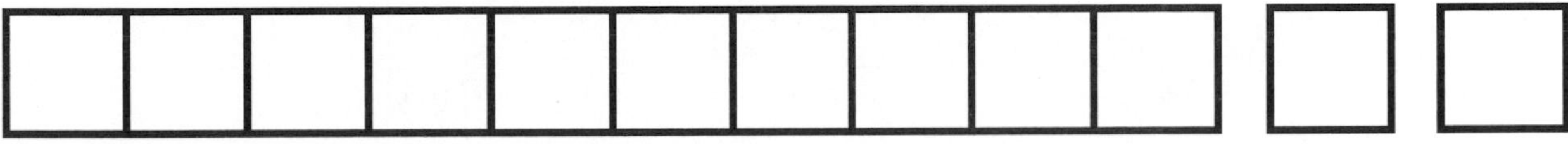

2 Draw lines to match the pictures with the number sentences.

I ten and I one = 11

I ten and 2 ones = 12

I ten and 3 ones =

I ten and 4 ones =

I ten and 5 ones =

I ten and 6 ones =

I ten and 7 ones =

I ten and 8 ones =

I ten and 9 ones =

2 tens = 20

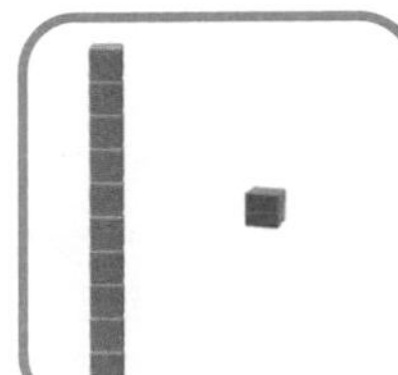
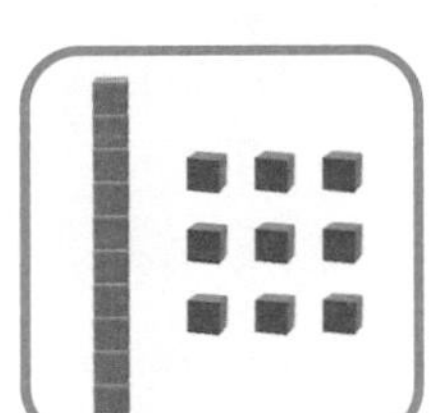
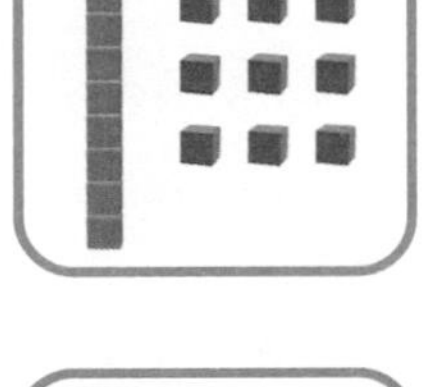

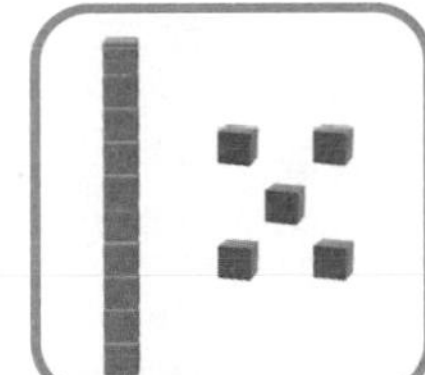
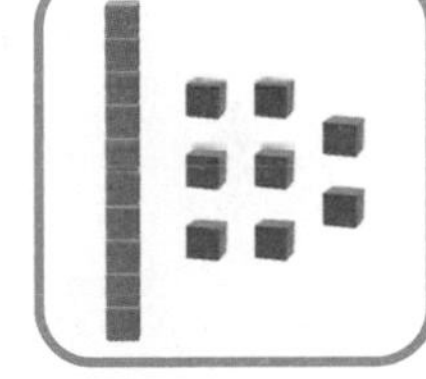
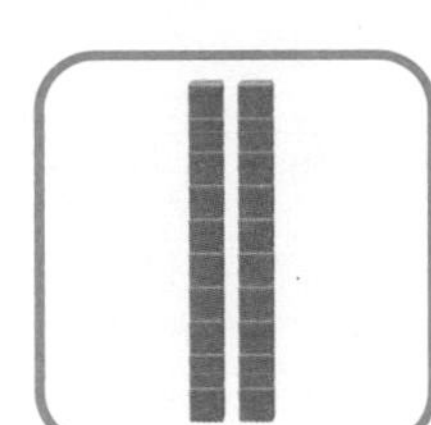

Tens and Ones

Trace the first problem, and then complete the others.

25 = [2] tens and [5] ones

25 = [20] + [5]

32 = [ ] tens and [ ] ones

32 = [ ] + [ ]

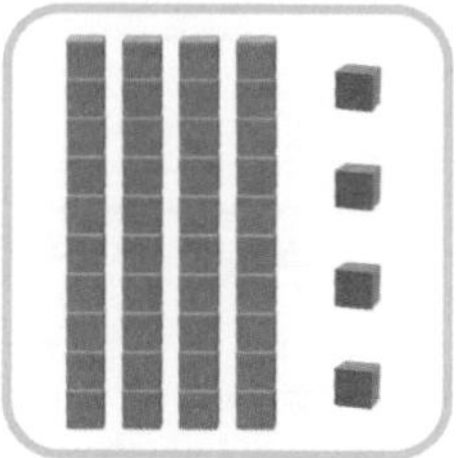

44 = [ ] tens and [ ] ones

44 = [ ] + [ ]

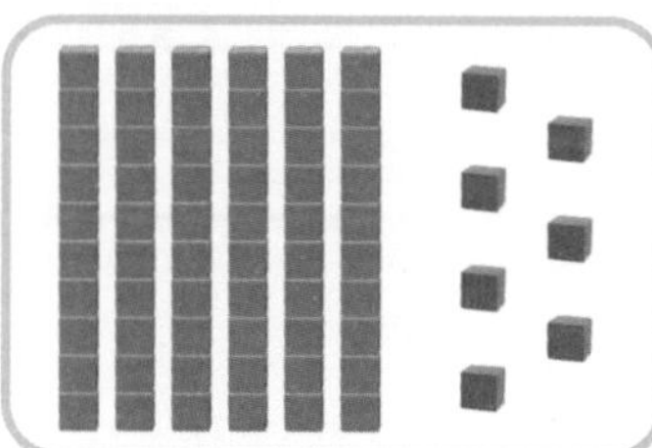

67 = [ ] tens and [ ] ones

67 = [ ] + [ ]

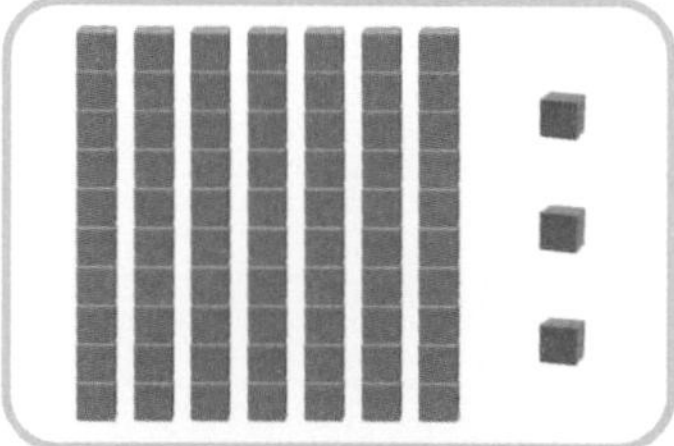

73 = [ ] tens and [ ] ones

73 = [ ] + 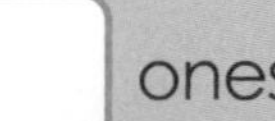

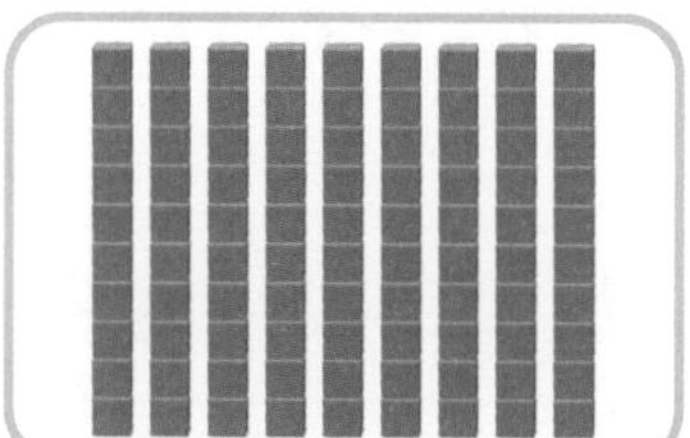

90 = [ ] tens and [ ] ones

90 = [ ] + 

Tens and Ones

1 Break down the numbers into tens and ones.

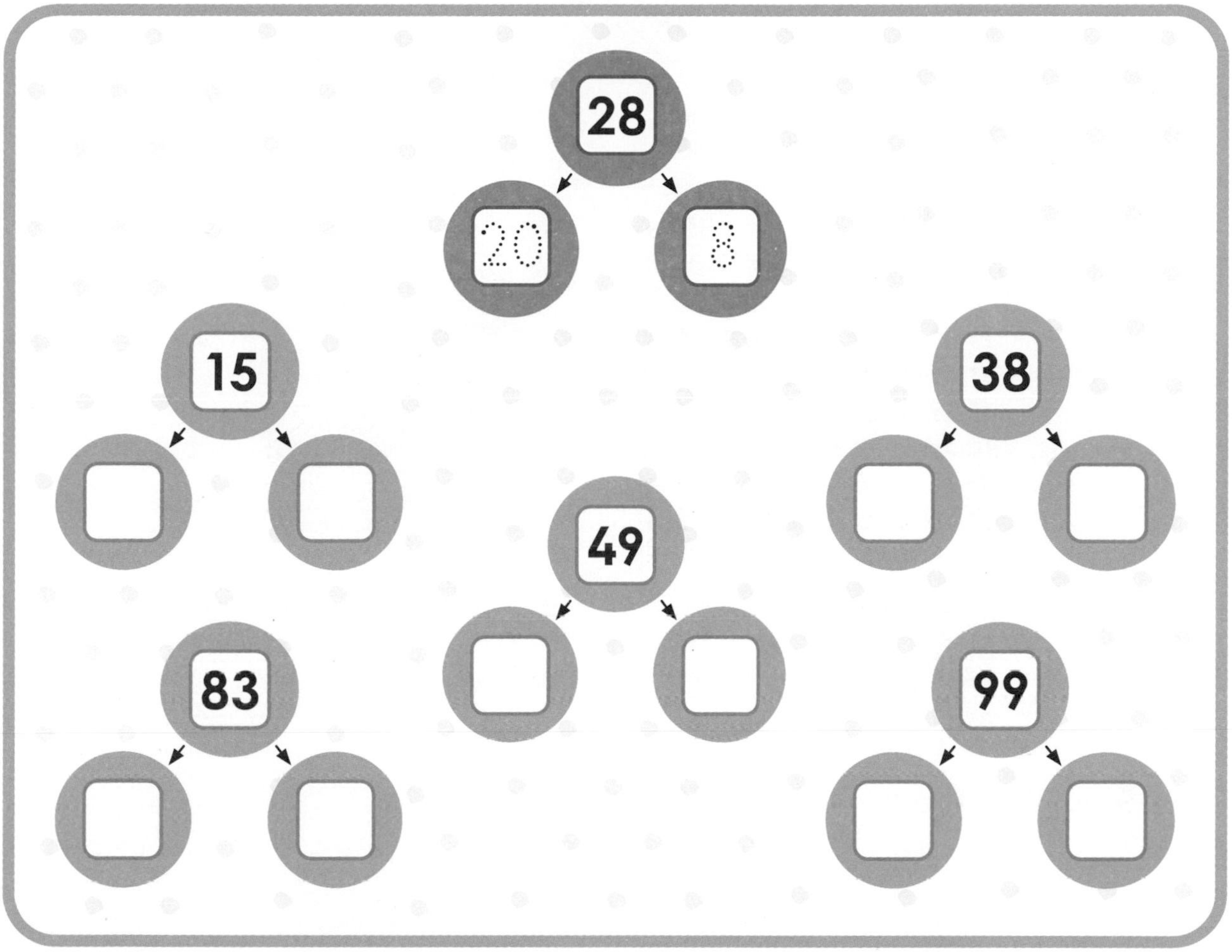

28 → 20, 8

15 → ☐, ☐

38 → ☐, ☐

49 → ☐, ☐

83 → ☐, ☐

99 → ☐, ☐

2 Complete the word problems.

56 is made of 5 tens and 6 ones.

29 is made of ☐ tens and ☐ ones.

12 is made of ☐ ten and ☐ ones.

21 is made of ☐ tens and ☐ one.

Hundred, Tens, and Ones

1 The number one hundred is made of 100 ones.
Trace the number sentence.

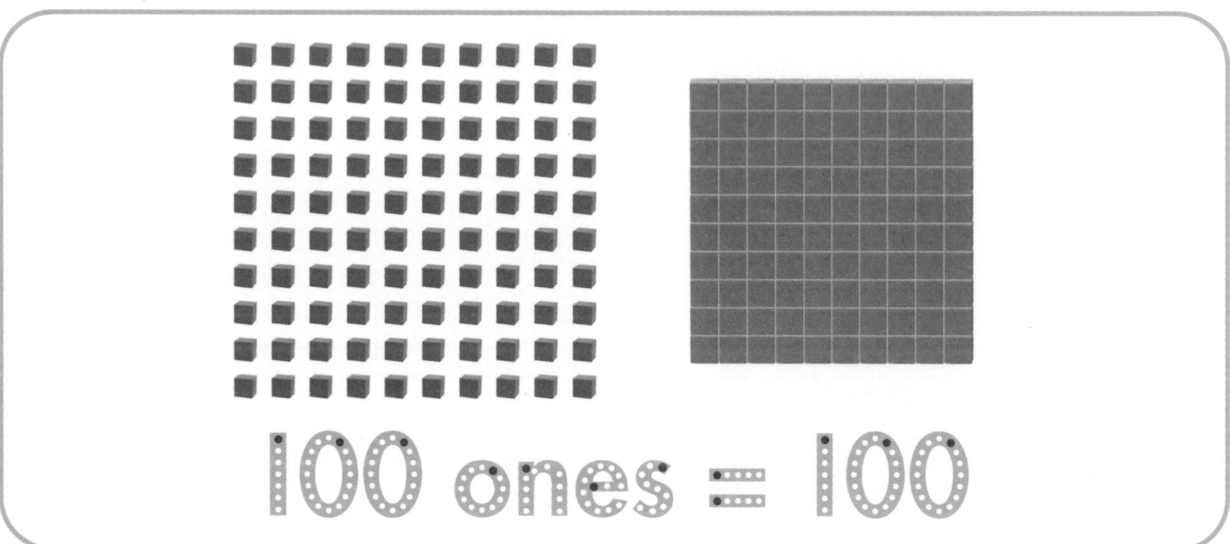

2 Complete the word problems. Where no blocks are shown, write 0 in the box. Zero is a placeholder.

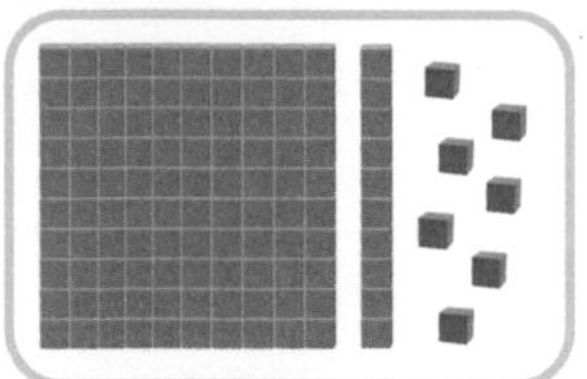

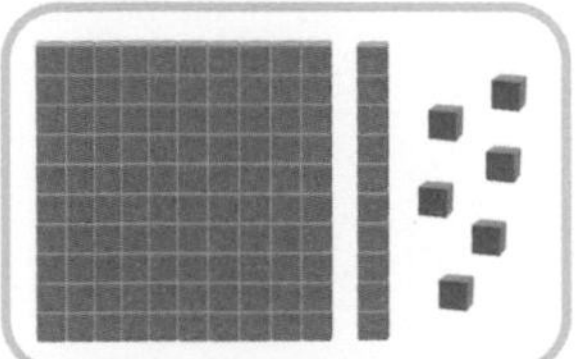

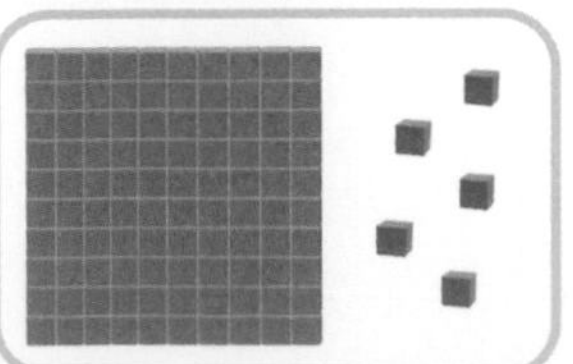

☐ hundred + ☐ tens + ☐ ones = 105

Place Value

Look at a number, and then write the place value for each numeral in the chart.

	hundreds	tens	ones
118	1	1	8
102	1	0	2
116			
106			
111			
117			
104			
120			
100			
109			

NUMBER SENSE

Ordering 1 to 120

Write the numbers on the carriages in order from smallest to biggest.

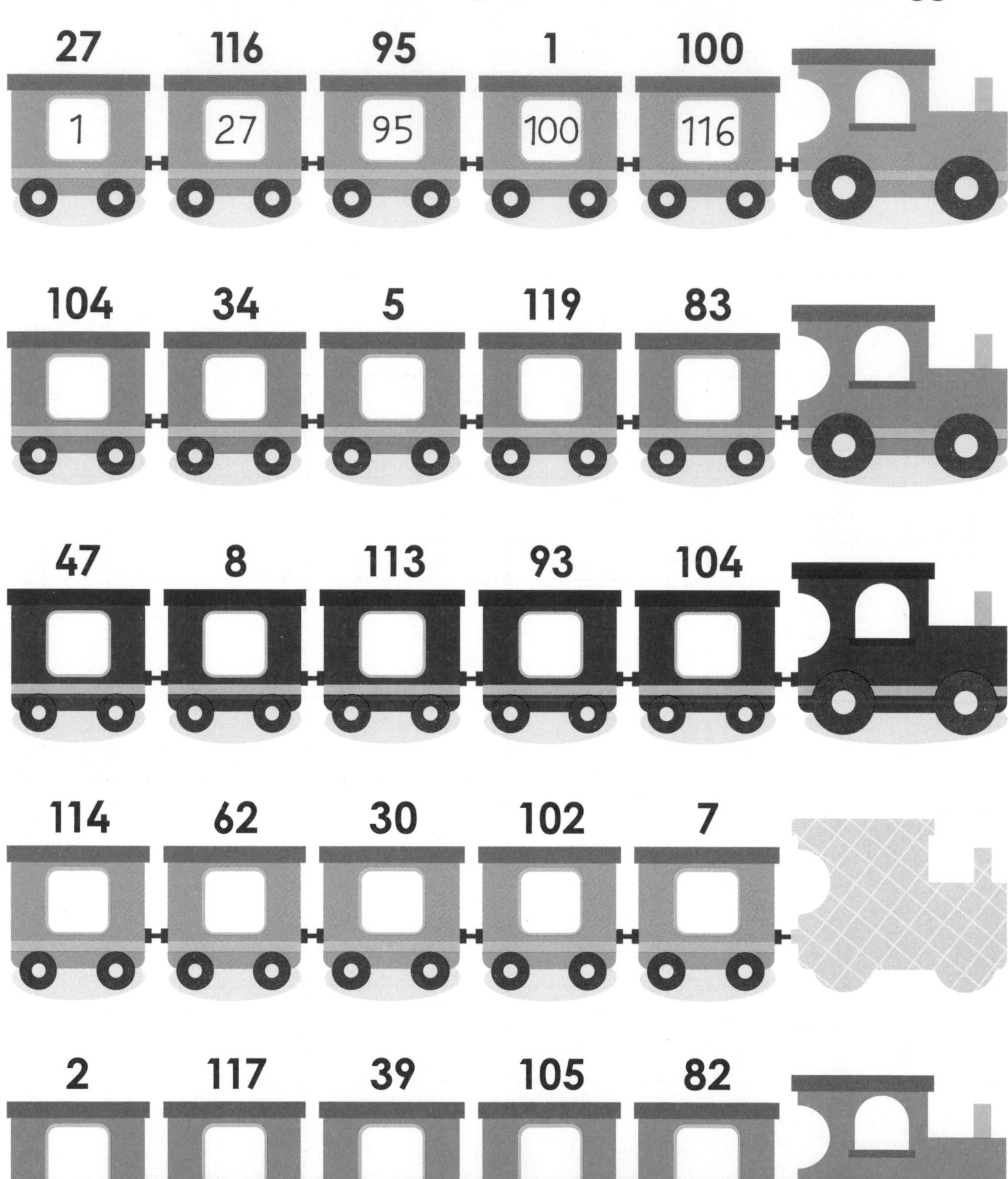

First Fractions

Color one half of each shape red and the other half green.

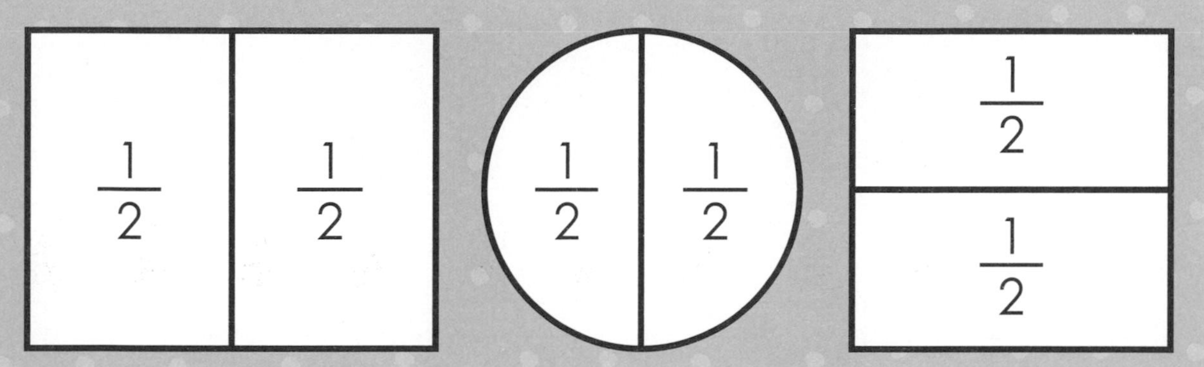

Color one third of each shape blue, one third orange, and one third pink.

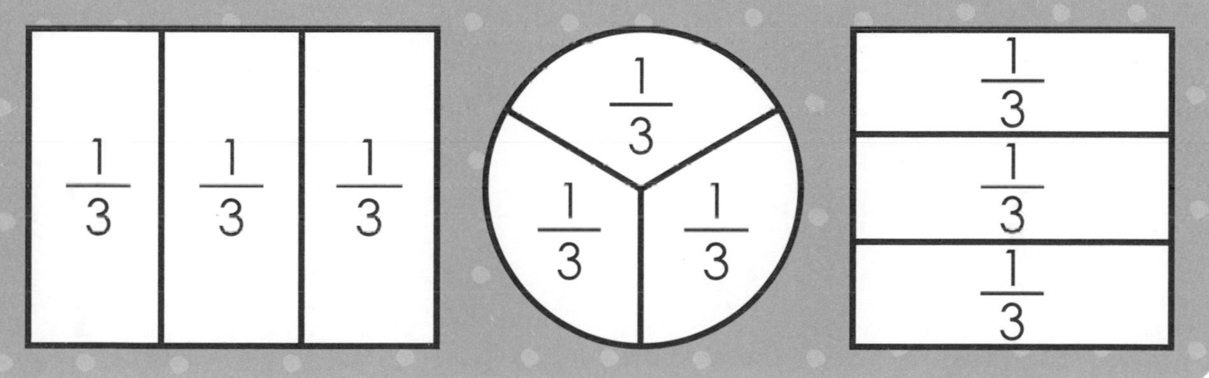

Color one quarter of each shape red, one quarter yellow, one quarter purple, and one quarter green.

$\frac{1}{4}$ $\frac{1}{4}$ $\frac{1}{4}$ $\frac{1}{4}$

$\frac{1}{4}$ $\frac{1}{4}$ $\frac{1}{4}$ $\frac{1}{4}$

$\frac{1}{4}$ $\frac{1}{4}$ $\frac{1}{4}$ $\frac{1}{4}$

Read a Graph

Each child in room 5 added a picture of their favorite pet to the graph. Use the graph to answer the questions.

Room 5's Favorite Pets									
cat	🐱	🐱	🐱	🐱	🐱	🐱			
dog	🐶	🐶	🐶	🐶	🐶	🐶	🐶	🐶	🐶
fish	🐟	🐟							
rabbit	🐰	🐰	🐰	🐰	🐰				
hamster	🐹	🐹	🐹	🐹					

1 Without counting, I think the most popular pet is the

....

2 Without counting, I think the least popular pet is the

....

3 By counting, I know that [6] children liked cats,

[ ] children liked dogs, [ ] liked fish,

[ ] liked rabbits, and [ ] liked hamsters.

4 Write the pet types in order from most popular to least popular.

....

NUMBER SENSE

Make a Graph

How many pieces of each type of fruit are in the box?
Count the fruit and write the numbers.

Room 5's Favorite Fruit

bananas	4
apples	
lemons	
pineapples	
oranges	

Color in one box for each piece of fruit to fill the graph.

bananas									
apples									
lemons									
pineapples									
oranges									

1 Which type of fruit is most popular? ....

2 Which type of fruit is least popular? ....

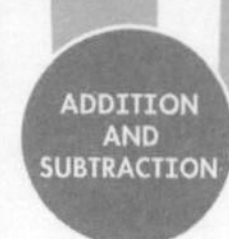

Drawing More

Draw more pictures in the boxes to help you solve the problems.

1 Tom has 3 blue T-shirts.
Then his dad buys him 2 red ones.
How many T-shirts does he have now?

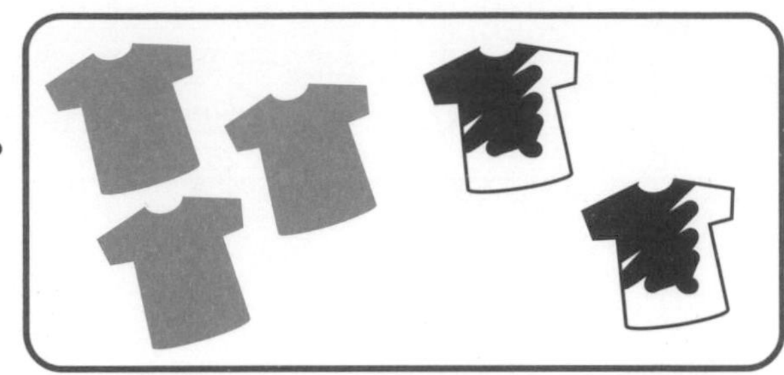

3 + 2 = ☐

2 Emma has 4 pencils. Then her mom gives her 3 more. How many pencils does she have now?

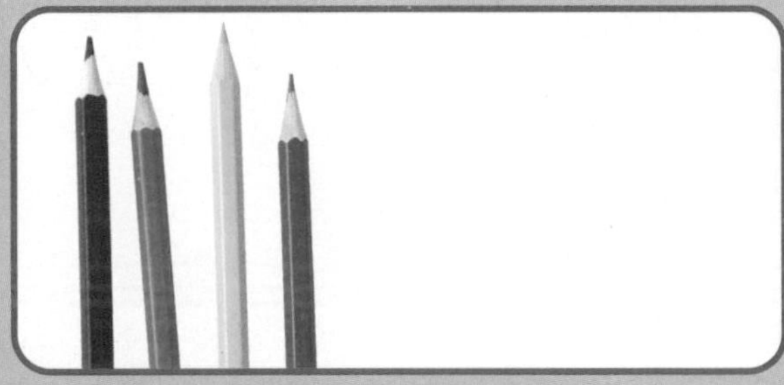

4 + 3 = ☐

3 Ben sees 10 stars in the sky.
Then 5 more come out.
How many stars are there now?

10 + 5 = ☐

4 Dad has 6 apples. Then he buys 6 more. How many apples does he have now?

6 + 6 = ☐

5 Luna sees 12 boats.
Then 4 more set sail.
How many boats are there now?

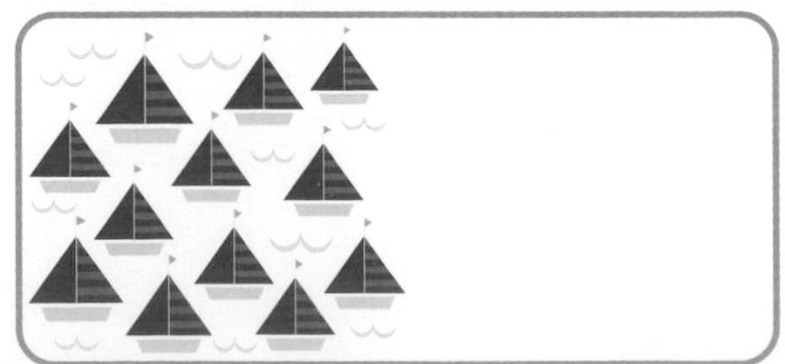

12 + 4 = ☐

Crossing Out

Cross out pictures to help you solve the problems.

1 A tree has 7 pears.
Then 2 fall off. How many pears are on the tree now?

$7 - 2 = \square$

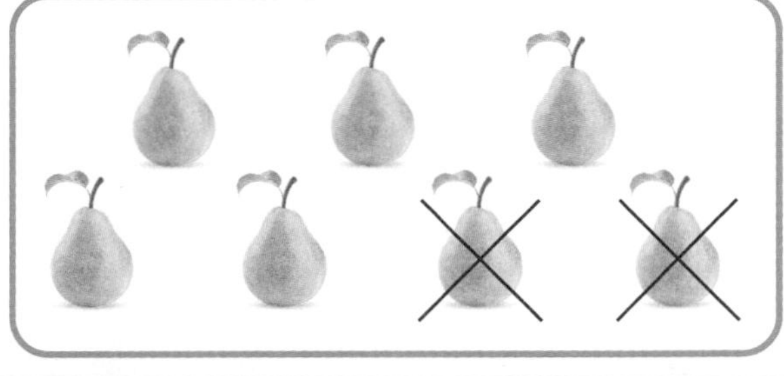

2 A mechanic has 9 cars to fix.
She fixes 3. How many cars does she have left to fix?

$9 - 3 = \square$

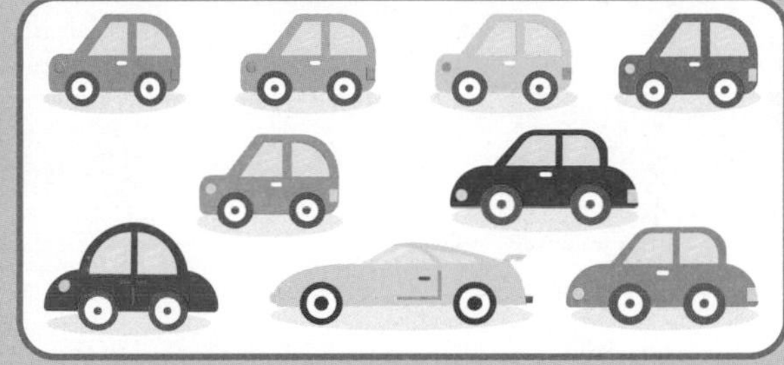

3 Jack has 14 candies. He eats 4.
How many candies does he have left?

$14 - 4 = \square$

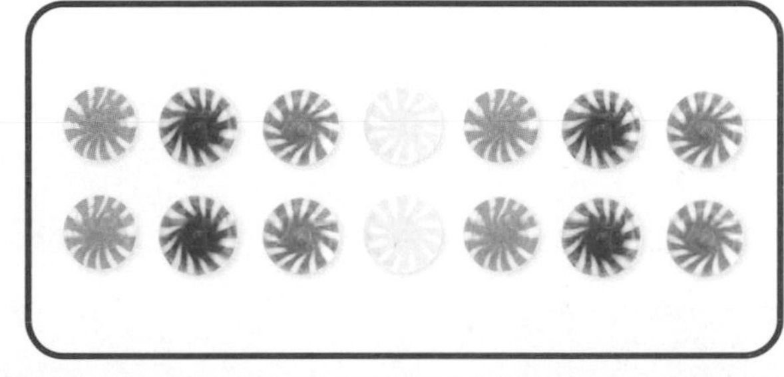

4 A farmer has 15 pigs.
He sells 10 of them.
How many pigs does he have left?

$15 - 10 = \square$

5 Daisy has 18 flowers.
She gives away 9.
How many does she have left?

$18 - 9 = \square$

Add to 10

Time how long it takes you to solve these addition problems.
Then, on another day, erase the answers and try to beat your time.

9 + 1 = ☐

4 + 2 = ☐

7 + 1 = ☐

1 + 1 = ☐

6 + 1 = ☐

5 + 4 = ☐

3 + 2 = ☐

5 + 1 = ☐

3 + 3 = ☐

4 + 1 = ☐

6 + 3 = ☐

5 + 5 = ☐

3 + 1 = ☐

7 + 2 = ☐

2 + 1 = ☐

8 + 2 = ☐

4 + 4 = ☐

6 + 4 = ☐

6 + 2 = ☐

5 + 2 = ☐

5 + 3 = ☐

7 + 3 = ☐

4 + 3 = ☐

8 + 1 = ☐

The first time I did this, my time was ....

The second time I did this, my time was ....

Subtract Below 10

Time how long it takes you to solve these subtraction problems. Then, on another day, erase the answers and try to beat your time.

10 – 1 = ☐	5 – 4 = ☐	7 – 3 = ☐
8 – 7 = ☐	9 – 5 = ☐	2 – 1 = ☐
10 – 4 = ☐	6 – 3 = ☐	9 – 2 = ☐
7 – 5 = ☐	8 – 3 = ☐	7 – 6 = ☐
3 – 2 = ☐	8 – 6 = ☐	10 – 3 = ☐
9 – 3 = ☐	4 – 2 = ☐	7 – 4 = ☐
10 – 7 = ☐	8 – 4 = ☐	5 – 3 = ☐
9 – 8 = ☐	10 – 6 = ☐	6 – 4 = ☐

The first time I did this, my time was ....

The second time I did this, my time was ....

The Meaning Of Equals

Write **T** for true if the two sides of the equation are equal.
Write **F** for false if the two sides of the equation are unequal.

5 = 5 [T]

7 = 8 [F]

25 = 25 [ ]

2 + 6 = 8 [ ]

15 + 3 = 18 [ ]

12 + 2 = 10 [ ]

14 = 10 + 5 [ ]

7 = 3 + 4 [ ]

6 + 3 = 3 + 6 [ ]

13 + 4 = 5 + 13 [ ]

2 + 3 = 2 + 2 [ ]

5 + 3 = 4 + 4 [ ]

12 + 3 = 8 + 5 [ ]

14 + 2 = 13 + 2 [ ]

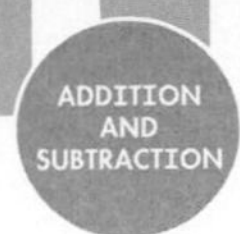

The Meaning Of Equals

Write **T** for true if the two sides of the equation are equal.
Write **F** for false if the two sides of the equation are unequal.

12 = 16 ☐

68 = 68 ☐

99 = 100 ☐

7 – 3 = 4 ☐

10 – 2 = 6 ☐

15 – 2 = 13 ☐

10 = 14 – 4 ☐

8 = 9 – 5 ☐

6 – 3 = 7 – 4 ☐

5 – 2 = 5 – 3 ☐

10 – 8 = 14 – 4 ☐

15 – 7 = 17 – 9 ☐

10 – 4 = 3 + 3 ☐

16 + 3 = 20 – 1 ☐

Addition Pairs

You can add numbers in any order. **2 + 3 = 5** and **3 + 2 = 5**.
Use this commutative property to solve problems.

2 + 3 = 5 so 3 + 2 = 5

5 + 3 = 8	so	3 + 5 = 8
4 + 2 = 6	so	2 + 4 = ☐
7 + 3 = 10	so	3 + 7 = ☐
10 + 8 = 18	so	8 + 10 = ☐
5 + 7 = 12	so	7 + 5 = ☐
11 + 4 = 15	so	4 + ☐ = 15
8 + 9 = 17	so	☐ + 8 = 17
7 + 6 = 13	so	6 + ☐ = 13
9 + 9 = 18	so	☐ + 9 = 18

Subtraction Pairs

Use the first subtraction problem in each row to help you solve the next one.

5 - 3 = 2 so 5 - 2 = 3

7 – 3 = 4	so	7 – 4 = [3]
6 – 5 = 1	so	6 – 1 = [ ]
10 – 8 = 2	so	10 – 2 = [ ]
12 – 3 = 9	so	12 – 9 = [ ]
15 – 6 = 9	so	15 – 9 = [ ]
8 – 5 = 3	so	8 – [ ] = 5
6 – 4 = 2	so	[ ] – 2 = 4
10 – 6 = 4	so	10 – [ ] = 6
12 – 3 = 9	so	[ ] – 9 = 3

Double Plus One

Use your doubles knowledge and add one to solve these problems.

5 + 5 = 10 so 5 + 6 = 11

7 + 7 = ☐ so 7 + 8 = ☐

2 + 2 = ☐ so 2 + 3 = ☐

4 + 4 = ☐ so 4 + 5 = ☐

3 + 3 = ☐ so 3 + 4 = ☐

1 + 1 = ☐ so 1 + 2 = ☐

8 + 8 = ☐ so 8 + 9 = ☐

6 + 6 = ☐ so 6 + 7 = ☐

9 + 9 = ☐ so 9 + 10 = ☐

10 + 10 = ☐ so 10 + 11 = ☐

Add and Subtract

Use the addition problems to help you solve the subtraction problems.

7 + 5 = 12 so 12 – 7 = 5

5 + 8 = 13 so 13 – 5 = ☐

8 + 3 = 11 so 11 – 8 = ☐

14 + 5 = 19 so 19 – 14 = ☐

6 + 3 = 9 so 9 – 3 = ☐

12 + 6 = 18 so 18 – 12 = ☐

9 + 5 = 14 so 14 – 5 = ☐

7 + 6 = 13 so 13 – 7 = ☐

5 + 4 = 9 so 9 – 4 = ☐

15 + 3 = 18 so 18 – 15 = ☐

Make 10 to Add

Use the ten frames to help you solve the problems.

Color the dots to show **8** + **4**.

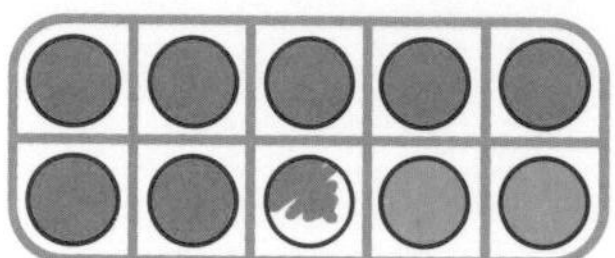

10 + 2 = 12

so 8 + 4 =

Color the dots to show **9** + **5**.

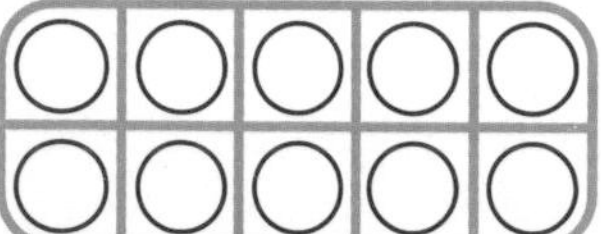

10 + 4 =

so 9 + 5 =

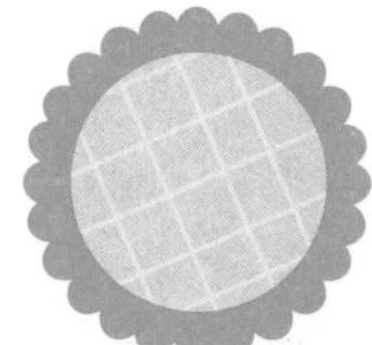

Color the dots to show **7** + **4**.

10 + 1 =

so 7 + 4 =

Color the dots to show **8** + **6**.

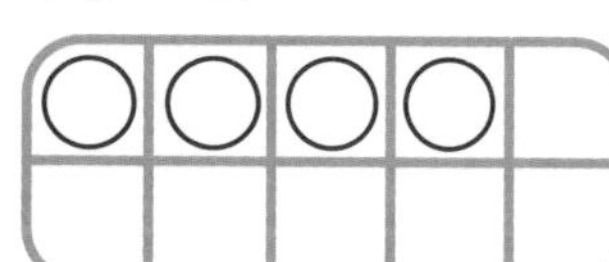

10 + 4 =

so 8 + 6 =

Color the dots to show **7** + **6**.

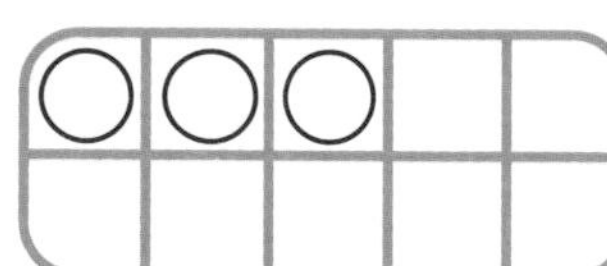

10 + 3 =

so 7 + 6 =

Color the dots to show **6** + **5**.

10 + 1 =

so 6 + 5 =

Color the dots to show **9** + **7**.

10 + 6 =

so 9 + 7 =

Make 10 to Add

Circle the two numbers in each problem that add up to make 10. Then add the remaining number to solve the problem.

③ + ⑦ + 5	=	10 + 5	=	15
4 + 6 + 2	=	10 + ☐	=	☐
2 + 1 + 8	=	10 + ☐	=	☐
5 + 8 + 5	=	10 + ☐	=	☐
6 + 7 + 3	=	10 + ☐	=	☐
6 + 4 + 3	=	10 + ☐	=	☐
9 + 1 + 4	=	10 + ☐	=	☐
7 + 5 + 3	=	10 + ☐	=	☐
8 + 2 + 7	=	10 + ☐	=	☐

Make 10 to Add

Break the second number into two so you'll be able to make 10.
Circle the numbers that make 10 to help solve the problem.

7 + 5	=	⑦ + ③	+ 2	=	10 +	2	=	12
9 + 2	=	9 + ☐	+ ☐	=	10 +	☐	=	☐
6 + 9	=	6 + ☐	+ ☐	=	10 +	☐	=	☐
4 + 7	=	4 + ☐	+ ☐	=	10 +	☐	=	☐
8 + 4	=	8 + ☐	+ ☐	=	10 +	☐	=	☐
3 + 9	=	3 + ☐	+ ☐	=	10 +	☐	=	☐
8 + 7	=	8 + ☐	+ ☐	=	10 +	☐	=	☐
5 + 8	=	5 + ☐	+ ☐	=	10 +	☐	=	☐
8 + 6	=	8 + ☐	+ ☐	=	10 +	☐	=	☐

Subtract to 10

Make subtraction easier by subtracting to 10 first. Cross out dots on the ten frames so you can see what you are taking away.

Cross out **9** to show **17 – 9**.

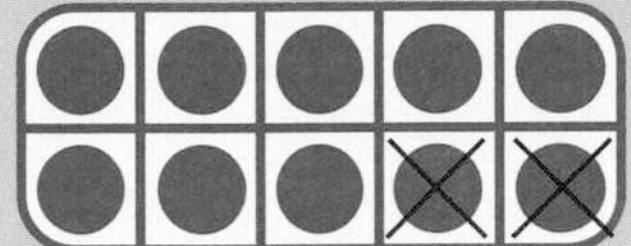
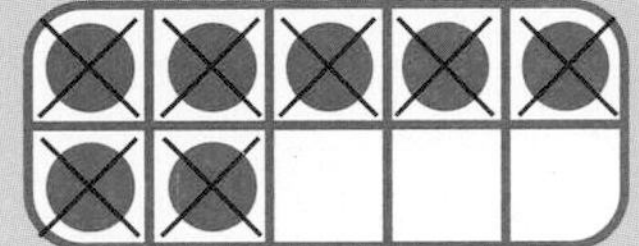

17 – 7 = 10
and 10 – 2 = 8
so 17 – 9 = 8

Cross out **6** to show **11 – 6**.

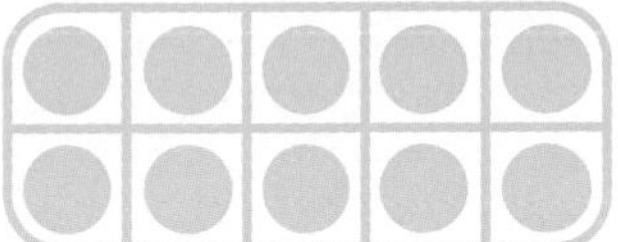

11 – ☐ = 10
and 10 – ☐ = ☐
so 11 – 6 = ☐

Cross out **5** to show **13 – 5**.

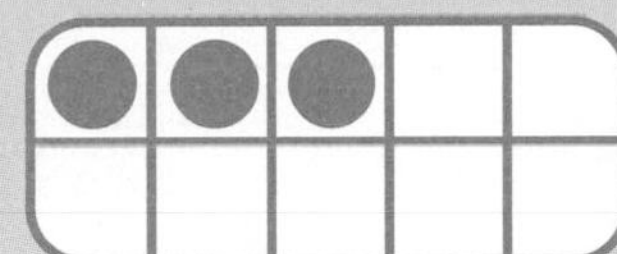

13 – ☐ = 10
and 10 – ☐ = ☐
so 13 – 5 = ☐

Cross out **6** to show **15 – 6**.

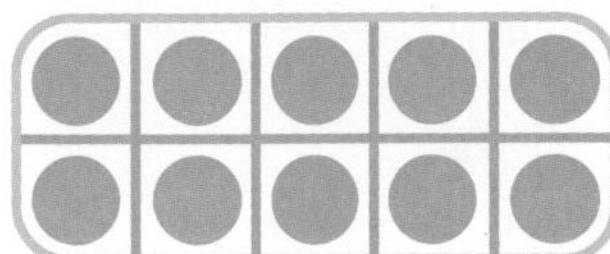
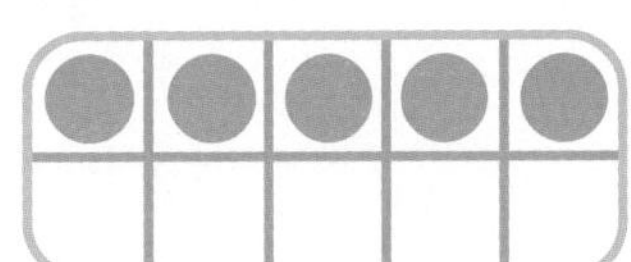

15 – ☐ = 10
and 10 – ☐ = ☐
so 15 – 6 = ☐

Cross out **8** to show **14 – 8**.

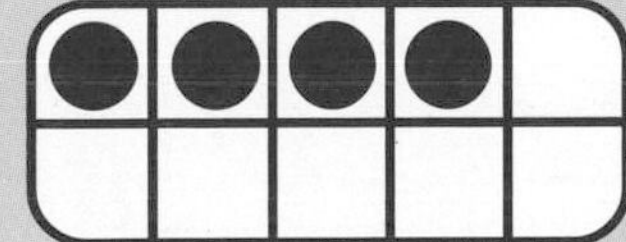

14 – ☐ = 10
and 10 – ☐ = ☐
so 14 – 8 = ☐

Cross out **9** to show **16 – 9**.

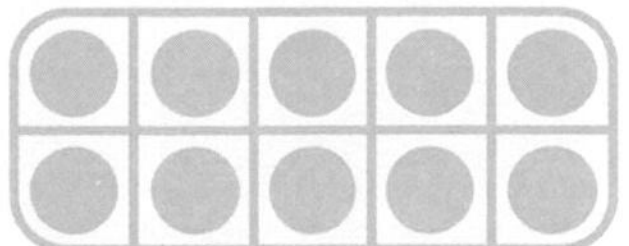
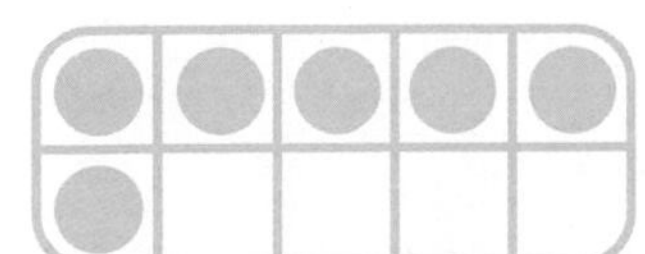

16 – ☐ = 10
and 10 – ☐ = ☐
so 16 – 9 = ☐

Subtract to 10

Break the second number into two so you'll be able to make 10. Circle the numbers that subtract to 10 to help solve each problem.

17 – 9 =	(17) –	(7) –	2 =	10 –	2 =	8
11 – 2 =	11 –	☐ –	☐ =	10 –	☐ =	☐
15 – 9 =	15 –	☐ –	☐ =	10 –	☐ =	☐
12 – 5 =	12 –	☐ –	☐ =	10 –	☐ =	☐
14 – 6 =	14 –	☐ –	☐ =	10 –	☐ =	☐
11 – 4 =	11 –	☐ –	☐ =	10 –	☐ =	☐
13 – 5 =	13 –	☐ –	☐ =	10 –	☐ =	☐
16 – 9 =	16 –	☐ –	☐ =	10 –	☐ =	☐
12 – 9 =	12 –	☐ –	☐ =	10 –	☐ =	☐

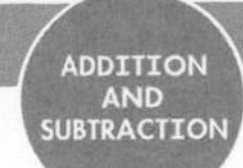

Addition Word Problems

Solve the word problems and show your work in the box.

1 Addison had 6 toy trains.
Then she got 4 more.
How many did she have now?

2 Max had 6 toy horses.
Then he won 5 more.
How many did he have now?

3 A teacher had 15 children in his class.
Then 4 more children joined.
How many did he have now?

4 On Saturday, Mom saw 6 geese fly past.
On Sunday, she saw 7 more.
How many did she see altogether?

5 Owen knew facts about 13 dinosaurs.
Then he found out about 5 more.
How many did he know about now?

6 Violet picked 10 peaches.
Then she picked the same number again.
How many did she pick altogether?

Subtraction Word Problems

Solve the word problems and show your work in the box.

1 Levi had 10 lollipops.
He gave 5 to his sister.
How many did he have left?

2 Penny counted 14 cars in the parking lot. 7 cars drove out.
How many were left?

3 Ollie opened a pack of 20 cookies.
He ate 3.
How many were left?

4 Harper saw 13 ladybugs.
6 ladybugs flew off.
How many were left?

5 There are 11 books in John's favorite series.
So far, he has read 5 of them.
How many more are left to read?

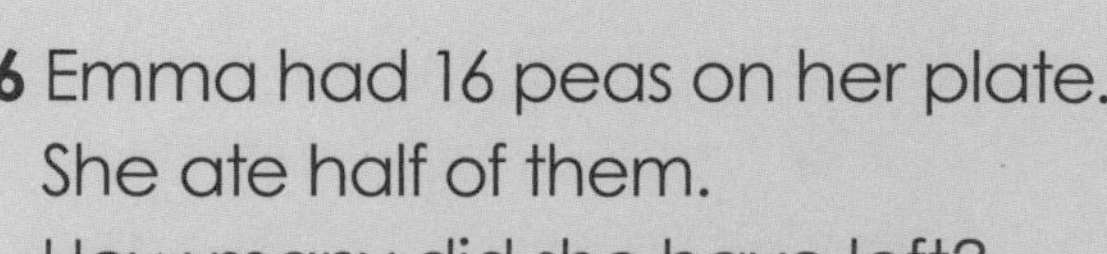

6 Emma had 16 peas on her plate.
She ate half of them.
How many did she have left?

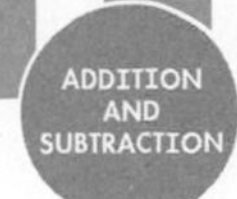

Three-Number Problems

Solve the word problems and show your work in the box.

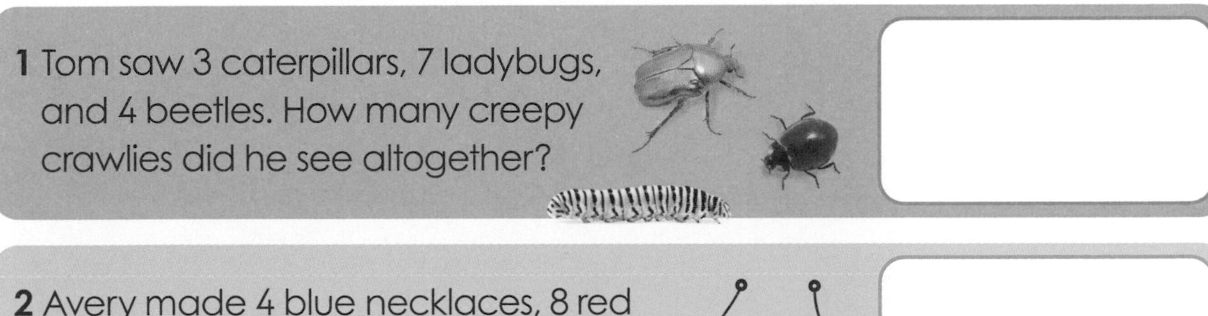

1 Tom saw 3 caterpillars, 7 ladybugs, and 4 beetles. How many creepy crawlies did he see altogether?

2 Avery made 4 blue necklaces, 8 red necklaces, and 6 orange necklaces. How many did she make altogether?

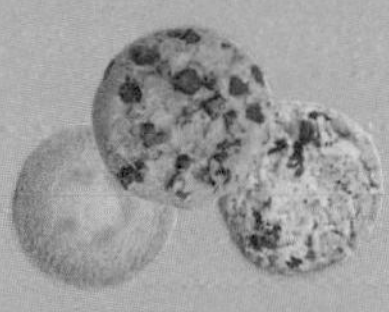

3 Ethan baked 7 chocolate cookies, 2 plain cookies, and 8 raisin cookies. How many did he bake altogether?

4 Amelia drew 10 cats, 4 dogs, and 6 rabbits. How many animals did she draw altogether?

5 Mason counted 9 oak trees, 7 beech trees, and 2 fir trees. How many trees did he count altogether?

6 Leah made cards for 5 aunts, 4 uncles, and 9 cousins. How many cards did she make altogether?

Finding Unknown Numbers

Fill in the boxes to finish the problems.

4 + ☐ = 10	7 + ☐ = 16	9 + ☐ = 15
☐ + 6 = 12	☐ + 9 = 14	☐ + 5 = 11
10 = 7 + ☐	18 = 8 + ☐	12 = 3 + ☐
8 = ☐ + 5	16 = ☐ + 5	9 = ☐ + 0
20 = 10 + ☐	20 = 2 + ☐	☐ + 5 = 5
7 + ☐ = 7	18 = ☐ + 7	☐ + 6 = 16

Finding Unknown Numbers

Fill in the boxes to finish the problems.

15 – ☐ = 10

14 – ☐ = 8

17 – ☐ = 12

☐ – 5 = 3

☐ – 7 = 7

☐ – 4 = 9

10 = 18 – ☐

16 = 19 – ☐

12 = 17 – ☐

8 = ☐ – 4

13 = ☐ – 6

4 = ☐ – 0

20 = 20 – ☐

10 = 20 – ☐

☐ – 0 = 3

7 – ☐ = 7

2D Shapes

Trace each two-dimensional shape and count its sides.

A square has 4 sides.

A rectangle has ☐ sides.

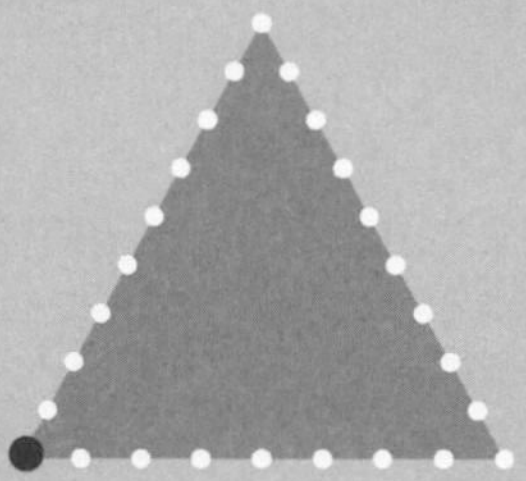

A triangle has ☐ sides.

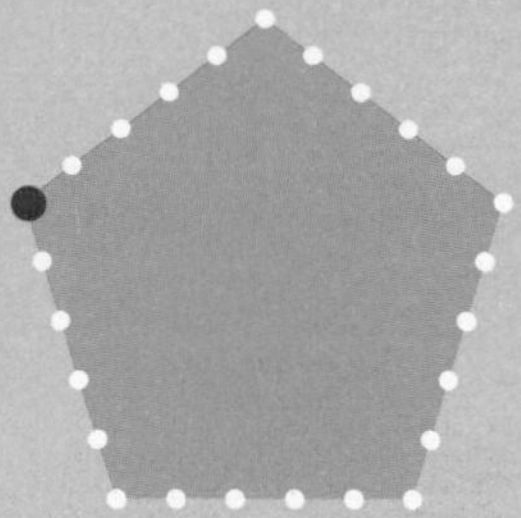

A pentagon has ☐ sides.

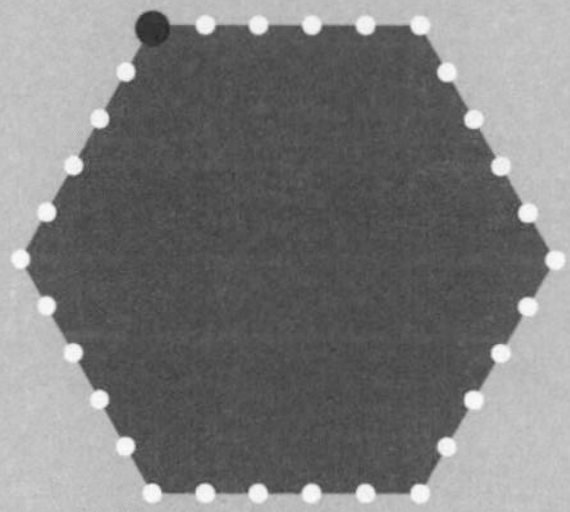

A hexagon has ☐ sides.

Draw the shapes.

square

hexagon

rectangle

triangle

pentagon

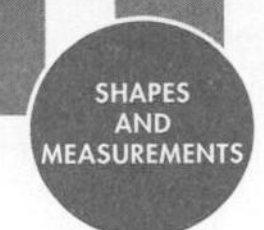

2D Shapes

Draw lines to match the shapes.

circle

triangle

square

rectangle

diamond

star

Finding Shapes

Shade the **square** objects **blue**.
Shade the **circular** objects **orange**.

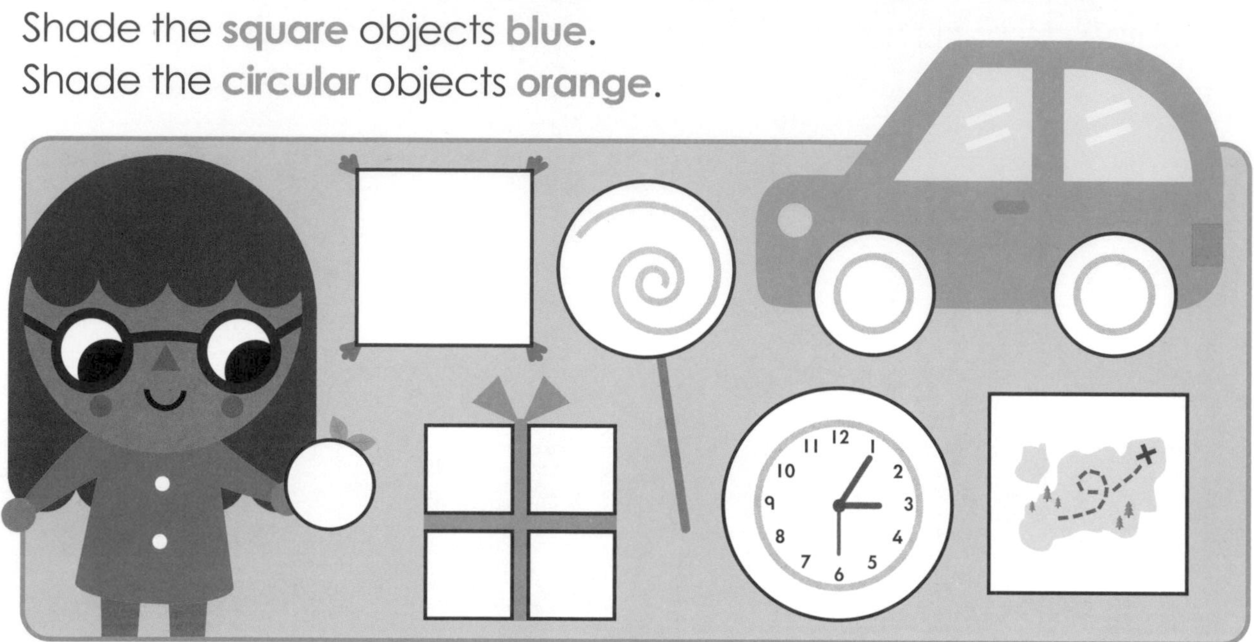

Count the triangles in each picture. Then write the number.

Count the rectangles in each picture. Then write the number.

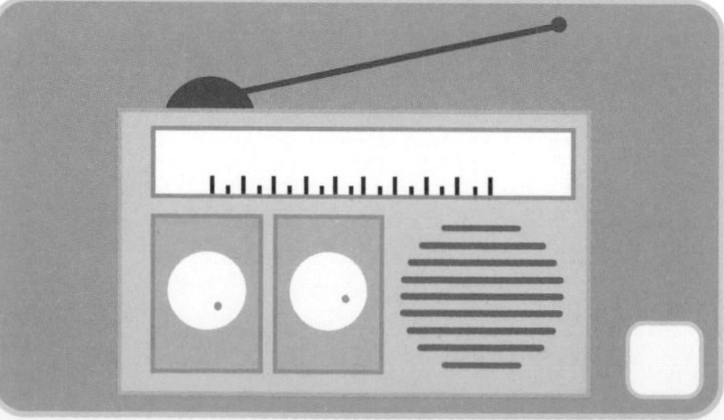

Counting Vertices

In a shape, the corner where two lines meet is called a vertex. Count the number of vertices in each shape.

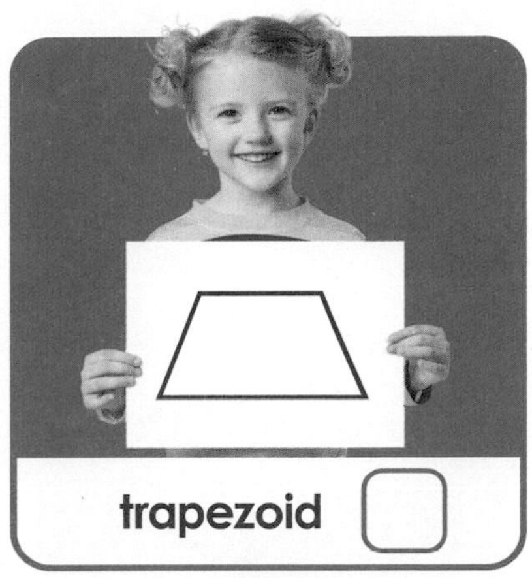

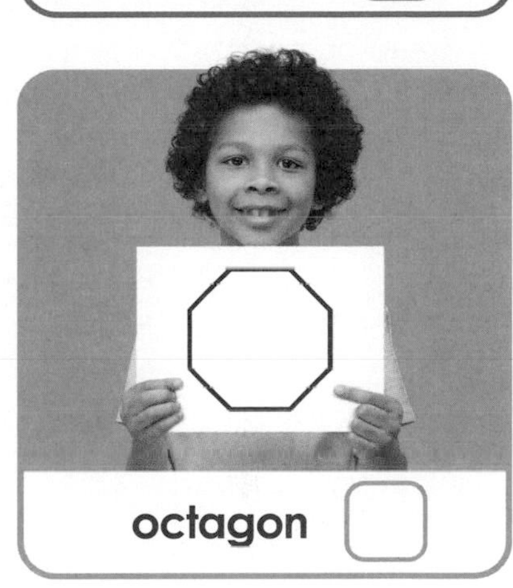

Draw lines to match the shapes with the vertex numbers.

3 vertices

4 vertices

5 vertices

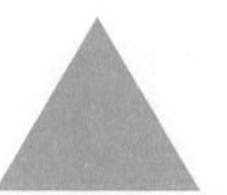

3D Shapes

Count the number of edges, faces (sides), and vertices (corners) on each three-dimensional shape.

CUBES

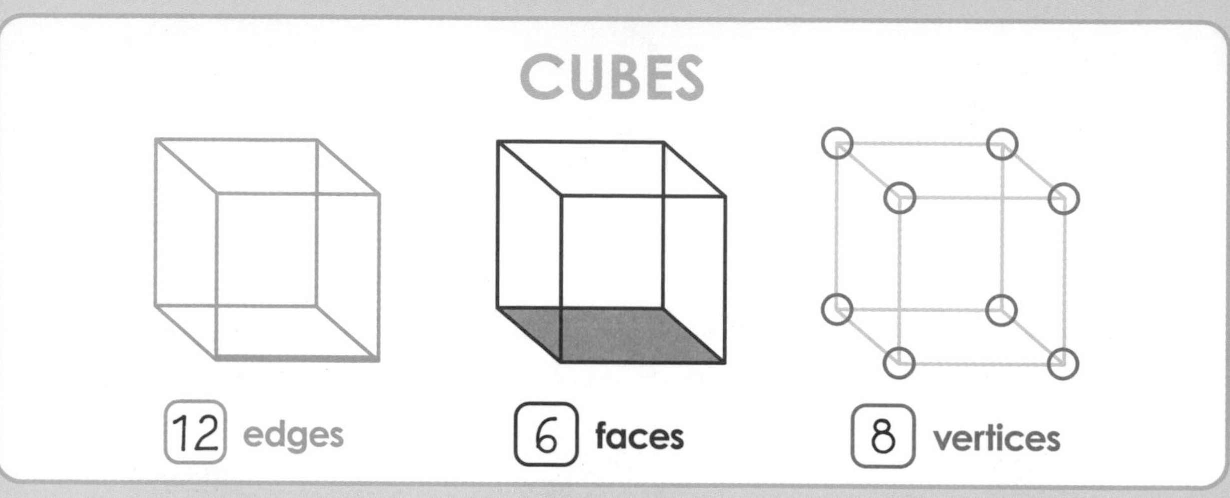

CUBOIDS

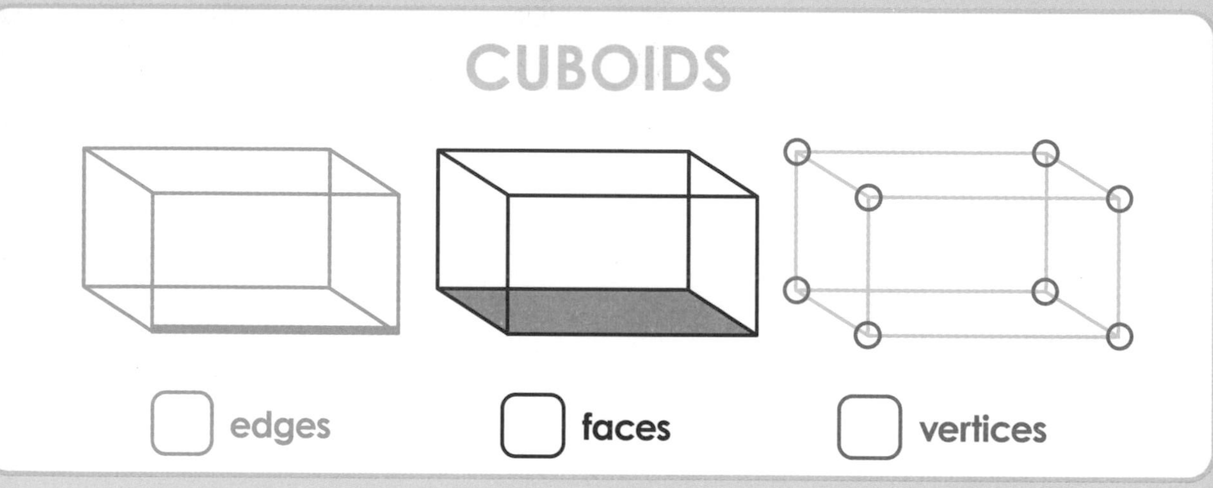

SQUARE PYRAMIDS

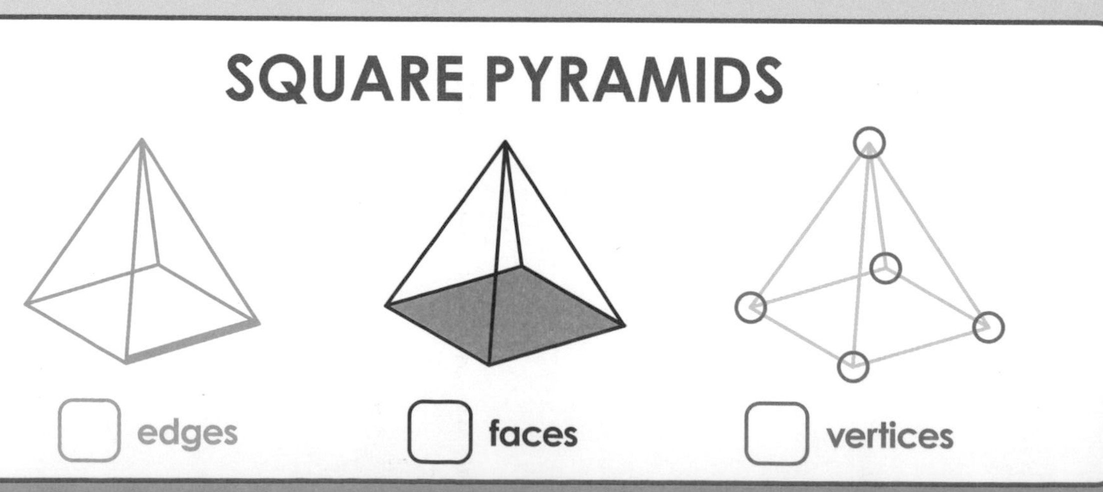

3D Shapes

Write **yes** or **no** after each question.

CONES

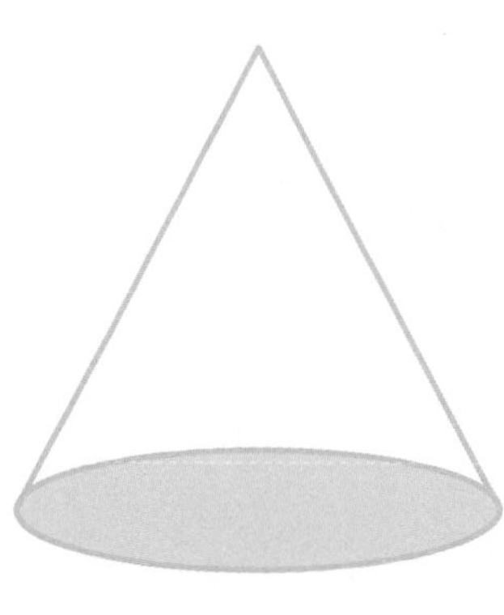

Does it have a pointed vertex? ....

Does it have a flat circular face? ....

Does it have a flat square face? ....

Does it have a curved face? ....

CYLINDERS

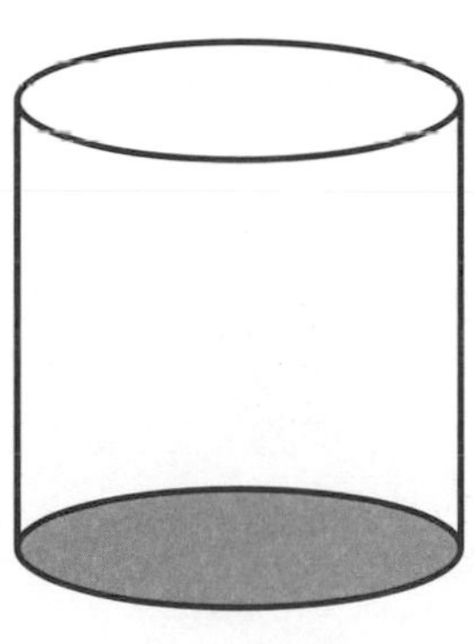

Does it have a curved face? ....

Does it have 2 flat circular faces? ....

Does it have a pentagon face? ....

Does it have 2 edges? ....

SPHERES

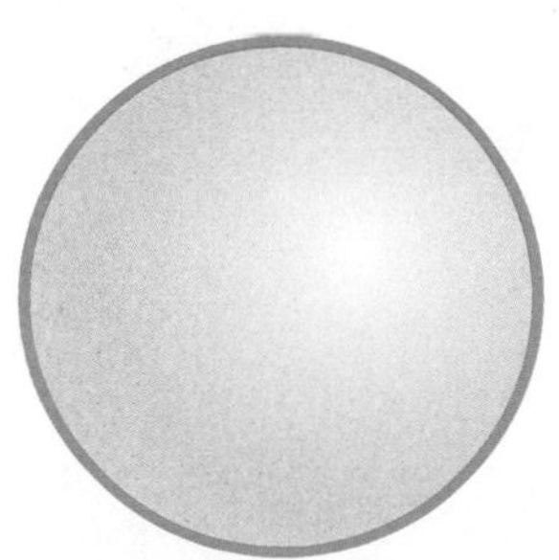

Does it have a flat face? ....

Does it have a curved face? ....

Does it have any vertices? ....

Does it have any edges? ....

Identifying Shapes

Sticker the shapes.

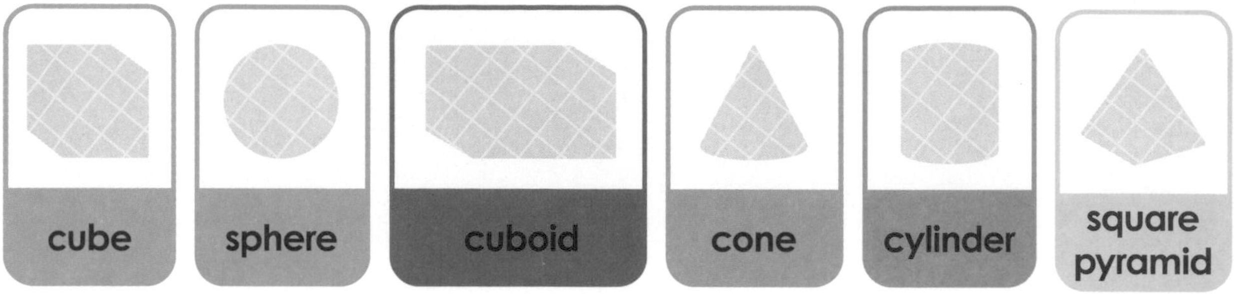

cube

sphere

cuboid

cone

cylinder

square pyramid

Count the 3D shapes.

There is ☐ sphere.

There are ☐ cones.

There are ☐ cylinders.

There are ☐ cubes.

There are ☐ other cuboids.

There are ☐ square pyramids.

2D or 3D?

2D shapes are flat. They have length and width.
3D shapes are not flat. They have length, width, and height.
Draw lines to sort the shapes into the categories.

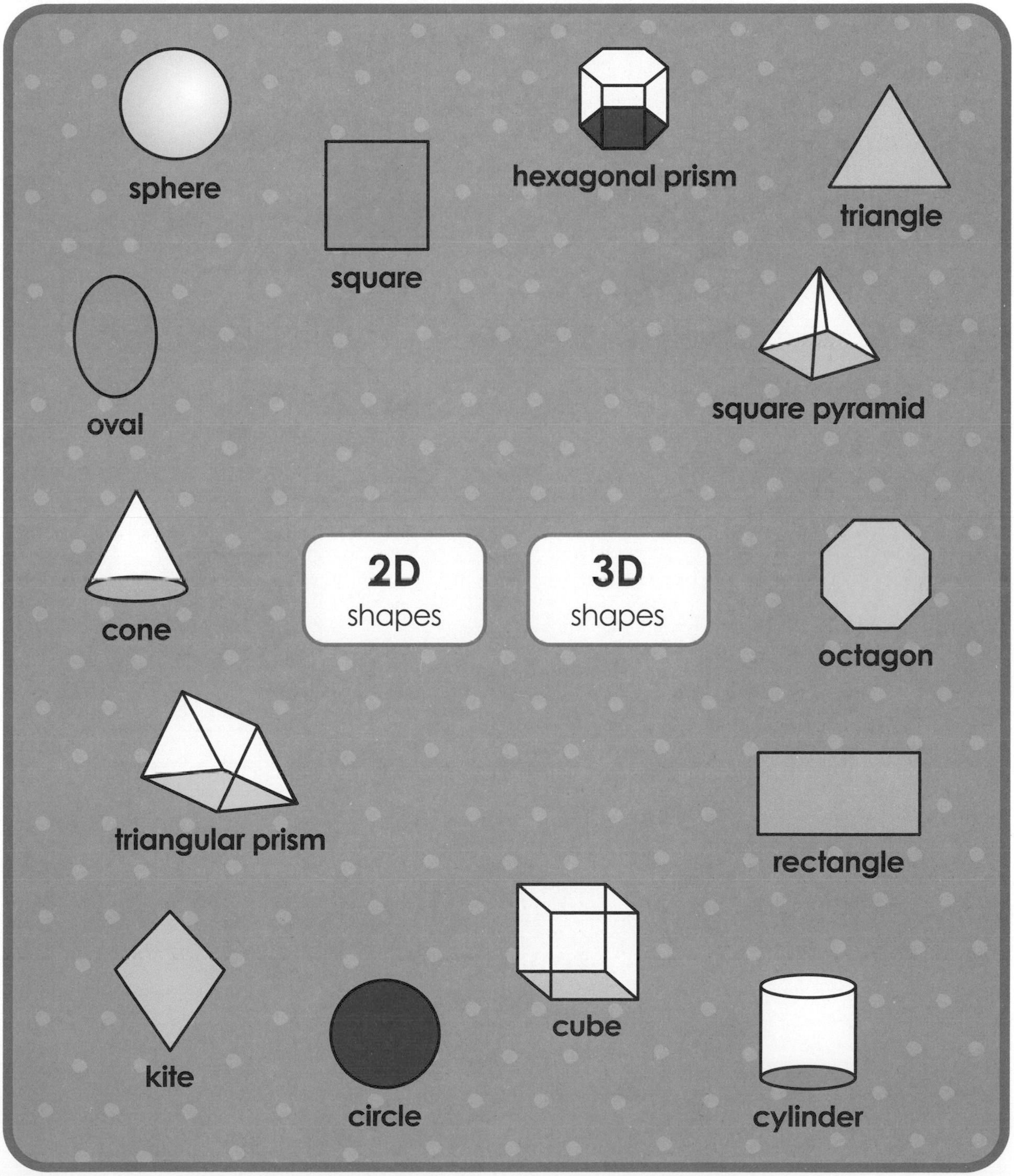

sphere

square

hexagonal prism

triangle

oval

square pyramid

cone

2D shapes

3D shapes

octagon

triangular prism

rectangle

kite

circle

cube

cylinder

Symmetry

Some shapes can be split up into halves that are mirror images of each other. These shapes are symmetrical. Circle the pictures that are symmetrical.

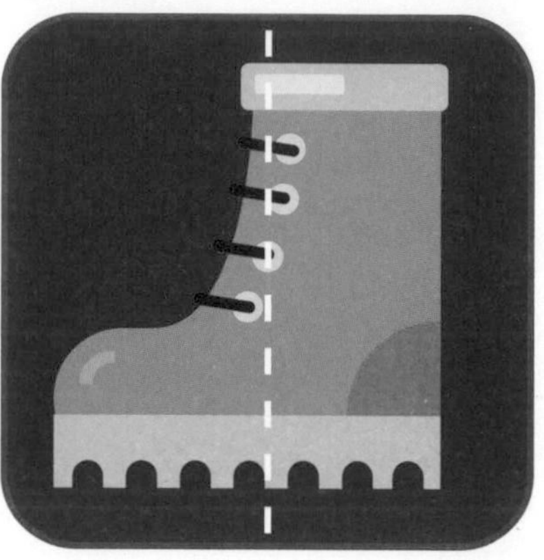

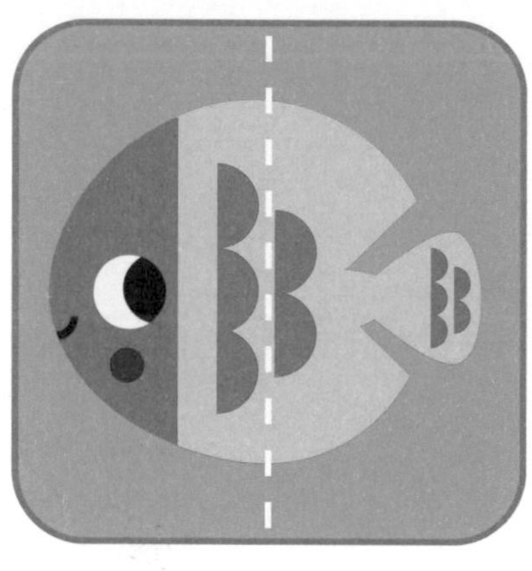

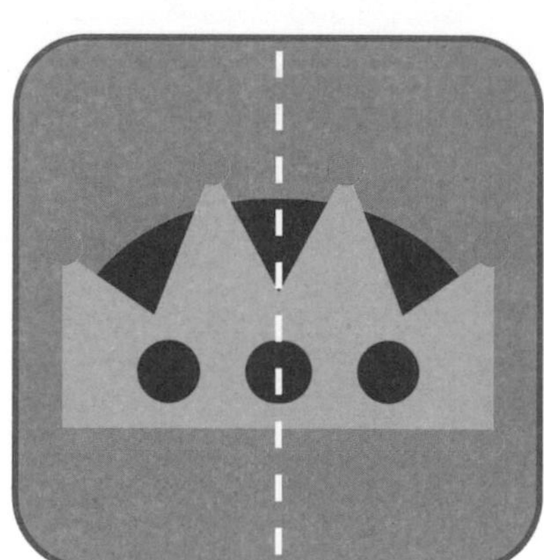

Symmetry

Use a ruler to draw a line of symmetry on each shape.

Use the grid to draw the other half of each picture. The final drawing should be symmetrical across the central black line.

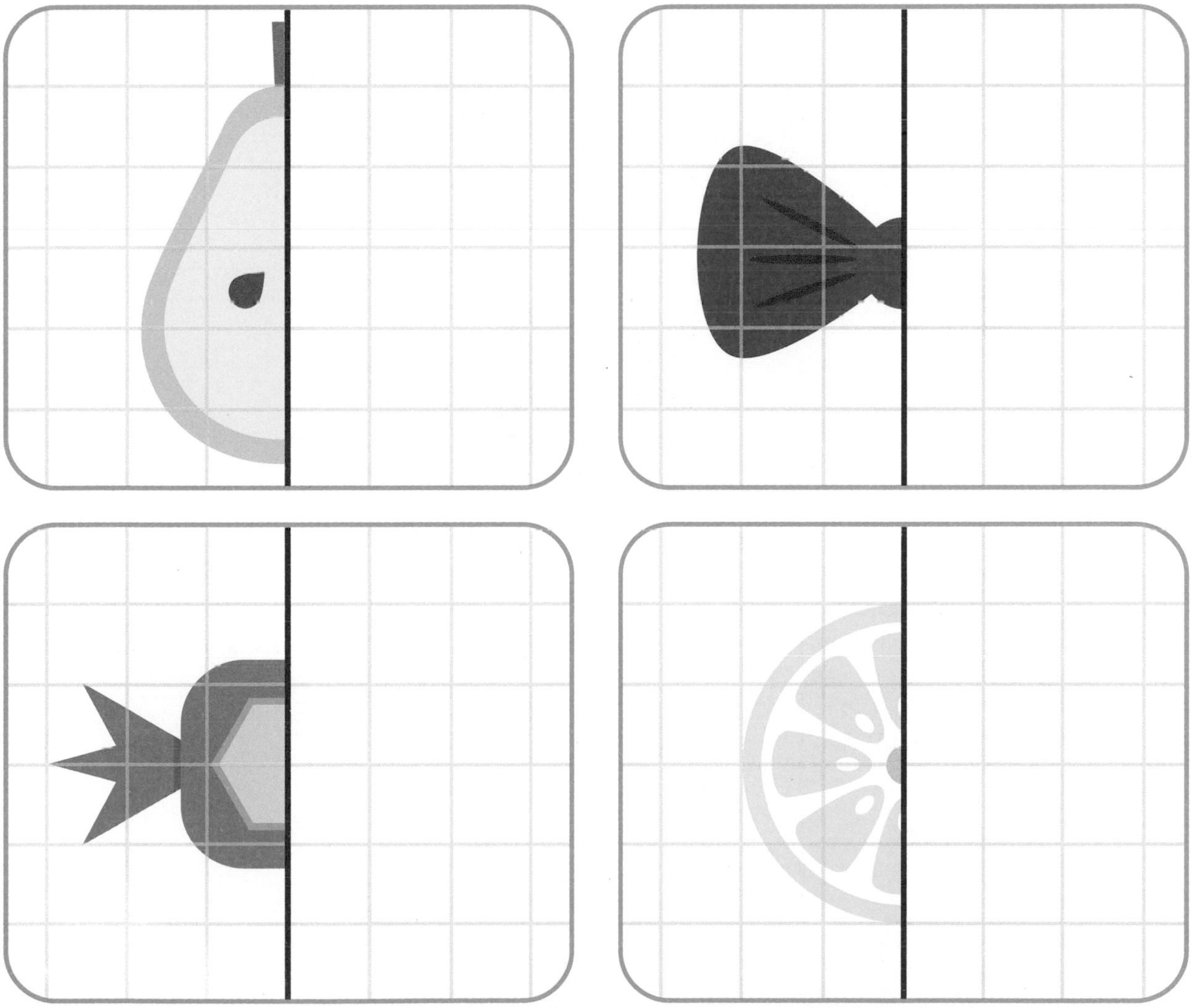

Measuring

Number the children from 1 to 3, from shortest to tallest.

We can measure the size of something by comparing it to something else. Use your hand to measure items.

How many hands high is your chair?

☐ hands

How many hands wide is your window?

☐ hands

How many hands long is your bed?

☐ hands

How many hands high is your kitchen sink from the ground?

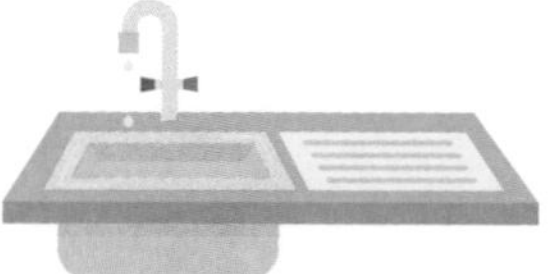

☐ hands

How many hands wide is your bedroom door?

☐ hands

How many hands long is your table?

☐ hands

Length

Draw lines to match objects that are the same length.

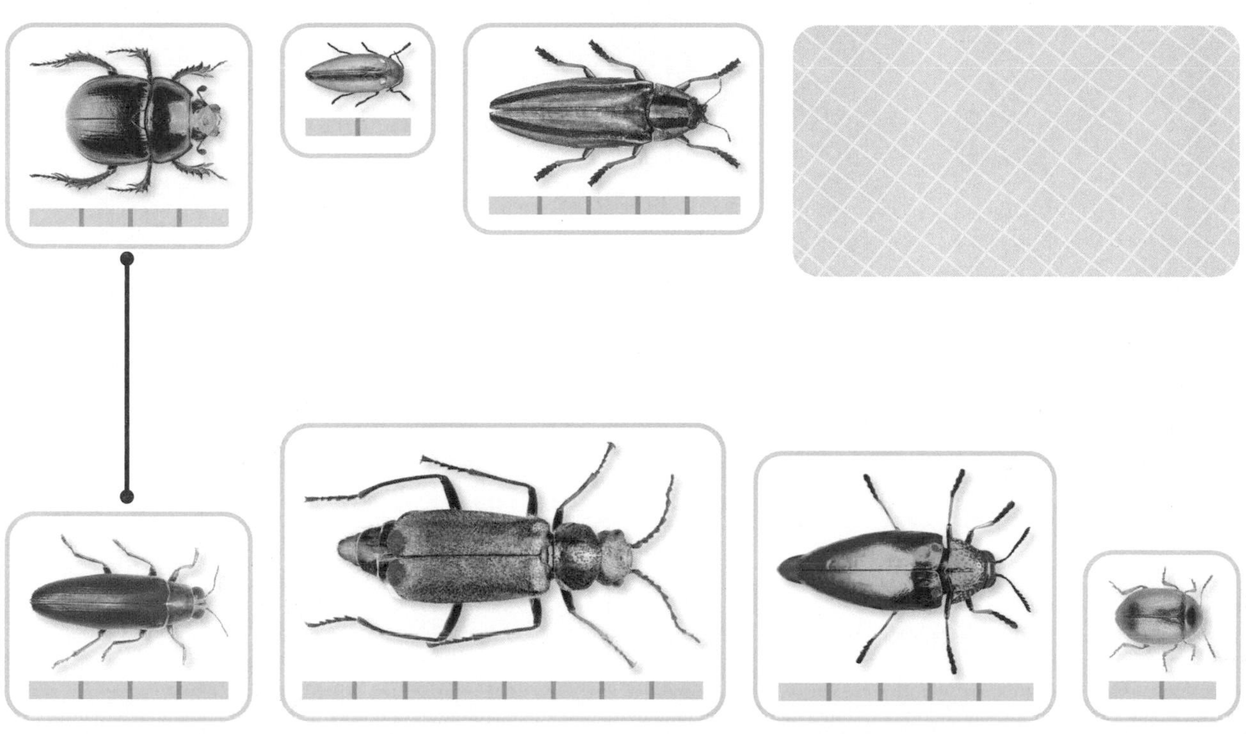

Color the crayons, and measure their lengths with the ruler.

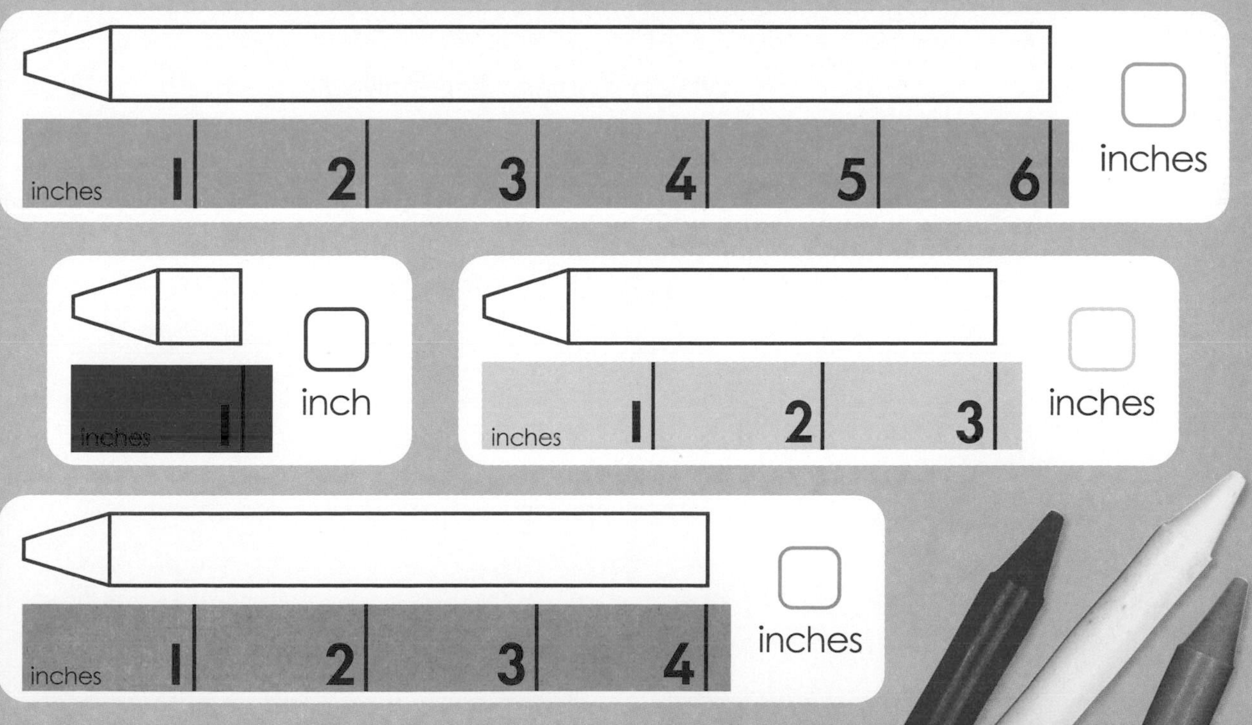

Height

Measure the height of each button with the ruler.

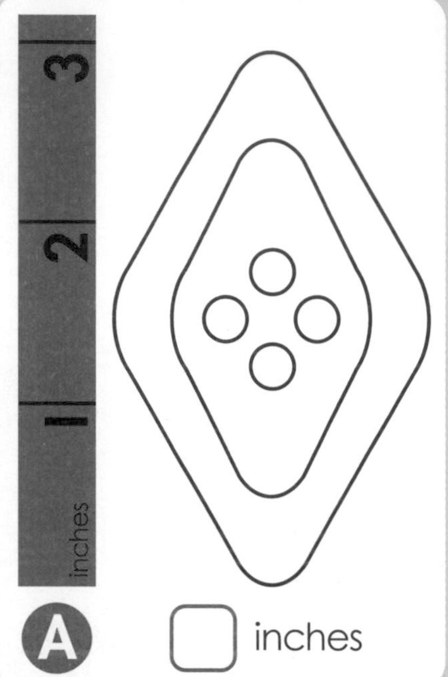

A ☐ inches

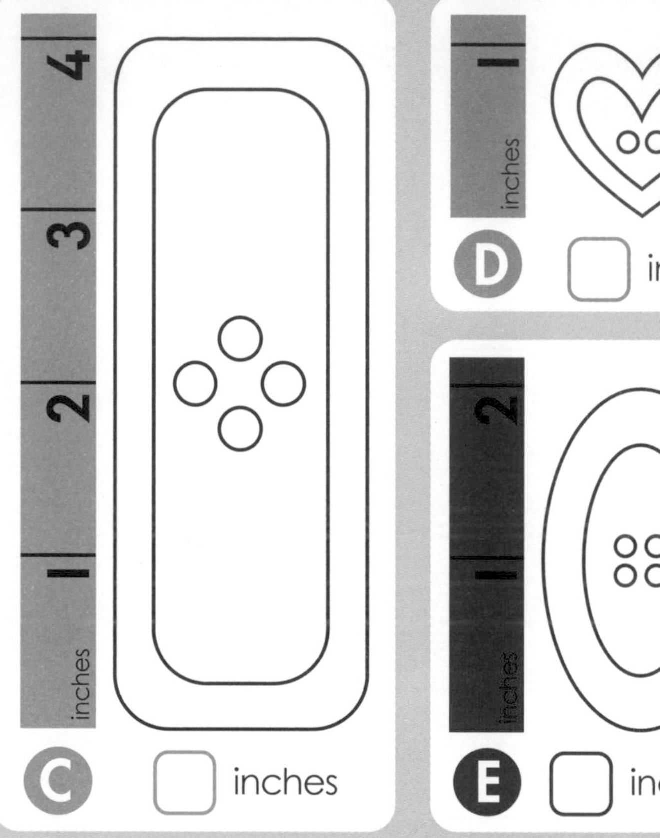

C ☐ inches

D ☐ inch

E ☐ inches

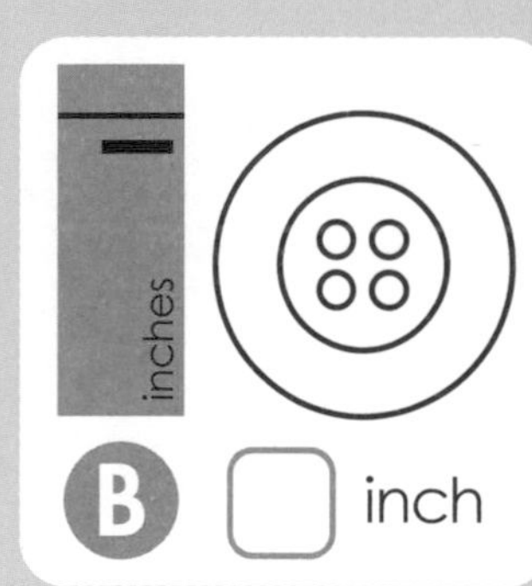

B ☐ inch

Which button is the tallest? ....

Which buttons are the shortest? ....

Cross out the incorrect word in each sentence.

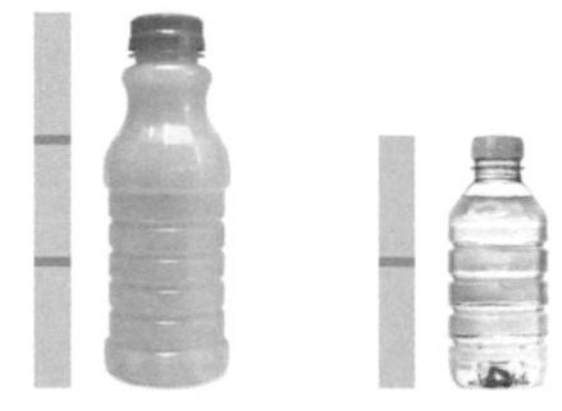

The juice bottle is **shorter / taller** than the water bottle.

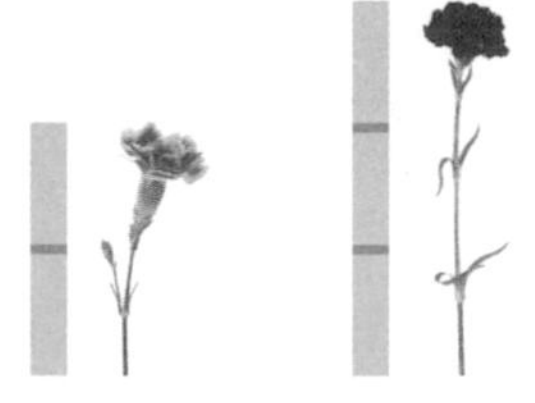

The pink flower is **shorter / taller** than the red flower.

Volume

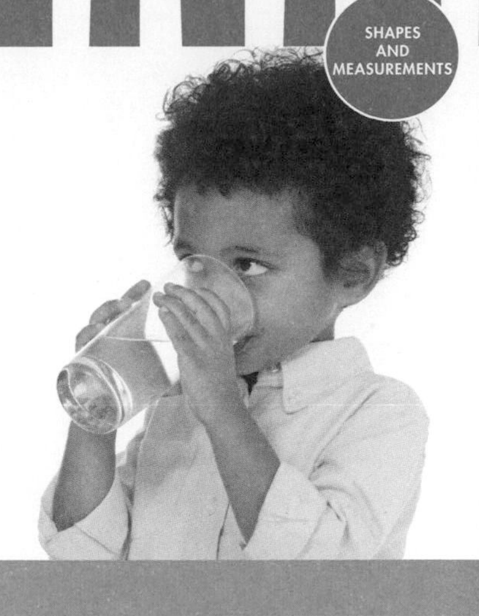

Number the cups from 1 to 3, from empty to full.

Check the answers.

Which box has the fewest eggs?

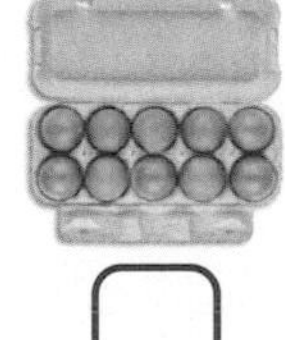

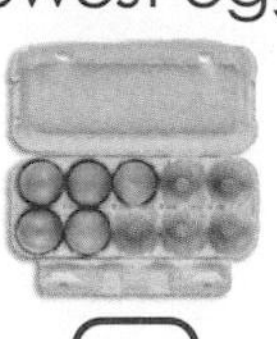

Which jar is less full?

Which bowl has the most fruit?

Which basket is empty?

How many cups of water are in each pitcher?

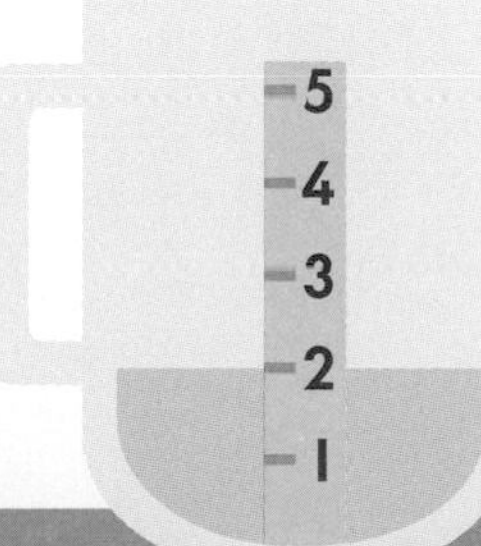

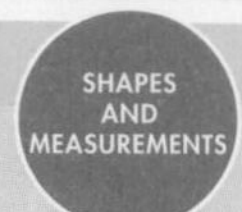

Weight

Circle the object in each pair that is heavier.

Circle the object in each pair that is lighter.

Fill in the missing word.

A **kite** is **lighter** than a **chair**.
A **truck** is **heavier** than a **chair**.

So, a **kite** is .... than a **truck**.

A **grape** is **lighter** than an **apple**.
An **apple** is **lighter** than a **melon**.

So, a **melon** is .... than a **grape**.

Weight

Circle the lightest item.

Circle the heaviest item.

Use addition to figure out the missing weights.

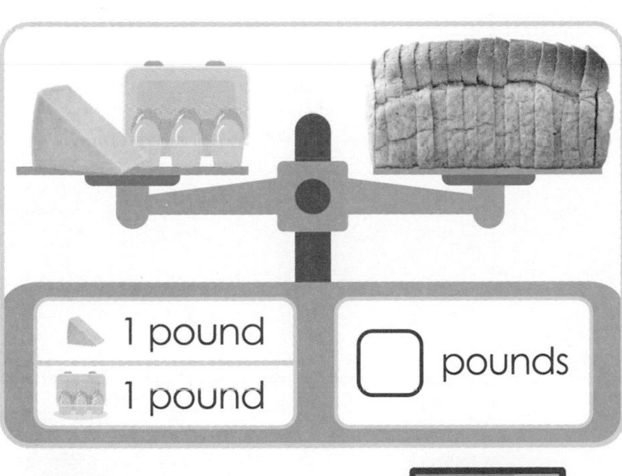

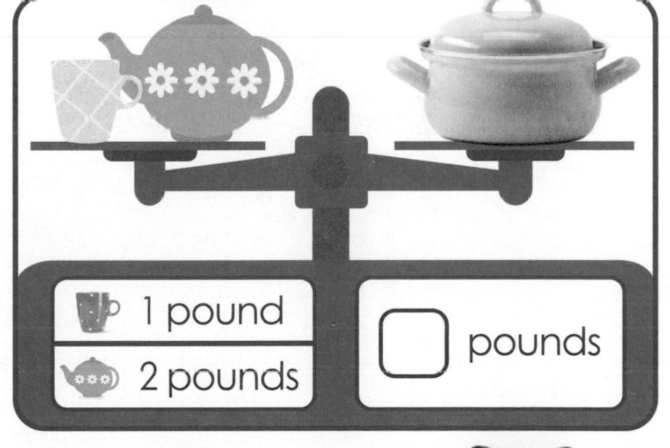

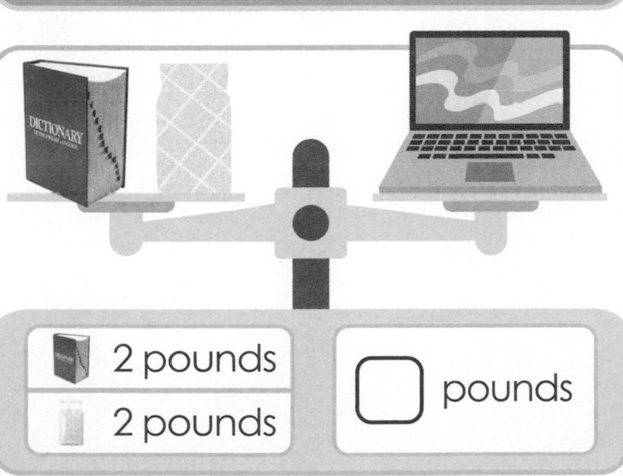

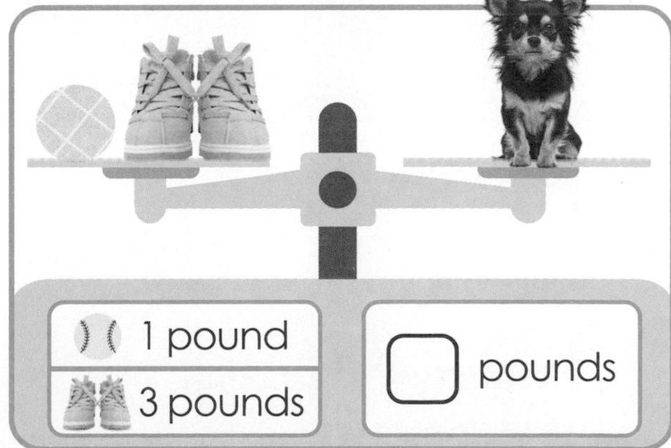

Clock Work

We use clocks to tell the time. The short hand shows the hour. What hour is each clock showing?

2 o'clock

☐ o'clock

☐ o'clock

☐ o'clock

☐ o'clock

☐ o'clock

The long hand on a clock shows the minutes. When the long hand points to 6, it is half past the hour. What time is each clock showing?

half-past 3

half-past ☐

half-past ☐

Draw the hands on the clocks.

4 o'clock

half-past 1

half-past 6

Digital Time

On a digital clock, the time is written in numbers.
12:00 means twelve o'clock, and 12:30 means half-past twelve.
What time do these digital clocks show?

01:00	06:30	12:00	07:30
[1] o'clock	half-past [6]	[ ] o'clock	half-past [ ]

11:00	10:30	03:00	05:00
[ ] o'clock	half-past [ ]	[ ] o'clock	[ ] o'clock

Fill in the digital clocks.

9 o'clock is **09:00** on a digital clock.

11 o'clock is **11:00** on a digital clock.

So, **10 o'clock** is

on a digital clock.

Half-past 5 is **05:30** on a digital clock.

Half-past 7 is **07:30** on a digital clock.

So, **half-past 9** is

on a digital clock.

Planet Earth

We live on planet Earth. The land is divided into continents and the water into oceans. Shade the oceans **blue** and the continents **green**.

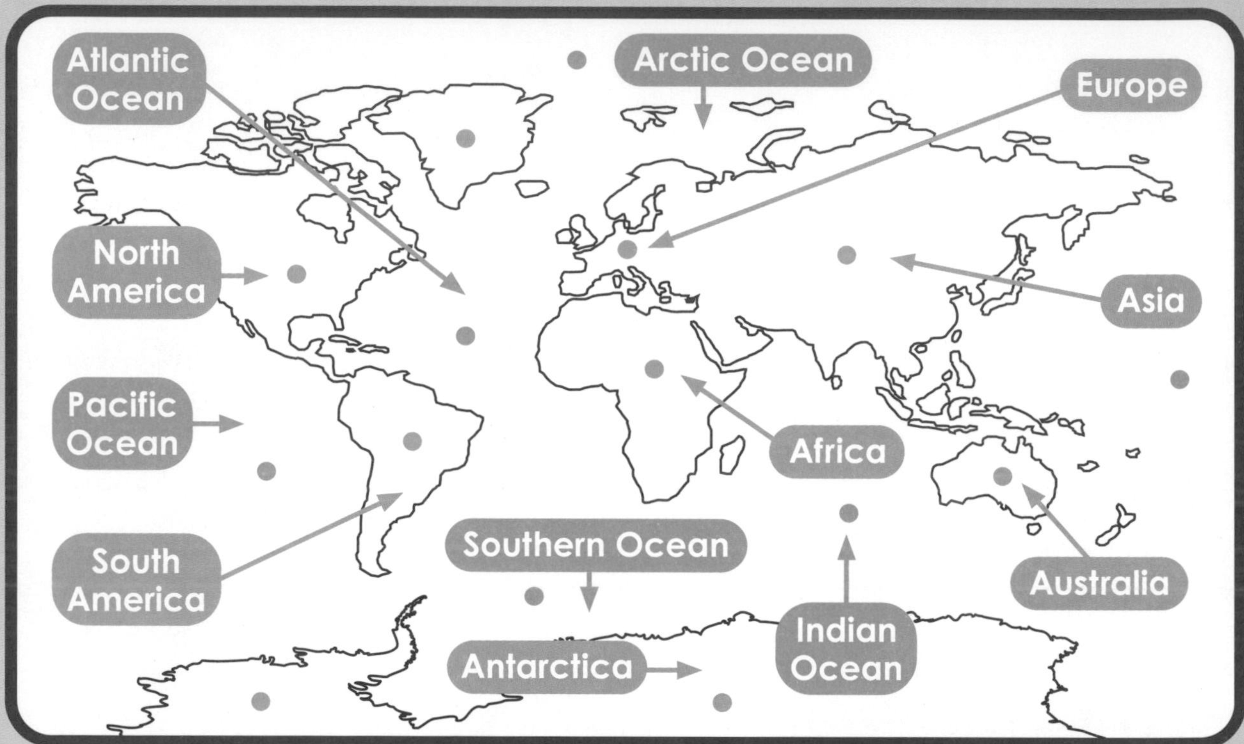

Fill in the missing words to describe where you live.

The continent I live on is called

....

The country I live in is called

....

My nearest ocean is

....

Inside the Earth

Earth is made up of three layers—the core in the center, then the mantle, and then the crust on the outside. Draw lines from the diagram to the correct labels.

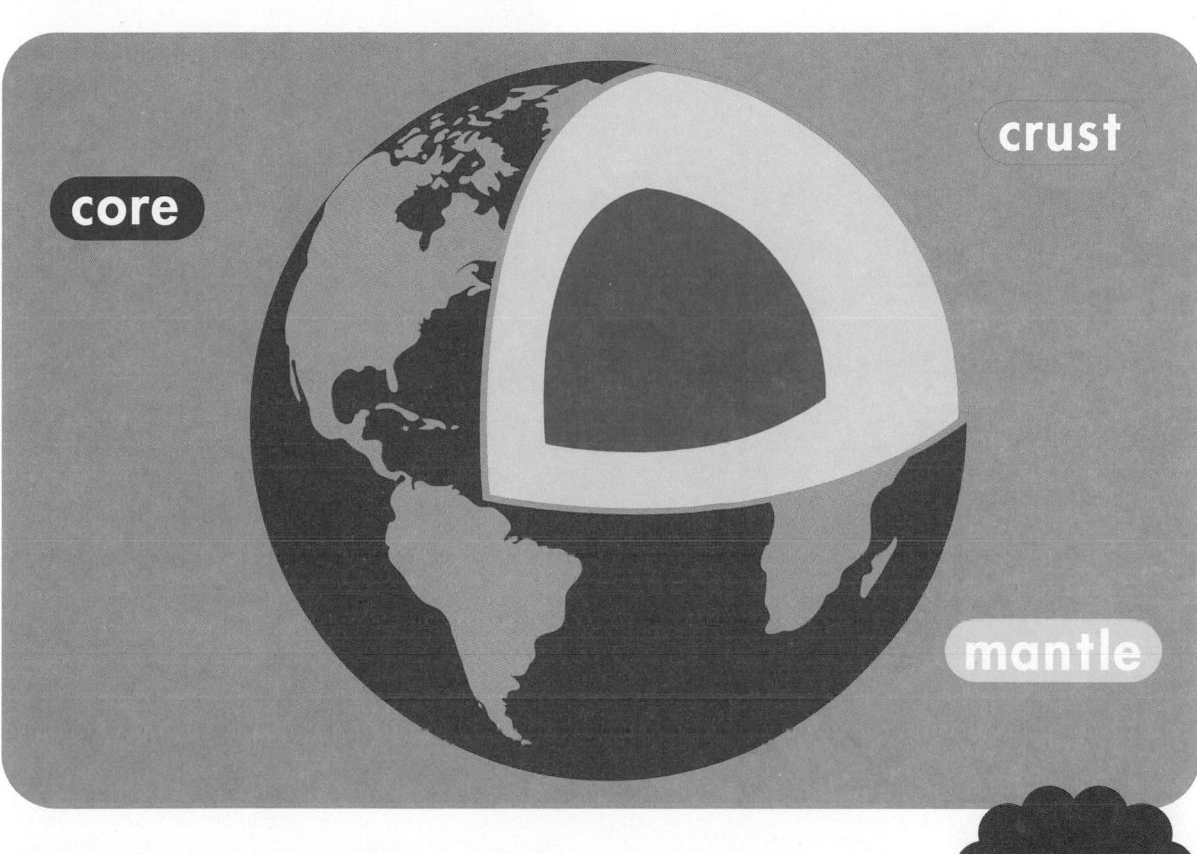

Write the missing words in these sentences.

core crust mantle three

Earth is made up of .... main layers.

At the center is the Earth's ....

The .... is in the middle, between the core and the crust.

The thinnest layer is the ...., which covers Earth's surface.

The Seasons

Many places have four seasons each year. Sticker the season name below each image.

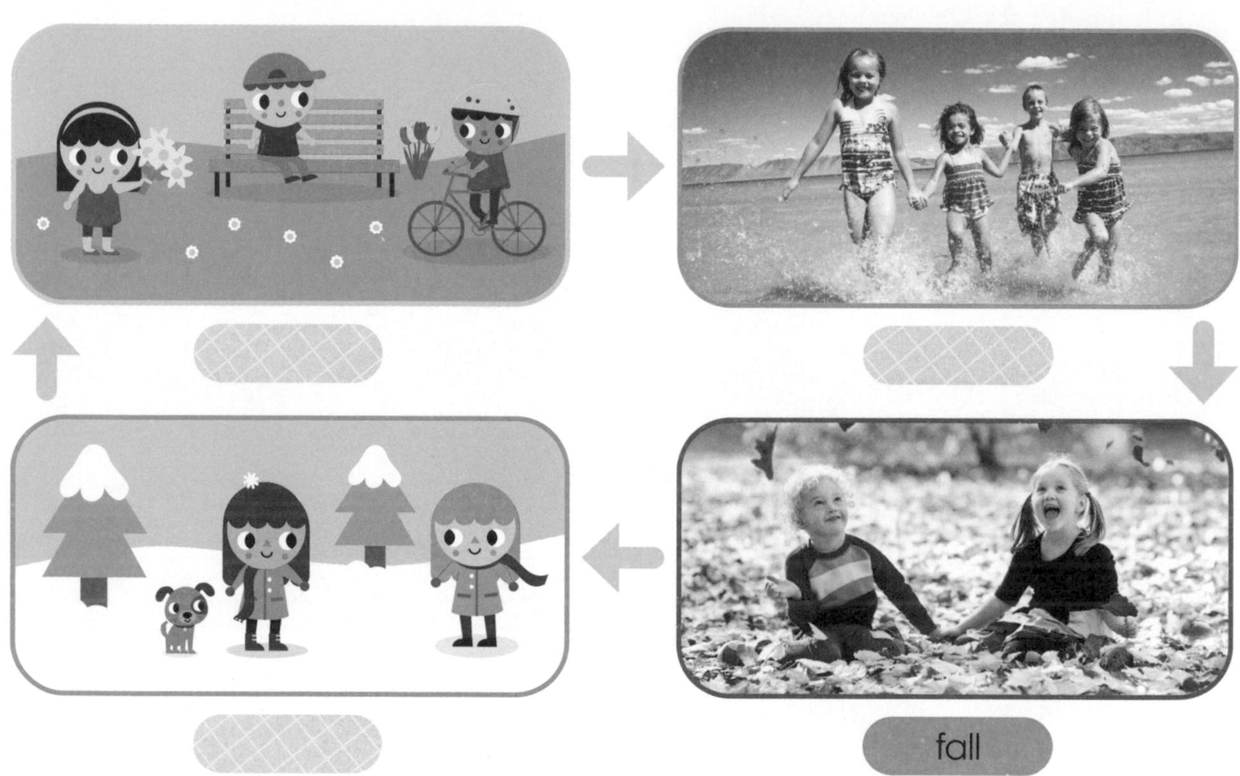

Check the activities that people do in summer.

Which is your favorite season? Why?

....

....

Weather

Fill in the missing words in these sentences.

Rain Wind Lightning

Sun Snow Thunder

.... is a flash of electricity that lights up the sky.

The .... is a giant star that gives us light and heat.

.... is moving air.

.... is drops of water that fall from clouds.

.... is made of white ice crystals with six sides.

.... is the sound that comes after lightning.

SCIENCE

Weather Log

Keep a weather log for a week. Each day, write words and use stickers to record the weather. You can use some of the words below.

cloudy sunny rainy windy

dry snowy hot cold

My Weather Log

Day	Weather words	Sticker
Monday	....	
Tuesday	....	
Wednesday	....	
Thursday	....	
Friday	....	
Saturday	....	
Sunday	....	

Plant Parts

Draw lines to match the labels to the parts of the plant. Then color the plant.

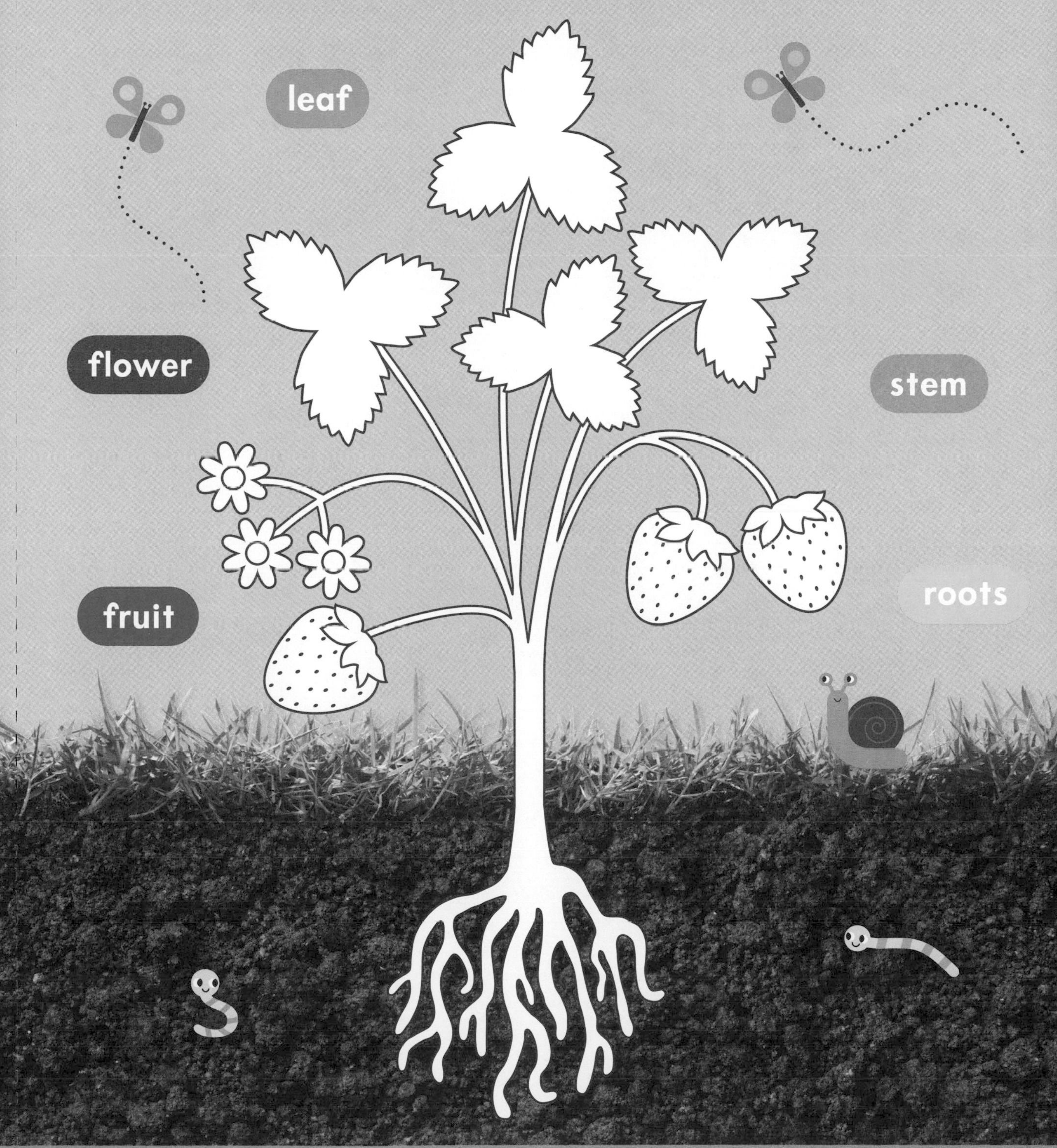

Plant Life Cycle

Sticker the labels on the diagram. Then add the numbers from 2 to 6.

The Life Cycle of a Pear Tree

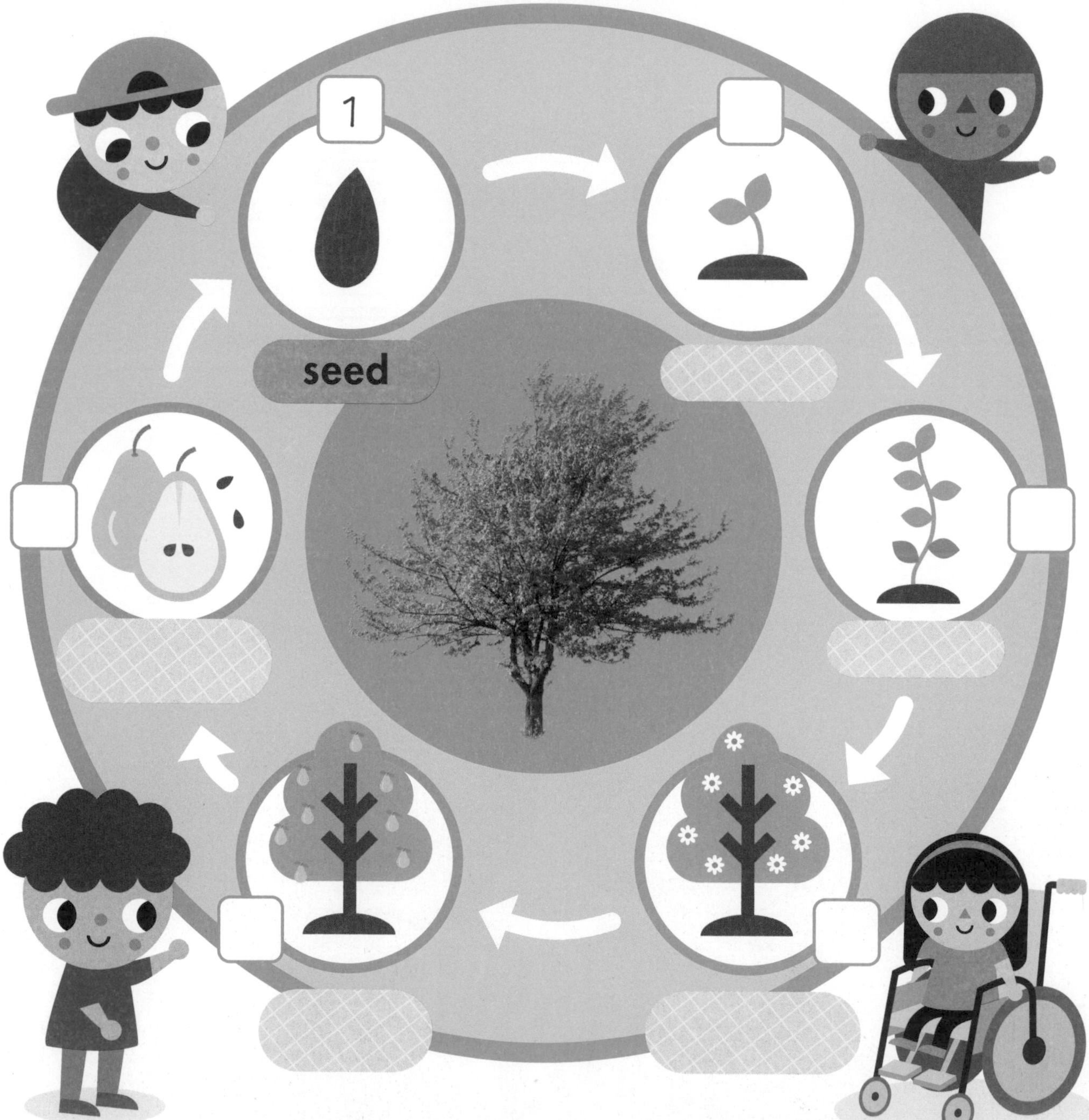

1

seed

SCIENCE

Interesting Insects

Most insects have the same body parts. Look at the beetle diagram. Then draw lines to join the correct labels to the bee.

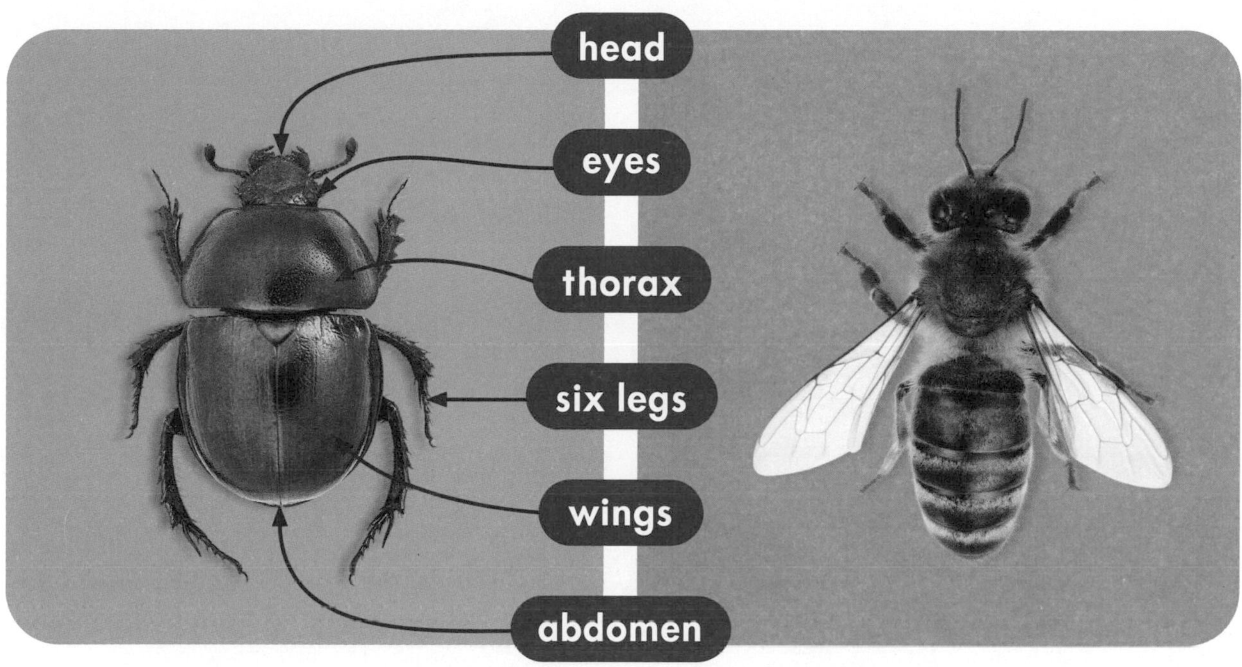

With an adult, search your yard or a park for insects. Check the ones you find. List any others that you also find.

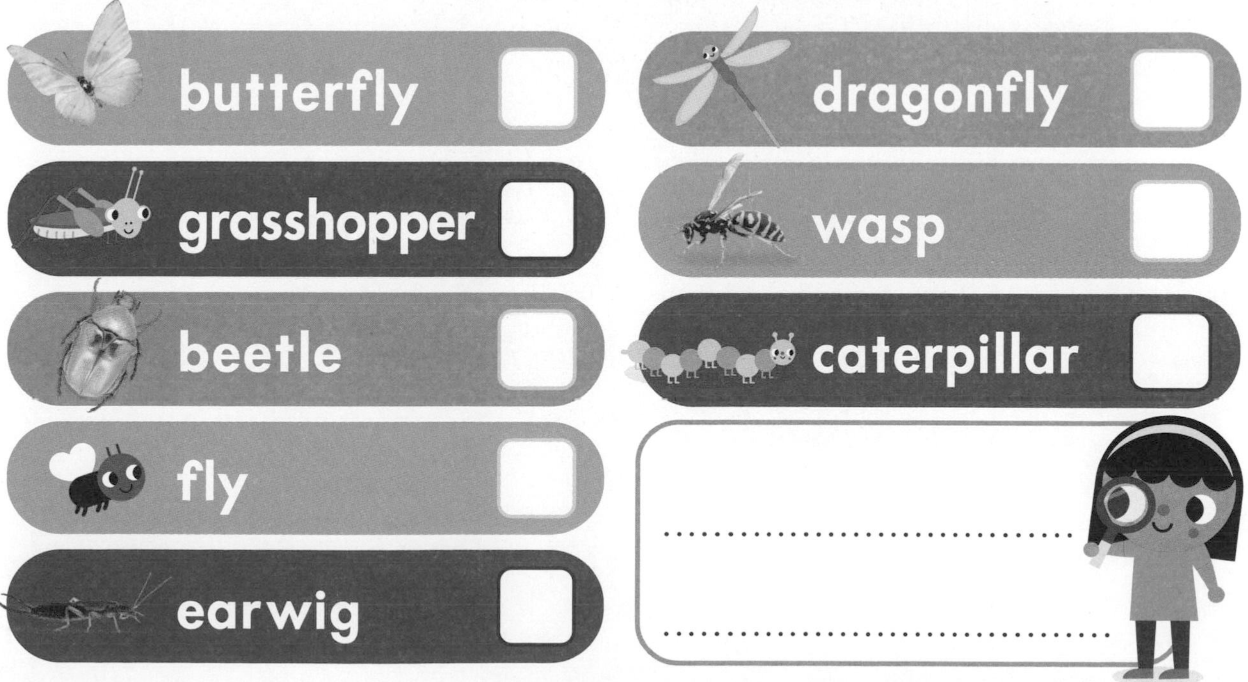

Butterfly Life Cycle

Match the pictures with the text. The first one has been done for you.

A butterfly lays an egg.

The fully grown caterpillar spins a chrysalis around itself.

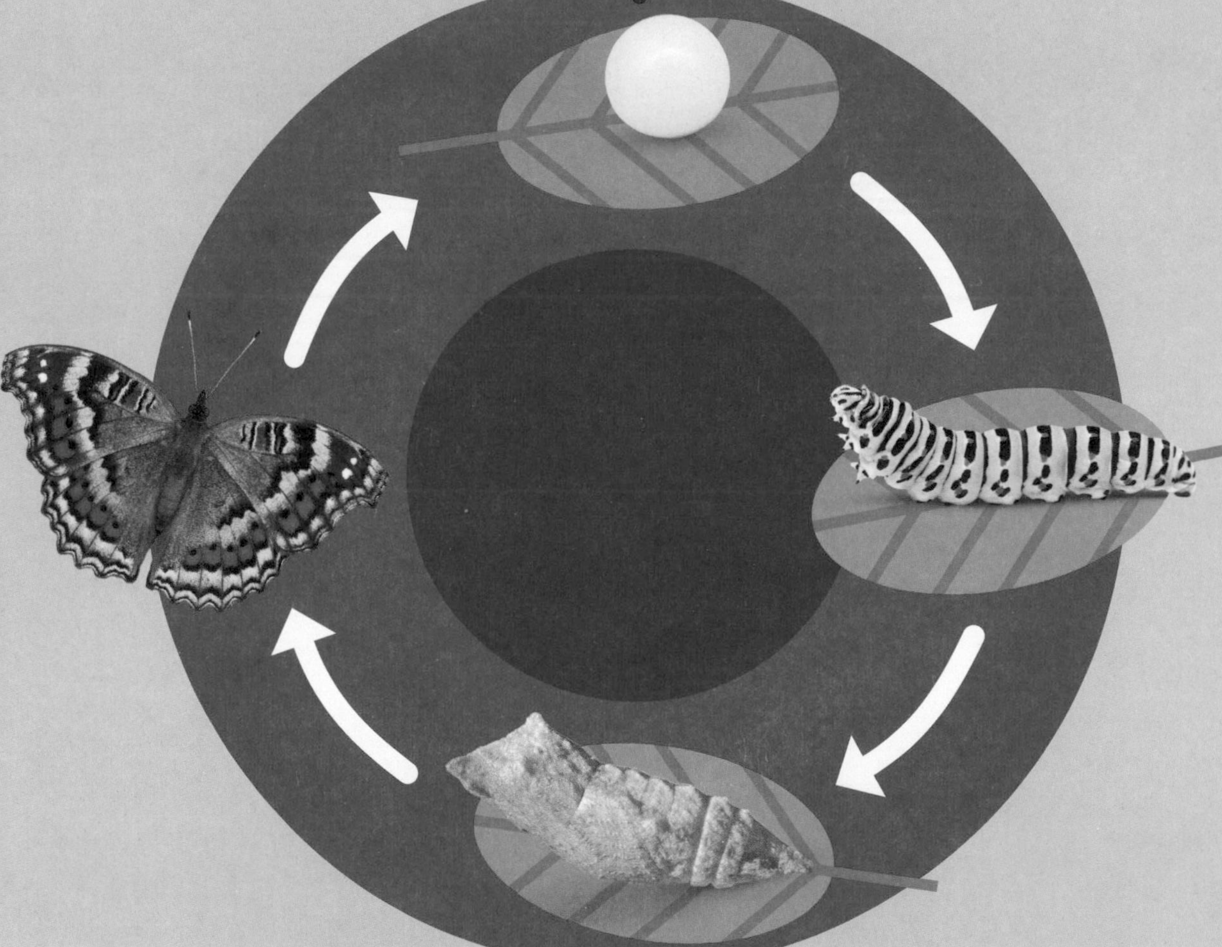

It comes out of the chrysalis as a butterfly.

The egg hatches into a caterpillar.

Animal Habitats

Different animals live in different habitats. Draw lines to match the animals with their habitats. Then write some words to describe that habitat.

....

....

....

....

SCIENCE

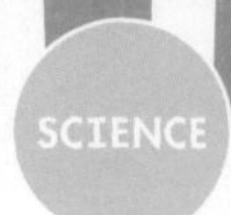

Food Chains

A food chain shows how animals need plants and other animals for food. Sticker the missing words into this food chain.

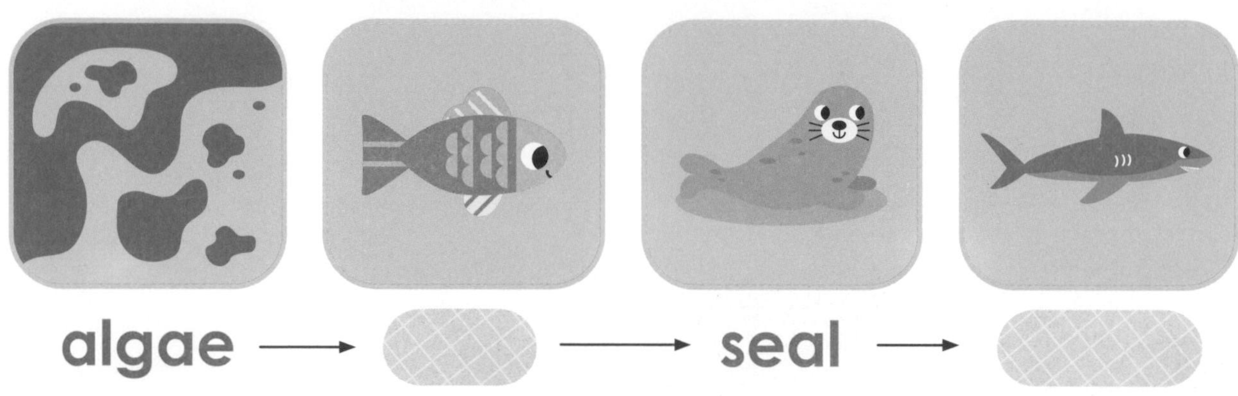

algae → ____ → seal → ____

Circle the animal that comes last in the food chain.

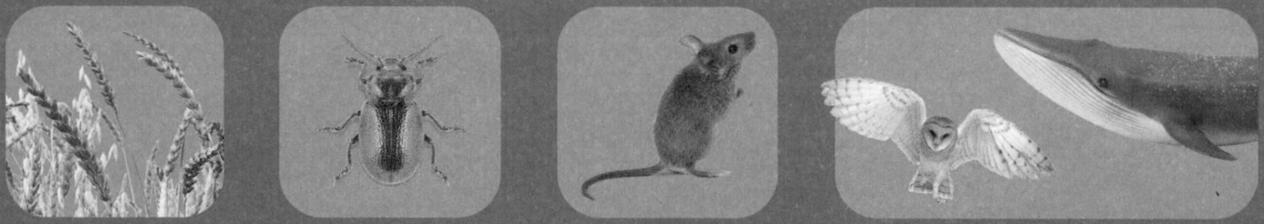

plant → insect → mouse → owl or whale?

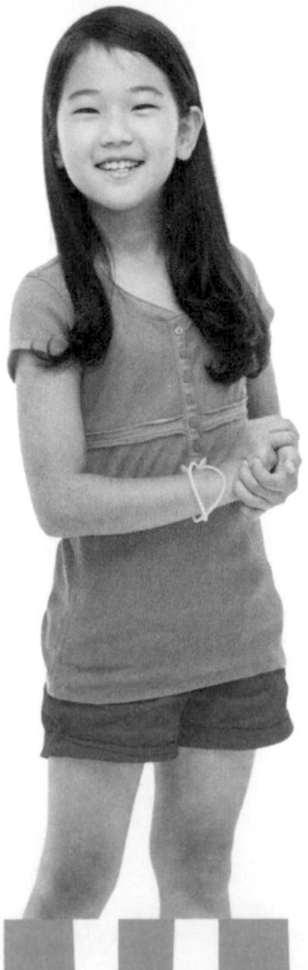

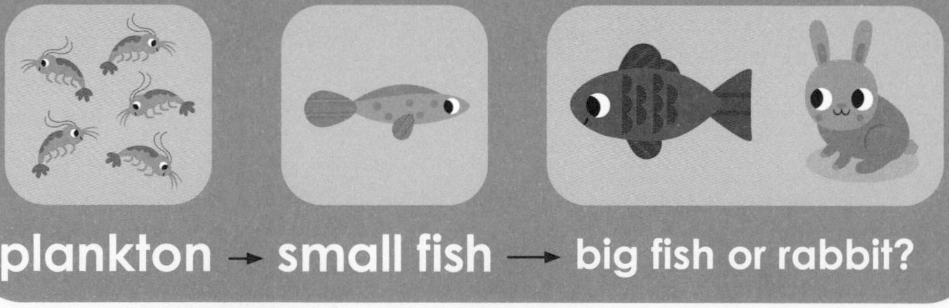

plankton → small fish → big fish or rabbit?

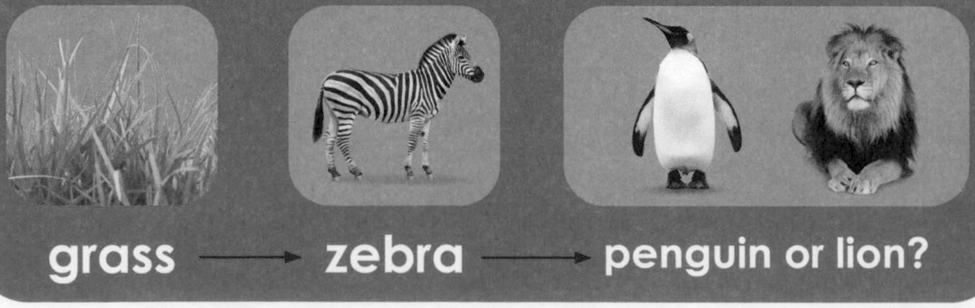

grass → zebra → penguin or lion?

What Animals Need

All animals need food, water, and shelter. Draw lines from the animal to the right food, water, and shelter.

food

water

shelter

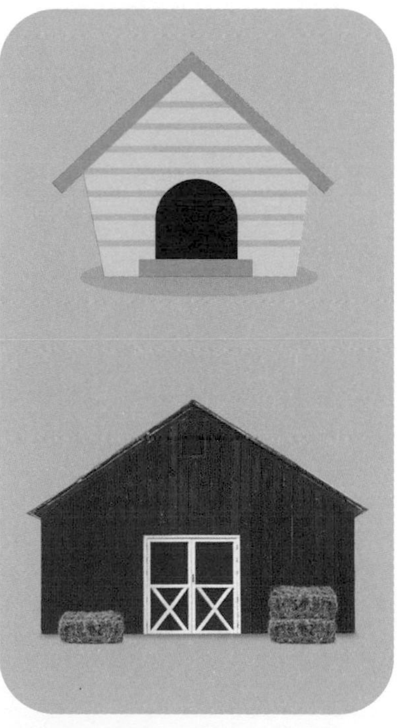

Growing Up

Number the pictures from 1 to 4 to show how we grow and age.

Draw yourself as a baby in the first box. Then draw yourself as you are now. Lastly, draw yourself as an adult.

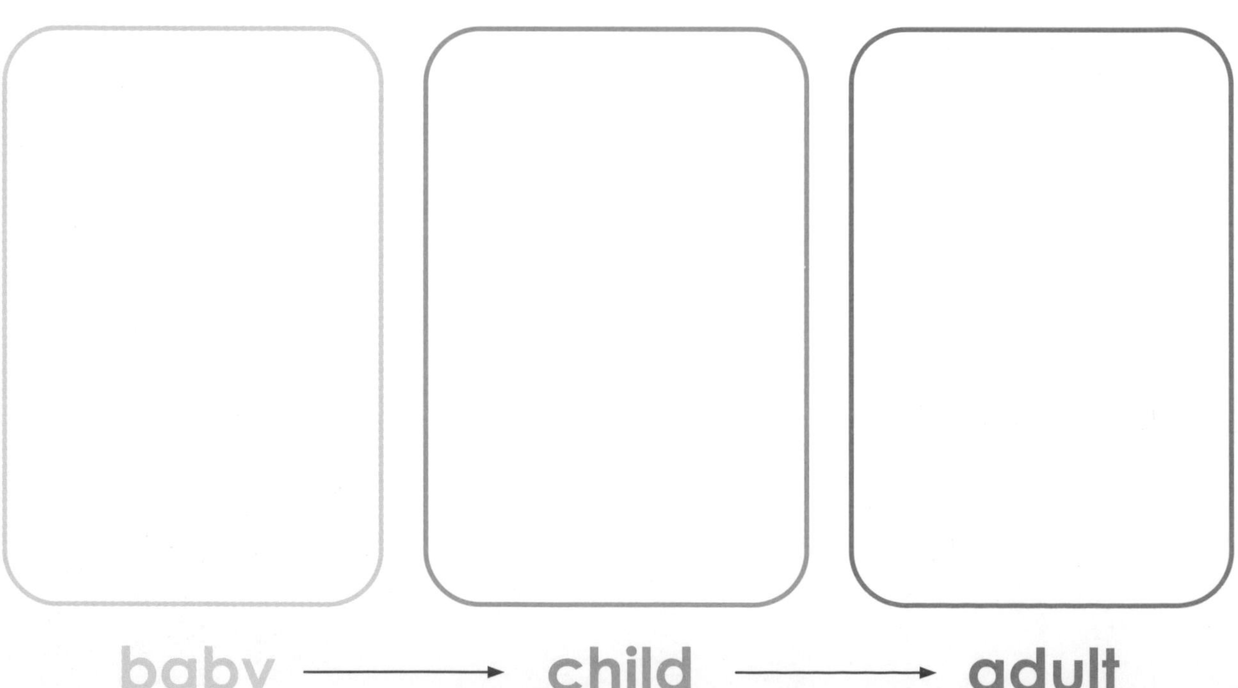

baby ⟶ child ⟶ adult

Solids and Liquids

A solid object holds its shape. A rock is a solid.
Liquids can flow and be poured. Water is a liquid.
Put an **S** beside the solids and an **L** beside the liquids.

Energy

Machines need energy to work. Write **B** by the items that get energy from batteries. Write **E** by the items that use mains electricity. Write **F** by the items that use fuel.

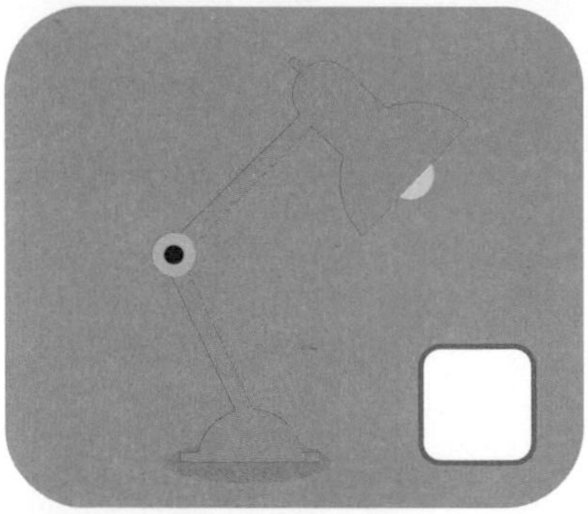

F

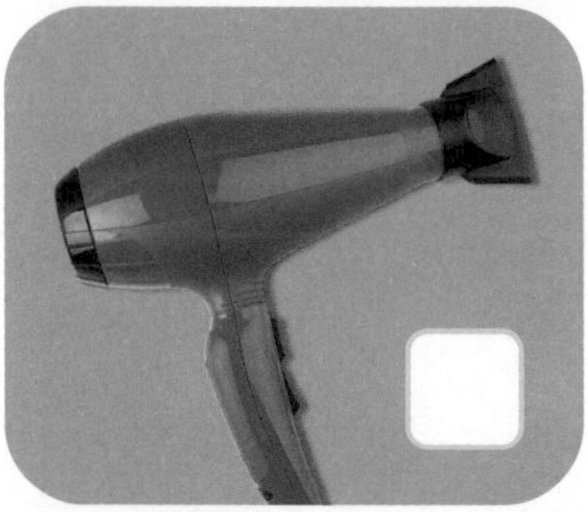

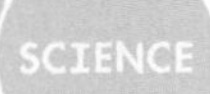

Keep Safe

Electricity is dangerous. It can hurt or even kill people.
Draw lines to join the sentences with the matching pictures.

Never put anything but a plug into an electric socket.

Don't touch or use a broken wire. Tell an adult about it.

Keep knives and forks out of toasters.

Keep electrical items, such as hair dryers, away from water.

Never play with batteries.

Unplug machines after using them.

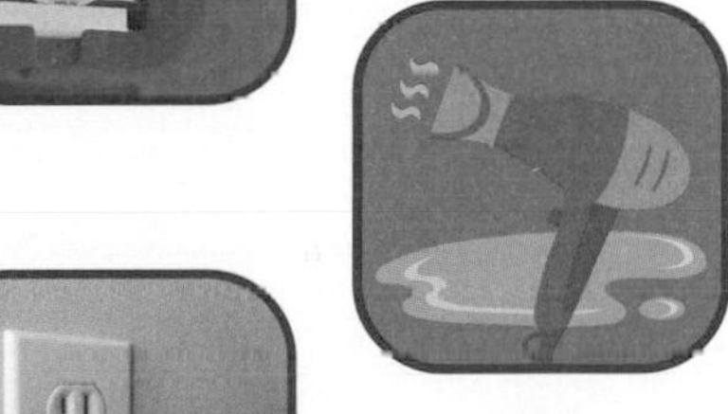

Cover the sentences above, and write 3 things you remember about keeping safe around electricity.

1 ....

2 ....

3 ....

All About Me

Finish these sentences about you.

My name is ....

I am .... years old. I have .... eyes

and .... hair.

I live in ....

Draw a picture of yourself here.

SOCIAL STUDIES

My Family

There are families all around the world.

What does your family look like?
Draw your family members here.

Who is in your family? Write their names here.

....

....

....

....

....

....

Differences and Similarities

Families are the same and different in many ways. Think of a friend. How is your friend's family different from yours?

....

....

How is your friend's family the same as yours?

....

....

Draw your friend's family here.

Family Events

Families celebrate special events. Fill in the calendar with special events in your family, such as birthdays, vacations, and holidays.

Calendar

January	February	March	April
May	**June**	**July**	**August**
September	**October**	**November**	**December**

Write about one of your favorite family events.

....

....

....

SOCIAL STUDIES

Family History

Families change and grow over time. Put the pictures in order to see how this family has changed. Write the letter of the picture that comes first next to **1**.

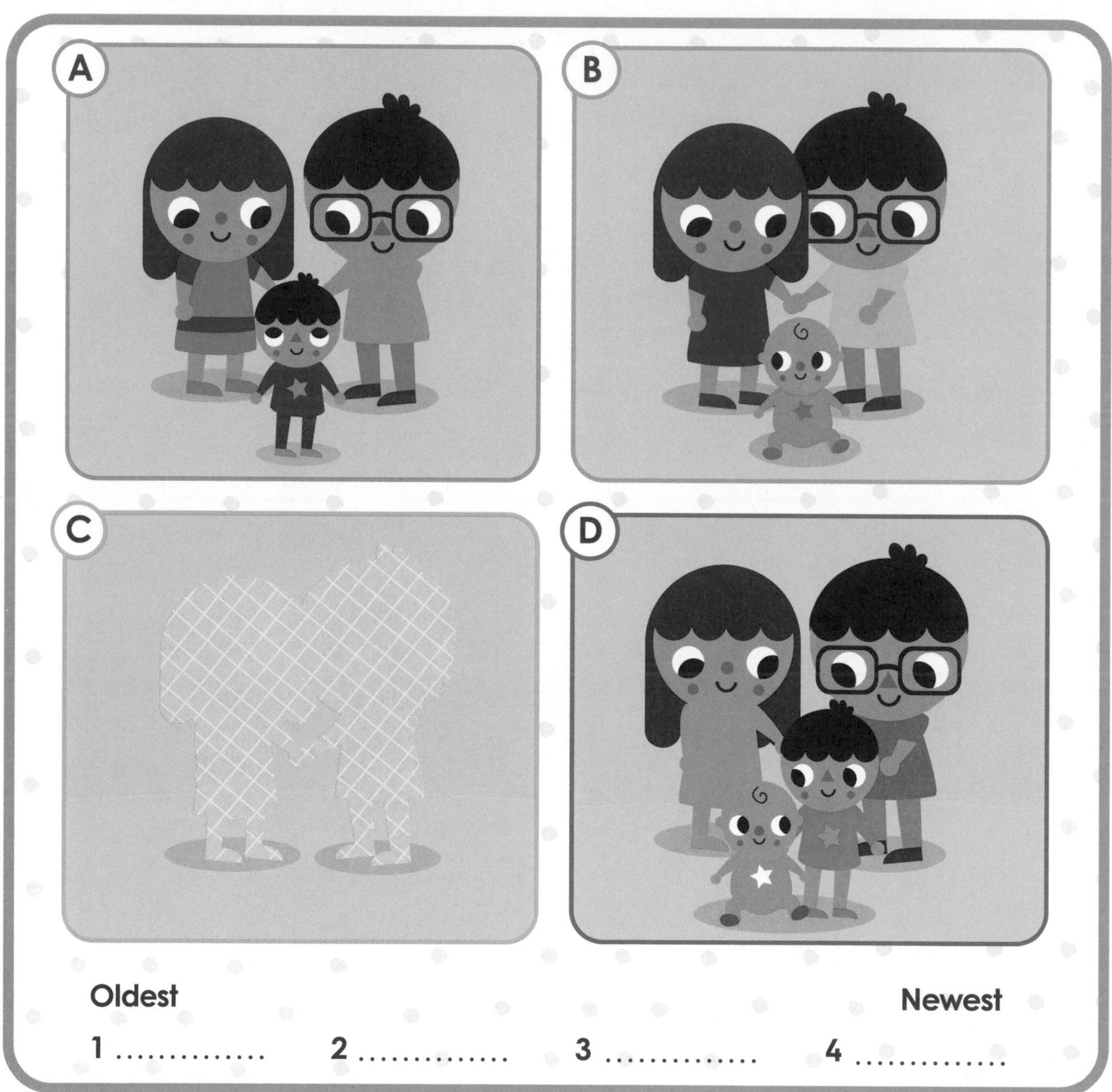

Oldest **Newest**

1 .... **2** .... **3** .... **4** ....

How has your family changed over time?

....

....

On the Move

Some families move to another home when they get bigger or smaller. Write the word **bigger** or **smaller** in each paragraph.

Grandma and Grandpa used to have four children living with them, but then their children grew up and left home. Now Grandma and Grandpa live in a big house with empty rooms.

They want to move to a .... home.

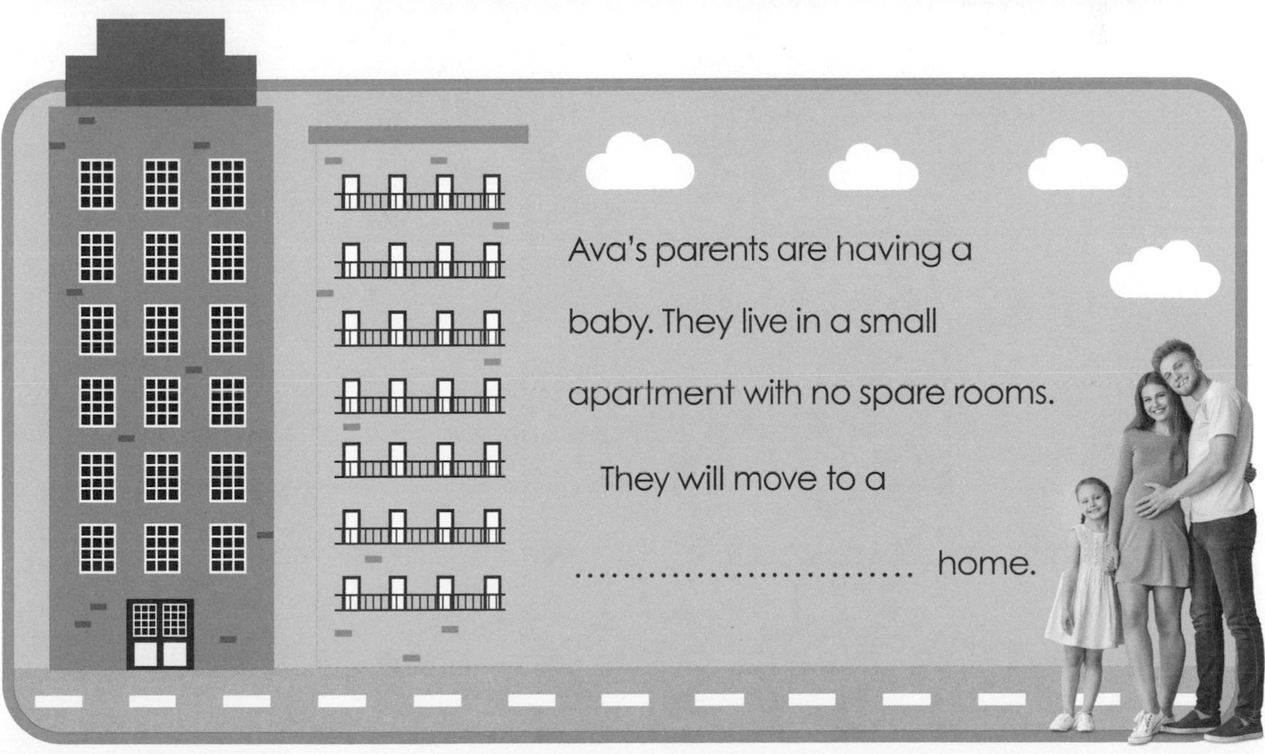

Ava's parents are having a baby. They live in a small apartment with no spare rooms.

They will move to a .... home.

Family Rules and Routines

Rules are guidelines for how people should behave. Routines are things we do in the same way each time. Every family has their own rules and routines. Circle the rules and routines that your family has.

Put away your toys after you've finished playing.

Read a story before bedtime.

Get dressed.

Play nicely.

Eat dinner at the table.

Have breakfast.

Say please.

Say thank-you.

Make your bed.

Brush your teeth before bed.

Write two more rules or routines that your family has.

1 ....

2 ....

Classroom Rules

Every school has different rules, such as no running in the halls. What rules does your school or your classroom have?

Draw a poster telling people about one of the rules.

SOCIAL STUDIES

Community Rules

Rules help keep people safe. Signs tell us the rules we need to follow. Draw a line to match the rules to the pictures.

Cars must stop.

Cars can go.

You can park here.

No bikes.

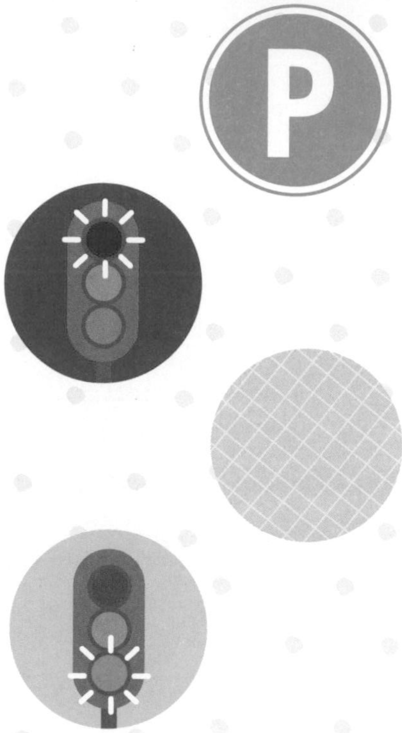

P

Think of a rule in your community. Design a sign to show this rule.

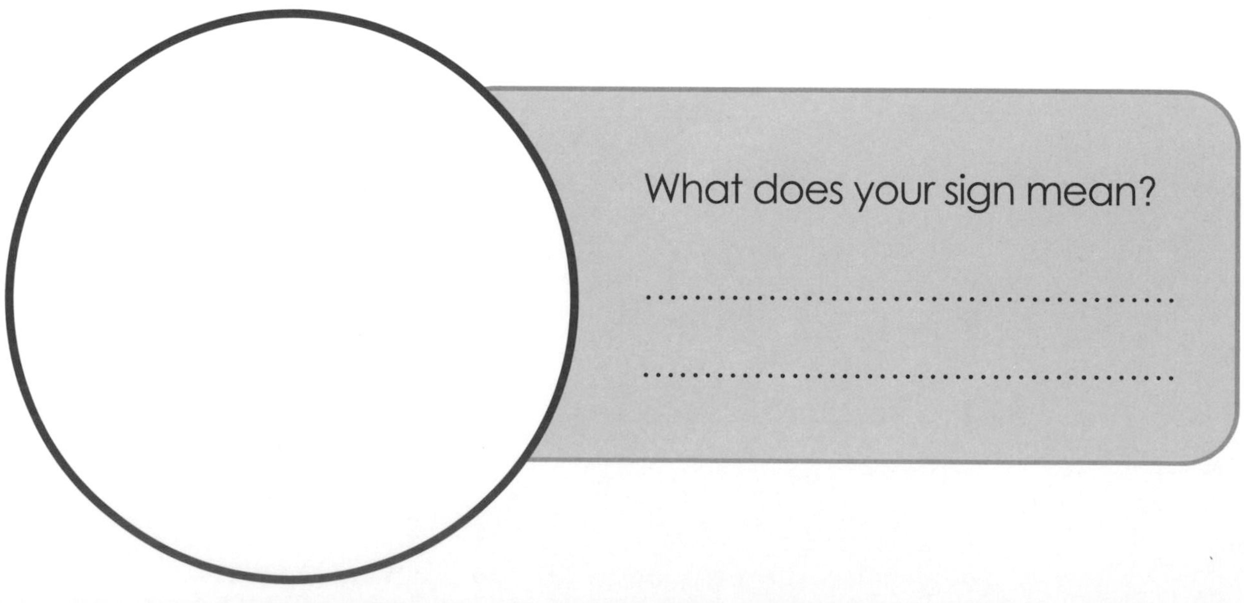

SOCIAL STUDIES

Places in the Community

Circle the places that are in your community.

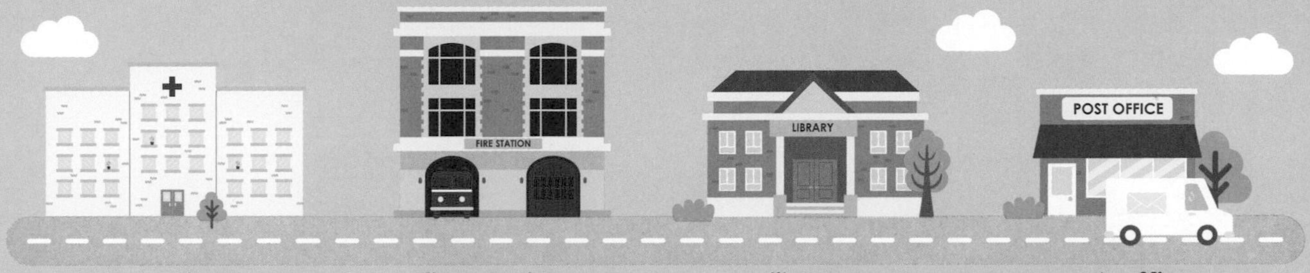

hospital

fire station

library

post office

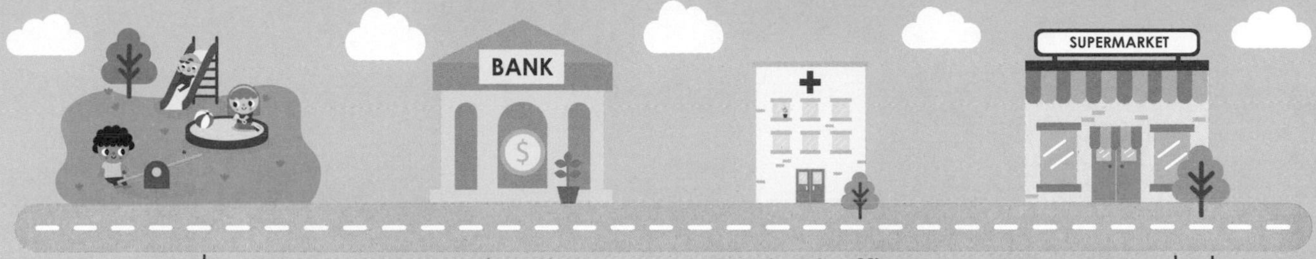

park

bank

doctors' office

supermarket

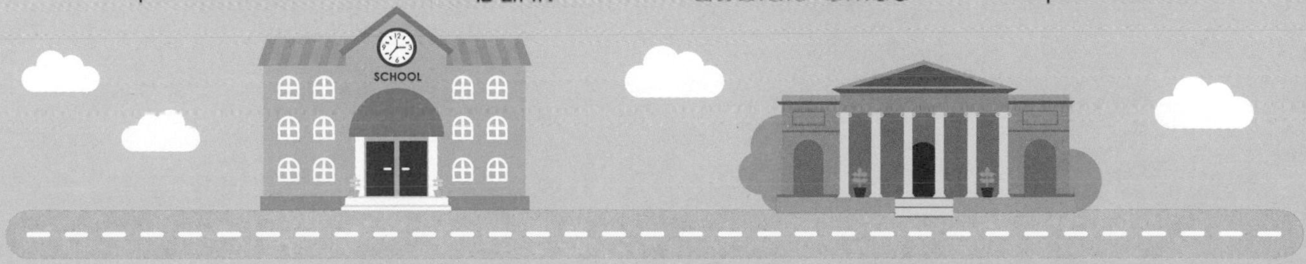

school

museum

Draw a line to match the question to the place in the community.

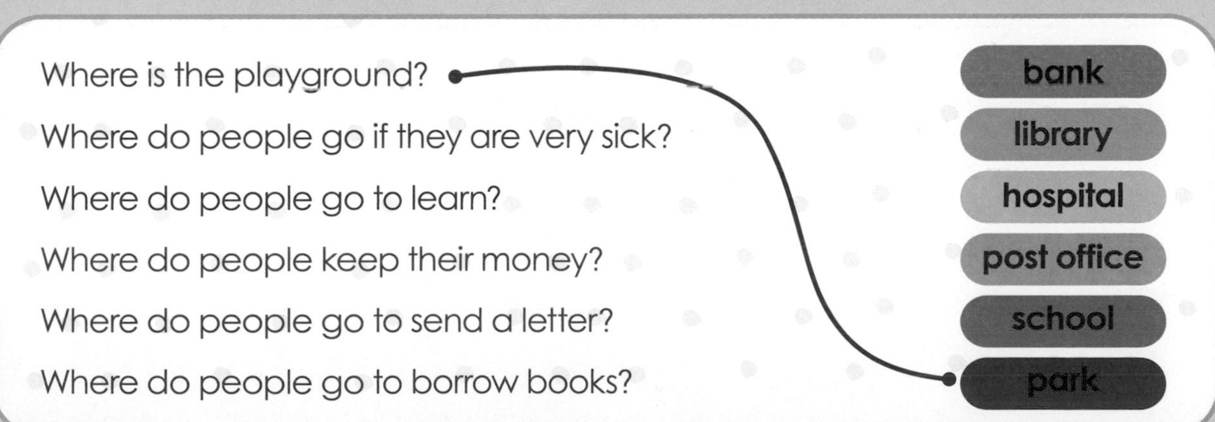

People in the Community

People in the community have different jobs. Trace the words under the community workers.

What do these people do for the community?

doctor: ....

librarian: ....

firefighter: ....

teacher: ....

Important People

Community workers help people in many ways. Draw someone in your community who is special or important to you, such as a postal worker or teacher.

postal worker

teacher

Who is this person? ....

What is their job? ....

Write a sentence about why you chose this person. ....

....

Map Symbols

Compasses show us where to find the directions of **north**, **east**, **south**, and **west**. Write the directions on the compass below.

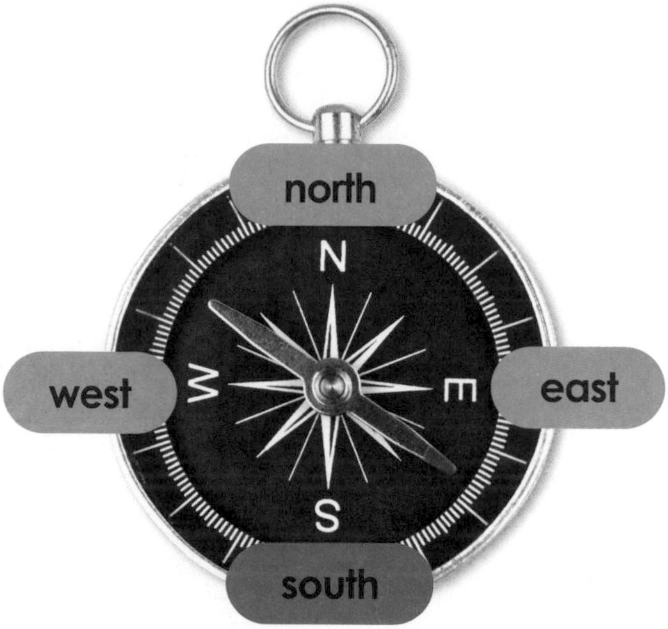

north
N
west
W
E
east
S
south

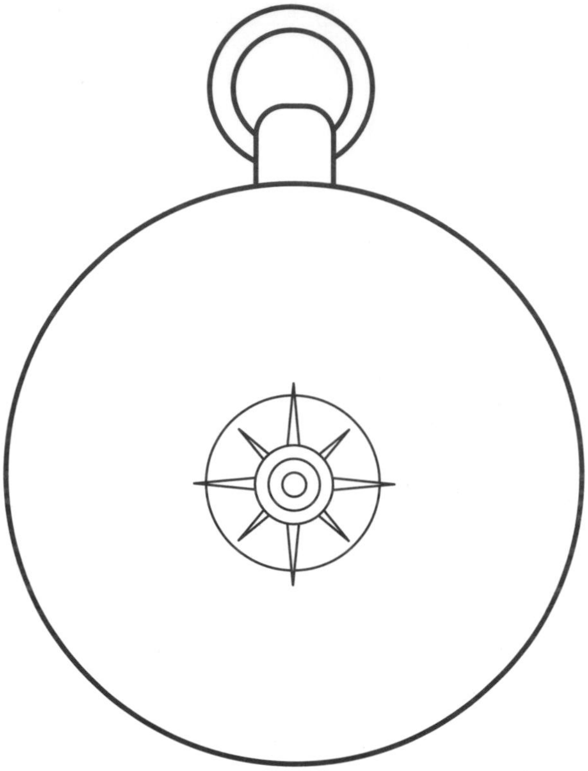

Some maps have symbols to mark important places. Find the sticker. Then draw a line to match the symbol to its meaning.

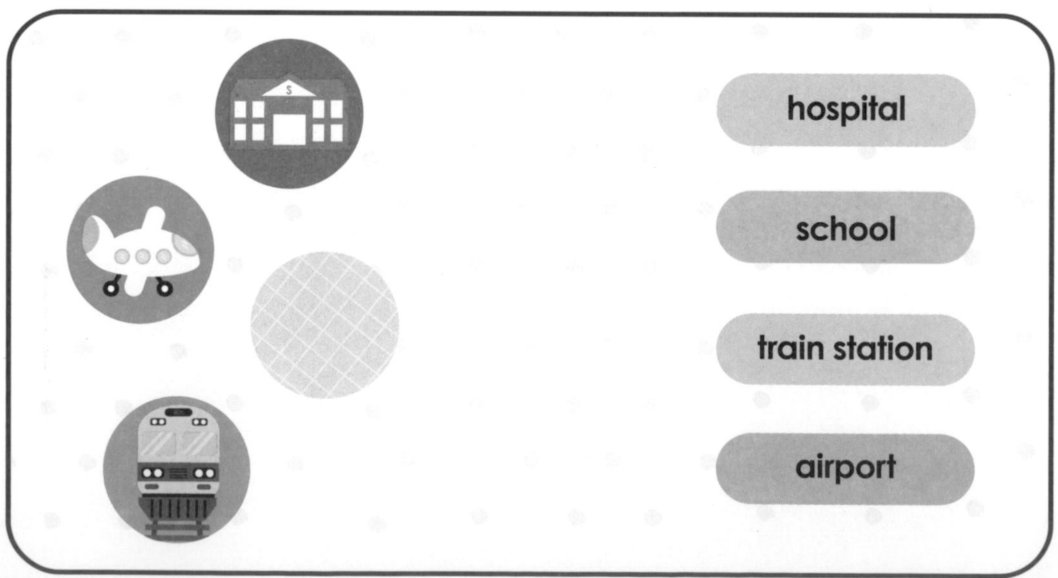

Local Map

We use maps to find our way to different places. Draw a line on the map to show how to go from the school to the park.

SCHOOL

LIBRARY

BANK

POST OFFICE

Map of the Zoo

Draw a line on the zoo map to show how to go from the entrance to the lions, and then to the zebras.

ZOO

Entrance

Monkeys

Giraffes

Tigers

Pandas

Elephants

Dolphins

Lions

Zebras

Penguins

Hippos

Human-Made and Natural Objects

Human-made objects are things that people have made.
Paint, plastic, glass, and paper are all human-made objects.
Natural objects are things that you find in nature.
Ice, stone, wood, sand, and feathers are natural objects.
Write the objects under the correct headings in the chart.

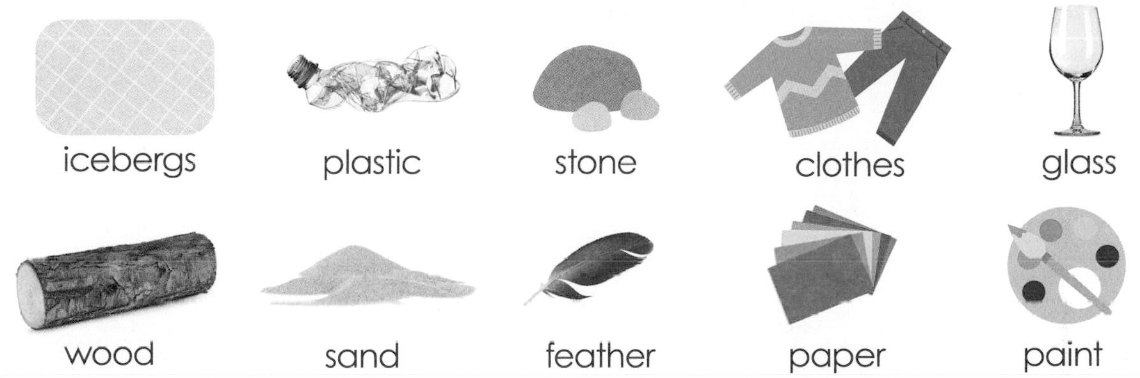

Human-Made Objects	Natural Objects
....	....
....	....
....	....
....	....
....	....
....	....
....	....

Goods and Services

Goods are things that we buy and sell that we can touch. Food, clothes, toys, and books are goods.
Services are jobs that we pay someone else to do, such as giving us a haircut. Decide if each thing in the chart is a **good** or a **service**. Then circle the correct word.

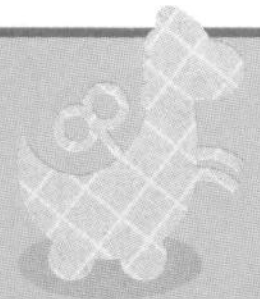 **toy**	**good**	or	**service**
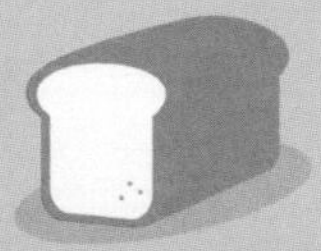 **bread**	**good**	or	**service**
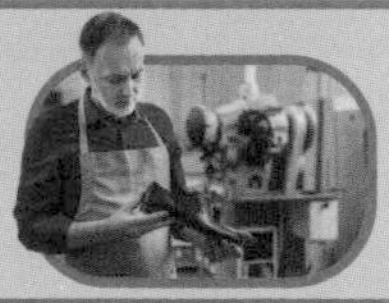 **shoe repair**	**good**	or	**service**
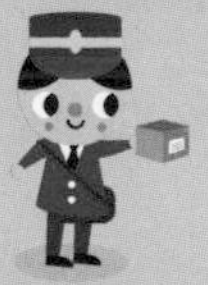 **package delivery**	**good**	or	**service**
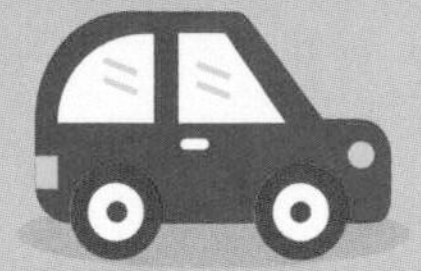 **car**	**good**	or	**service**
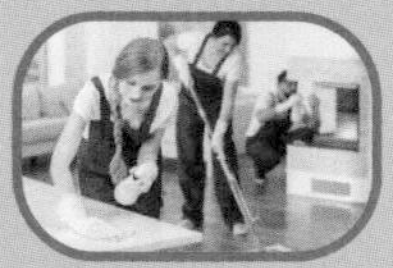 **house cleaning**	**good**	or	**service**
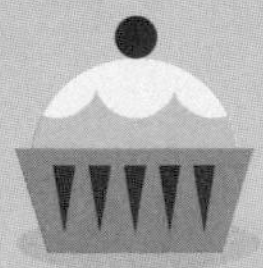 **cupcake**	**good**	or	**service**
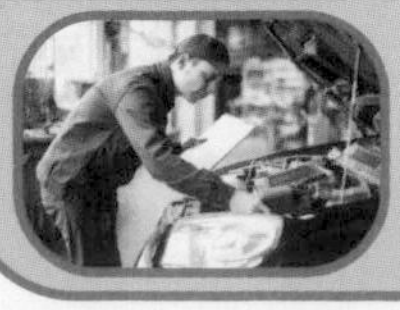 **car repair**	**good**	or	**service**

Producers and Consumers

Producers are people who sell goods or services.
Consumers are people who buy goods or services.
Number the pictures from 1 to 4 showing how the strawberries get from the farm to the supermarket.

Write the word **consumer** or **producer** next to each image.

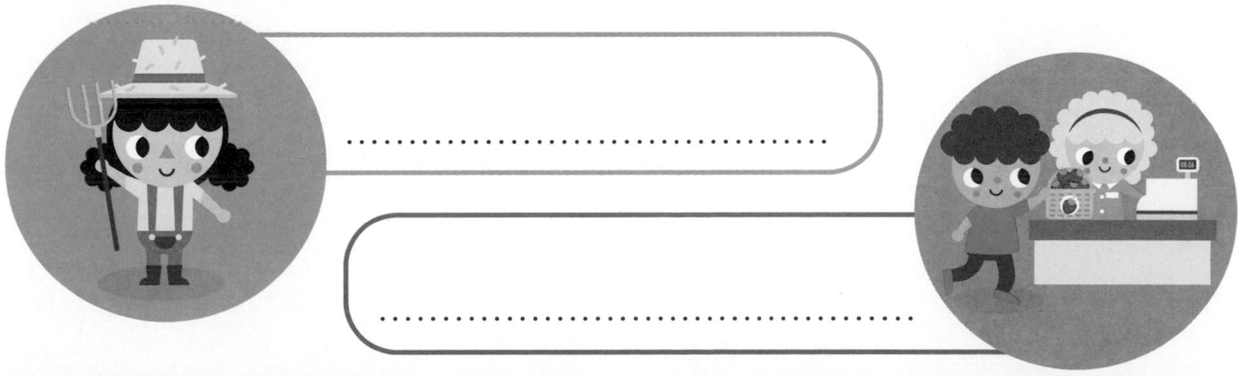

SOCIAL STUDIES

Needs and Wants

Needs are things we cannot live without. **Wants** are things we don't need but would like to have. Write an **N** by the objects that are **needs**, and write a **W** by the objects that are **wants**.

sunshine ☐

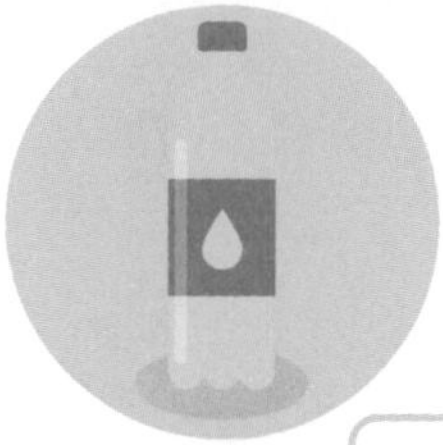

water ☐

bicycle ☐

computer ☐

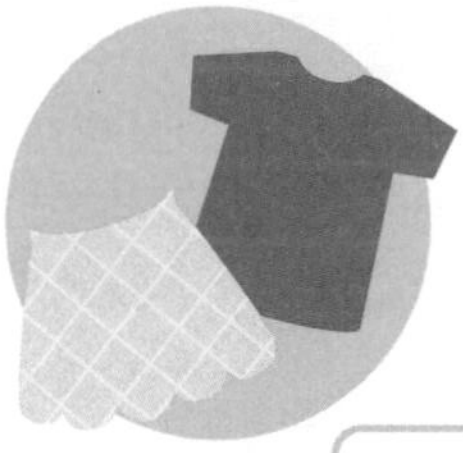

clothes ☐

television ☐

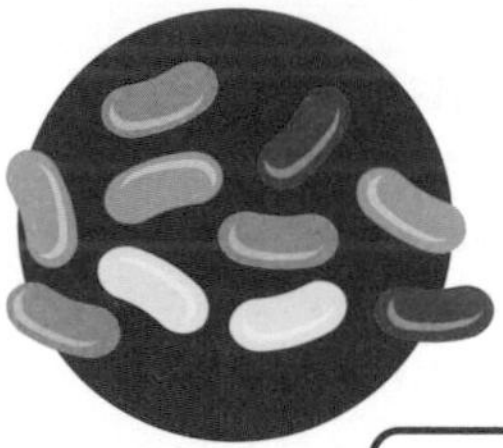

candy ☐

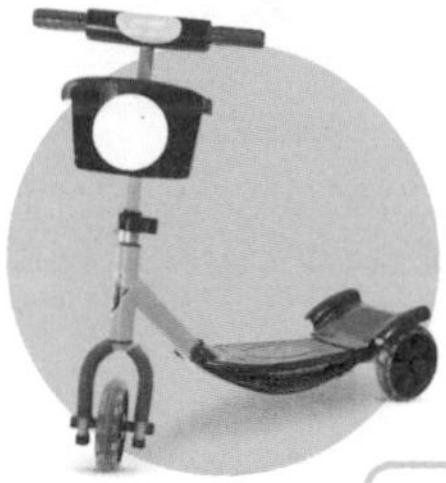

scooter ☐

vegetables ☐

home ☐

donuts ☐

toys ☐

fruit ☐

shoes ☐

books ☐

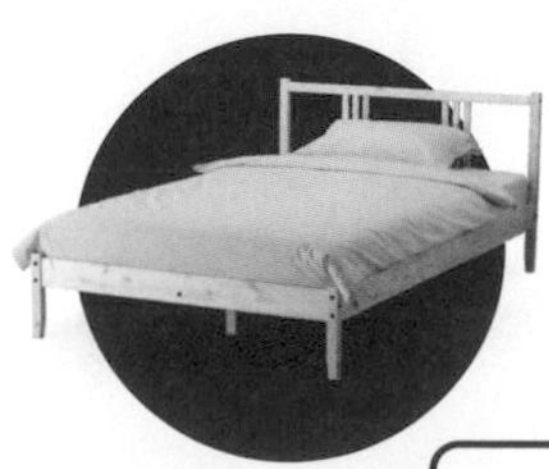

bed ☐

The Environment

Actions that help the environment are called **positive** actions. Actions that harm the environment are called **negative** actions.

negative action

Write **positive** or **negative** next to each behavior.

Littering ....

Cutting down forests ....

Cleaning lakes, rivers, and seas ....

Pollution from cars ....

Recycling plastic ....

Growing your own vegetables ....

Protecting endangered animals ....

Write down two positive ways you can help the environment.

1 ....

2 ....

SOCIAL STUDIES

What Is Recycling?

We recycle old things into new things. Materials such as paper, fabrics, glass, metals, and some plastics can be recycled. Food waste can be made into compost for plants.

empty can | newspaper | soda bottle | jelly jar | old sneakers | carrot tops

aluminum | cardboard box | yogurt cup | dress | glass bottle | apple

Draw or write each object in its correct recycling group.

paper and card

glass

plastic

compost

metals

clothes

Getting Involved

Children can help solve problems and make decisions in their families, schools, and communities.

Write two ways you could help your school.

1 ....

2 ....

Design a poster to encourage children to help your school.

ANSWERS

Answers

HANDWRITING

Alphabetical order exercises:

p4	aardvark	ape	April	avocado
p5	bamboo	bluebird	Boston	bubble
p6	Canada	castle	circle	clock
p7	dad	December	dodge	dragon
p8	Earth	eel	elephant	energy
p10	Hawaii	hero	high	hip-hop
p11	icing	India	inside	island
p13	likely	lion	London	lunch
p14	mammal	Mars	mother	museum
p15	nest	none	Norway	number
p16	October	onion	ooze	owl
p17	paper	Paris	parrot	people
p19	Saturday	shark	shorts	sports
p20	text	tiptoe	truck	Tuesday
p21	uncle	under	Uranus	useful
p22	vanilla	video	Viking	vivid
p23	walk	walrus	Wednesday	willow
p25	zany	Zanzibar	zero	zilch

READING

p26 Blue: Pete the Panda; Yellow: How to Play the Drums; Orange: Tom Gets a Puppy; Purple: Grade 1 Math; Red: Dinosaurs From Long Ago; Green: Let's Bake Cakes

p27 **1** sports **2** Children play all sorts of sports.
3 start

p28 **1** tigers **2** scaly **3** pigs **4** trees

p29 **1** a huge fire **2** very small
3 a railroad bridge **4** very large
5 heavy rain

p30 **1** James flapped his arms and flew up into the sky.
2 Freddie the fire truck was scared of fires.
3 There was a dinosaur in Lucy's backyard.
4 Fifi the fairy waved her magic wand.

p31 Beginning: Once upon a time …
Middle: Jack's mother was angry …
End: When Jack got to the bottom …
Fairy tales often start with these four words:
One upon a time
Fairy tales often end with these six words:
They all lived happily ever after

p32 eagle (B) rabbit (M) turtle (R) tiger (M)
parrot (B) lizard (R) owl (B) dog (M)
4 birds and reptiles

p33 **1** to make her drop the cheese
2 to show off her voice
3 She dropped the cheese.
4 Do not trust people who flatter you.

p34 A god granted Midas a wish. ✘
Midas was kind but greedy. ✔
Everything Midas touched turned to gold. ✘
Midas had a daughter. ✔
His daughter turned to gold. ✘

p35 **1** a capital letter
2 stalk
3 The caterpillar spins a cocoon around itself.
4 I hope no toads see you.

p36

	Sophy	Aria	Neither girl
Has older brothers	✔		
Has younger brothers		✔	
Has brothers	✔	✔	
Has sisters			✔
Likes to ride bikes	✔	✔	
Likes to play with dolls		✔	
Has a best friend	✔	✔	

p37 **Who** Zoe
What a poster
When on her birthday
Where on her bedroom wall
How with sticky tack
Why because they were painted in glow-in-the-dark paint

p38 What happens next: 2nd picture down
Who do you think will help the children?
The museum guard

p39 **1** sticky **2** warm bread **3** the timer beep
4 golden brown **5** fresh

p40 Top to bottom: Cinderella, Puss in Boots, Little Red Riding Hood, Goldilocks and the Three Bears, The Gingerbread Man, The Little Mermaid

p42 **1** bus driver **2** dinner
3 fall **4** she walked
5 reading a book **6** on the table

p43 **1** angry **2** He had fallen down.
3 just her friend **4** He had slipped on the ice.
5 no **6** in a car

WRITING

p44 Pink: Poems about Pets
Blue: Mia the Mountain Climber
Yellow: How to Bake Cakes

p46 1B **2**A **3**B **4**A

p51 look, hear, smelled, tasted, felt

p53 It was an exciting day. **First** we climbed into our rocket. **Then** it blasted off and zoomed into space. **When** we reached Mars, the rocket landed. **After that**, the door opened, and we stepped out. **At last**, we were on the red planet.

p57 **tomato** sauce
grated **cheese**
1 pita bread **2** spinach
5 pizzas **6** cheese

p62 **A** still, hill
B blue, you
C cat, rat fail, tail

WORD STUDY

p66 hand nest
pig milk dog
sock jump rug

p67 hen mix
map best slug
drip jog frost fun
pond brush
twins flag shell

p68 tent drum crab
book mug

r	a	b	l	y	a	l	w	d	k
a	i	e	o	w	r	n	x	a	u
b	v	e	w	j	k	c	s	t	w
e	n	m	l	f	j	f	u	d	z
s	n	a	k	e	h	i	v	d	f
b	s	h	e	e	p	s	o	l	d
t	e	s	n	q	g	h	b	i	l
s	m	r	z	e	b	r	a	o	i
a	o	s	x	r	t	f	k	n	s
b	d	k	y	r	a	b	b	i	t

Hidden word: elephant

p69 mop bed
hat red plant
lamp home shelf

p70 circle = 2 syllables
rectangle = 3 syllables
triangle = 3 syllables
bub|ble let|ter po|ta|to pud|dle
di|no|saur ap|ple kan|ga|roo
ro|bot hip|po|pot|a|mus

p72 blue words: unwell, unfair, unclean, untrue, unlock
red words: dishonest, dislike, disappear, disconnect, disappoint
untie unlucky disbelieve unfold disobey
dispose unkind uneven

p73 green words: redo, replay, reappear, remove, refill
yellow words: incorrect, incomplete, inspect, incredible, inside
invisible react rewind include invent reopen
reread inform

p74

careless	hopeless
talked	looked
friendly	softly
brightest	biggest
kindness	darkness
excitement	amazement
adorable	enjoyable
faster	lighter
noisy	grumpy

p75 **-let**
piglet, booklet, droplet, owlet, bracelet
-ful
hopeful, cheerful, truthful, playful, powerful, wonderful
-less
powerless, helpless, hopeless

p76

bicycle		cycle
painter		paint
imaginary		imagine
unfair		fair
opened		open
disagree		agree
wishful		wish
care	**careful**	**caring**
hope	**hopefully**	**hopeless**
friend	**friendship**	**friendly**
joy	**enjoy**	**joyful**

p77 hand, leg
coat, jeans, socks
book, doll, kite
blue, green, red, yellow
ride, run, skip
sad, shocked, sleepy
pear, pineapple, plum

p79 basketball, butterfly, sunglasses, strawberry, cupcake, paintbrush

p80 funny **amusing**
small **little**
big **large**
fast **quick**
start **begin**
tired **sleepy**
easy **simple**

p81 hard **soft**
empty **full**
light **dark**
hot **cold**

p82 **1** green **2** cold **3** sheep **4** run **5** smell **6** cats

GRAMMAR AND PUNCTUATION

p84 Adjectives: happy, fast, slow, big, sweet, tall, soft, noisy, sleepy, hot, kind

p85 Adjectives: speedy, lazy, fluffy, clumsy new, clever huge, hungry green

p86 Activity 1: swim, sleep, slide, play, paint
Activity 2: hops, ride, play sleep, dances sings

p87 Circled: walked, played, chased, wanted, watched, cooked, listened, closed

p88 **b** rockets, **c** book, **a** pizza

p89 lamb's, cat's, boy's, shark's, bird's

p90 Activity 1: We, They, I They, It, He me, I It, She her, She them
Activity 2: he, me, They, I, She, them

p91 ours, hers, his, yours, its, mine

p92 can't: can not
that's: that is
doesn't: does not
they're: they are
don't: do not
what's: what is
you're: you are
how's: how is
let's: let us

p93 party, parties; baby, babies; girl, girls; hen, hens; tree, trees; ball, balls; puppy, puppies; house, houses; game, games
green words: strawberry, flower, apple, crayon
red words: apples, flowers, crayons, strawberries

p94 Proper nouns: England, Paris, Friday, July, Sophia, London, Isaac Newton
Common nouns: city, park, building, medal, farm, sock, house, pear, dentist, book

p95 What is **the** time?
A mouse ate some cheese.
I would like **an** orange.
The helicopter flies up high.
Can I have **a** pencil please?
An alligator has sharp teeth.

a	k	d	a	u	v	t	h	e	b
c	j	w	i	m	a	r	o	d	a
t	z	g	a	l	n	f	x	p	n
h	l	m	s	t	g	i	m	a	i
e	v	a	o	h	x	a	o	z	c
o	d	n	d	e	c	n	l	g	o
r	z	r	p	r	j	w	t	h	e
w	f	z	p	a	o	s	q	f	p
a	o	d	f	p	g	m	d	j	f
n	g	t	r	o	m	t	h	e	b

p96 on, in, under, in, on, behind, in front of, between, beside, on

p97 Let's go swimming.
I can sing.
My dog barks.
Here are my shoes.
The lion roars.

p98 My friends are Kim, Pedro, and Mia.
We eat red, green, and purple grapes.
I play hockey, tennis, and basketball.
I have a pen, a pencil, and some paper.
I like strawberry, chocolate, and vanilla ice cream.
Let's buy bread, milk, and eggs.
The farm has sheep, cows, and pigs.
My T-shirt is blue, white, and yellow.

p99 3 sentences in each

p100 What is your name**?**
How old are you**?**
I have a pet kitten**.**
The baby is crying**.**
Where do you live**?**
I saw an alien**.**
Which animal do you like best**?**

p101 **What** are we eating for lunch?
Who wants to play outside?
Why is the dog barking?
When is your birthday?

p102 Bike: Ouch! Apple: Yuck! Fireworks: Wow! Thumbs up: Yes!

p103 **Exclamation!**
Oh, no! Phew! Hi! Yippee!
Question?
Why not? Who is it? How are you? Where is it?

SPELLING

p107

d	c	i	e	a	p	o	h
z	s	u	n	y	i	x	p
d	v	f	o	h	g	l	e
o	e	c	a	t	m	r	i
g	k	j	w	u	b	e	d

p110

ch	th	wh
much	that	whale
cheese	the	where
each	they	why

p116

talk	talks	talked	talking
stay	stays	stayed	staying
kick	kicks	kicked	kicking

SORTING AND SEQUENCING

p120 Odd numbers: 1, nineteen, 𝍸III, 5-dot ten frame, 15, 3-dot ten frame, nine
Even numbers: 20, 𝍸𝍸, IIII, 10-dot ten frame, 𝍸𝍸II, 6, 2-dot ten frame, eight

p121 Left: woman's hand, fish, girl pointing
Right: child with binoculars, yellow-and-black arrow

p122 circle triangle
circle square rectangle
square triangle hexagon

p123 cube cone
cone cylinder cuboid
cylinder sphere cube

p124 Letters with curved lines: a b c d e f g h j m n o p q r s u
Letters with straight lines: a b d e f g h i j k l m n p q r t u v w x y z
Letters with dots above them: i j
Letters with slanted straight lines: k v w x y z

p126

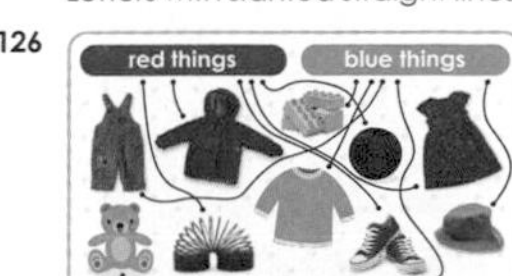

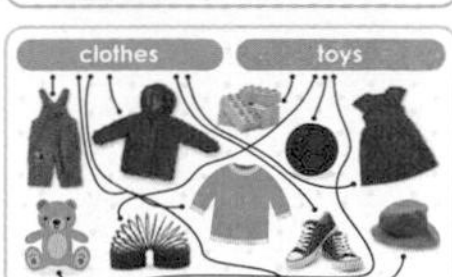

p127

p128 Top: 2 6
Middle: 3 1
Bottom: 4 5

p129 Top: 5 3
Middle: 1 6
Bottom: 4 2

p132

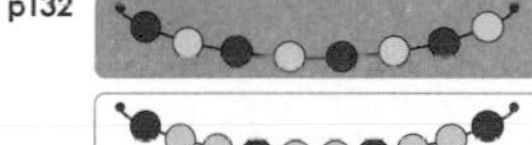

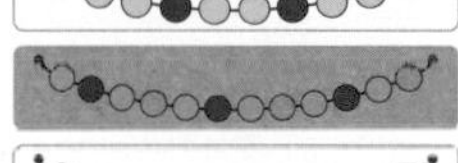

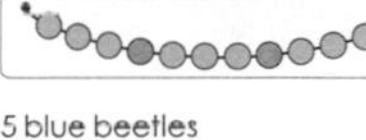

p133 5 blue beetles
4 green beetles
2 pink beetles
3 orange beetles

p134

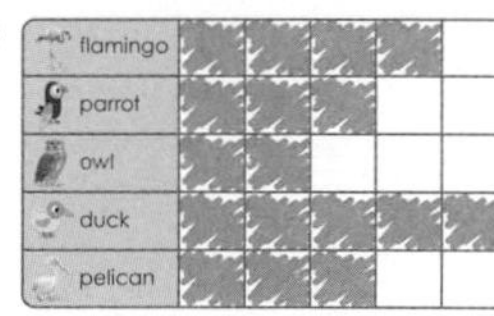

Which bird is most common? duck
Which bird is least common? owl

p136 Tallies: 4 10 2
1 4 **2** small fish **3** octopuses **4** 9 **5** 5

p137 **1** 3 **2** strawberry **3** lemon lime **4** strawberry **5** 10 **6** 20

NUMBER SENSE

p138 1 one I
2 two II
3 three III
4 four IIII
5 five 𝍸
6 six 𝍸I
7 seven 𝍸II

8 eight 卌|||
9 nine 卌||||
10 ten 卌卌

p139 11 卌卌|
12 卌卌||
13 卌卌|||
14 卌卌||||
15 卌卌卌
16 卌卌卌|
17 卌卌卌||
18 卌卌卌|||
19 卌卌卌||||
20 卌卌卌卌

p140 9th, 8th, 7th, 6th, 5th, 4th, 3rd, 1st

p141

p142

p143 1 pineapples **8** oranges **6**
There are **2** more pineapples than oranges
pears **10** strawberries **14**
There are **4** more strawberries than pears.
2 Popsicles **10** ice-cream cones **14**
There are **4** fewer Popsicles than ice-cream cones.
donuts **7** cupcakes **5**
There are **2** fewer cupcakes than donuts.
orange candies **11** green candies **15**
There are **4** fewer orange candies than green candies.

p144 tractors =, green cars <, blue buses >
5 > 1 11 < 15 10 > 8
8 = 8 18 > 8 11 = 11
11 > 10 1 < 4 18 < 20

p145 10, 20, 30, 40, 50, 60, 70, 80, 90, 100

p146 Missing numbers: 3, 8, 14, 20, 22, 24, 28, 31, 39, 45, 57, 60, 61, 67, 72, 73, 89, 90, 96, 100

p147 Socks: 6, 8, 10, 12, 14, 16, 18, 20, 22, 24, 26, 28, 30

p148 Hands: 20, 30, 35, 40, 45, 50

p149 **1** 30, 40, 60, 70, 80, 100
2 20, 30, 50, 60, 70, 90, 100, 110, 120

p150 **2** 40, 50, 80, 100

p151 13, 14, 15, 16, 17, 18, 19

p152 32 = **3** tens and **2** ones
32 = **30** + **2**
44 = **4** tens and **4** ones
44 = **40** + **4**
67 = **6** tens and **7** ones
67 = **60** + **7**
73 = **7** tens and **3** ones
73 = **70** + **3**
90 = **9** tens and **0** ones
90 = **90** + **0**

p153 **1** 15 (10, 5), 38 (30, 8), 49 (40, 9), 83 (80, 3), 99 (90, 9)
2 29 (2, 9), 12 (1, 2), 21 (2, 1)

p154 **1** hundred + **1** ten + **6** ones = **116**
1 hundred + **0** tens + **5** ones = 105

p155

	hundreds	tens	ones
118	1	1	8
102	1	0	2
116	1	1	6
106	1	0	6
111	1	1	1
117	1	1	7
104	1	0	4
120	1	2	0
100	1	0	0
109	1	0	9

p156 blue train: 5, 34, 83, 104, 119
red train: 8, 47, 93, 104, 113
green train: 7, 30, 62, 102, 114
blue train: 2, 39, 82, 105, 117

p157

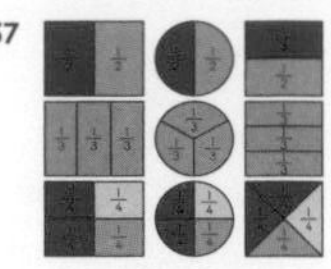

p158 **1** dog **2** fish **3** 9, 2, 5, 4
4 dog, cat, rabbit, hamster, fish

p159 apples **7**, lemons **3**, pineapples **1**, oranges **5**

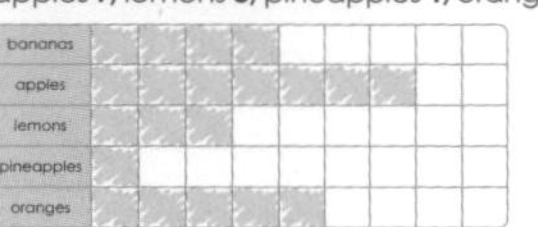

1 apples **2** pineapple

ADDITION AND SUBTRACTION

p160 **1** 5 **2** 7 **3** 15 **4** 12 **5** 16

p161 **1** 5 **2** 6 **3** 10 **4** 5 **5** 9

p162 9 + 1 = 10, 4 + 2 = 6, 7 + 1 = 8, 1 + 1 = 2, 6 + 1 = 7, 5 + 4 = 9, 3 + 2 = 5, 5 + 1 = 6, 3 + 3 = 6, 4 + 1 = 5, 6 + 3 = 9, 5 + 5 = 10, 3 + 1 = 4, 7 + 2 = 9, 2 + 1 = 3, 8 + 2 = 10, 4 + 4 = 8, 6 + 4 = 10, 6 + 2 = 8, 5 + 2 = 7, 5 + 3 = 8, 7 + 3 = 10, 4 + 3 = 7, 8 + 1 = 9

p163 10 − 1 = 9, 5 − 4 = 1, 7 − 3 = 4, 8 − 7 = 1, 9 − 5 = 4, 2 − 1 = 1, 10 − 4 = 6, 6 − 3 = 3, 9 − 2 = 7, 7 − 5 = 2, 8 − 3 = 5, 7 − 6 = 1, 3 − 2 = 1, 8 − 6 = 2, 10 − 3 = 7, 9 − 3 = 6, 4 − 2 = 2, 7 − 4 = 3, 10 − 7 = 3, 8 − 4 = 4, 5 − 3 = 2, 9 − 8 = 1, 10 − 6 = 4, 6 − 4 = 2

p164 25 = 25 T, 2 + 6 = 8 T, 15 + 3 = 18 T, 12 + 2 = 10 F, 14 = 10 + 5 F, 7 = 3 + 4 T, 6 + 3 = 3 + 6 T, 13 + 4 = 5 + 13 F, 2 + 3 = 2 + 2 F, 5 + 3 = 4 + 4 T, 12 + 3 = 8 + 5 F, 14 + 2 = 13 + 2 F

p165 12 = 16 F, 68 = 68 T, 99 = 100 F, 7 − 3 = 4 T, 10 − 2 = 6 F, 15 − 2 = 13 T, 10 = 14 − 4 T, 8 = 9 − 5 F, 6 − 3 = 7 − 4 T, 5 − 2 = 5 − 3 F, 10 − 8 = 14 − 4 F, 15 − 7 = 17 − 9 T, 10 − 4 = 3 + 3 T, 16 + 3 = 20 − 1 T

p166 6, 10, 18, 12, 11, 9, 7, 9

p167 5, 8, 3, 6, 3, 6, 4, 12

p168 7 + 7 = 14, 7 + 8 = 15, 2 + 2 = 4, 2 + 3 = 5, 4 + 4 = 8, 4 + 5 = 9, 3 + 3 = 6, 3 + 4 = 7, 1 + 1 = 2, 1 + 2 = 3, 8 + 8 = 16, 8 + 9 = 17, 6 + 6 = 12, 6 + 7 = 13, 9 + 9 = 18, 9 + 10 = 19, 10 + 10 = 20, 10 + 11 = 21

p169 8, 3, 5, 6, 6, 9, 6, 5, 3

p170 12, 14, 14, 11, 11, 14, 14, 13, 13, 11, 11, 16, 16

p171 10 + 2 = 12, 10 + 1 = 11, 10 + 8 = 18, 10 + 6 = 16, 10 + 3 = 13, 10 + 4 = 14, 10 + 5 = 15, 10 + 7 = 17

p172 9 + 2 = 9 + **1** + **1** = 10 + **1** = **11**
6 + 9 = 6 + **4** + **5** = 10 + **5** = **15**
4 + 7 = 4 + **6** + **1** = 10 + **1** = **11**
8 + 4 = 8 + **2** + **2** = 10 + **2** = **12**
3 + 9 = 3 + **7** + **2** = 10 + **2** = **12**
8 + 7 = 8 + **2** + **5** = 10 + **5** = **15**
5 + 8 = 5 + **5** + **3** = 10 + **3** = **13**
8 + 6 = 8 + **2** + **4** = 10 + **4** = **14**

p173 11 − **1** = 10, 10 − **5** = **5**, 11 − 6 = **5**
13 − **3** = 10, 10 − **2** = **8**, 13 − 5 = **8**
15 − **5** = 10, 10 − **1** = **9**, 15 − 6 = **9**
14 − **4** = 10, 10 − **4** = **6**, 14 − 8 = **6**
16 − **6** = 10, 10 − **3** = **7**, 16 − 9 = **7**

p174 11 − **1** − **1** = 10 − **1** = **9**
15 − **5** − **4** = 10 − **4** = **6**
12 − **2** − **3** = 10 − **3** = **7**
14 − **4** − **2** = 10 − **2** = **8**
11 − **1** − **3** = 10 − **3** = **7**
13 − **3** − **2** = 10 − **2** = **8**
16 − **6** − **3** = 10 − **3** = **7**
12 − **2** − **7** = 10 − **7** = **3**

p175 10, 11, 19, 13, 18, 20

p176 5, 7, 17, 7, 6, 8

p177 14, 18, 17, 20, 18, 18

p178 4 + 6 = 10, 7 + 9 = 16, 9 + 6 = 15, 6 + 6 = 12, 5 + 9 = 14, 6 + 5 = 11, 10 = 7 + 3, 18 = 8 + 10, 12 = 3 + 9, 8 = 3 + 5, 16 = 11 + 5, 9 = 9 + 0, 20 = 10 + 10, 20 = 2 + 18, 0 + 5 = 5, 7 + 0 = 7, 18 = 11 + 7, 10 + 6 = 16

p179 15 − 5 = 10, 14 − 6 = 8, 17 − 5 = 12, 8 − 5 = 3, 14 − 7 = 7, 13 − 4 = 9, 10 = 18 − 8, 16 = 19 − 3, 12 = 17 − 5, 8 = 12 − 4, 13 = 19 − 6, 4 = 4 − 0, 20 = 20 − 0, 10 = 20 − 10, 3 − 0 = 3, 7 − 0 = 7

SHAPES AND MEASUREMENTS

p180 Rectangle: 4
Triangle: 3
Pentagon: 5
Hexagon: 6

p181

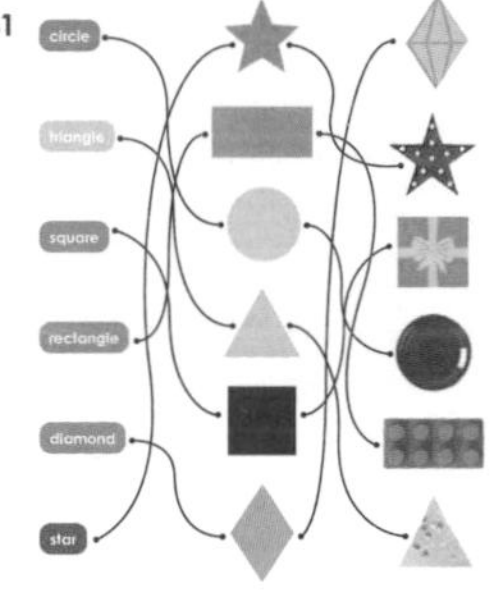

p182 Triangles: 4, 6
Rectangles: 7, 4

p183 4 4
5 6 8

p184 12 6 8
8 5 5

p185 Cones: Yes, Yes, No, Yes
Cylinders: Yes, Yes, No, Yes
Spheres: No, Yes, No, No

p186 1 4
2 3
3 5

p187

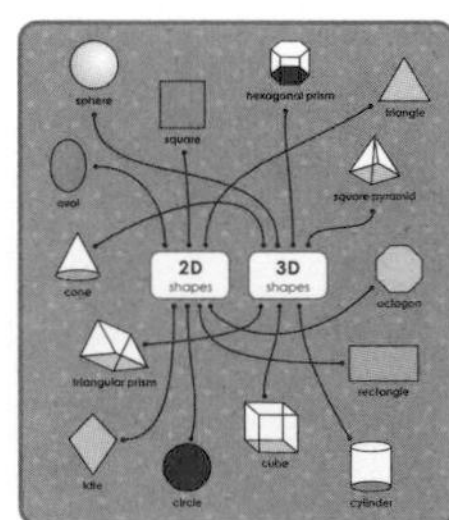

p188 Symmetrical images: flower, plane, crown, rainbow

p190 Activity 1: 3, 1, 2

p191 Crayon lengths: 6, 1, 3, 4

p192 A **3** B **1** C **4** D **1** E **2**
Tallest: C
Shortest: B and D
The juice bottle is **taller** than the water bottle.
The pink flower is **shorter** than the red flower.

p193 Cups: 2, 3, 1
Box 2 Jar 2
Bowl 1 Basket 1
Pitcher: 1, 4, 2, 5

p194 Circled: microwave, bus, dog
key, teddy, lemon
So, a kite is **lighter** than a truck.
So, a melon is **heavier** than a grape.

p195 Lightest: balloon dog
Heaviest: sofa
2 pounds **3** pounds
4 pounds **4** pounds

p196 **5** o'clock **1** o'clock
4 o'clock **7** o'clock **10** o'clock
half-past **9** half-past **7**

4 o'clock

half-past 1

half-past 6

p197 **12** o'clock half-past **7**
11 o'clock half-past **10**
3 o'clock **5** o'clock
10:00
09:30

SCIENCE

p199 Earth is made up of **three** main layers.
At the center is the Earth's **core**.
The **mantle** is in the middle, between the core and the crust.
The thinnest layer is the **crust**, which covers Earth's surface.

p200 Stickers: spring, summer, winter
Pictures **1** and **4**

p201 **Lightning** is a flash of electricity that lights up the sky.
The **Sun** is a giant star that gives us light and heat.
Wind is moving air.
Rain is drops of water that fall from clouds.
Snow is made of white ice crystals with six sides.
Thunder is the sound that comes after lightning.

p203

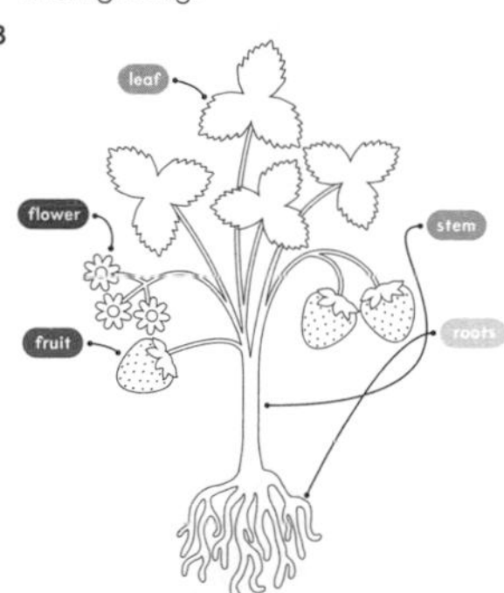

p204

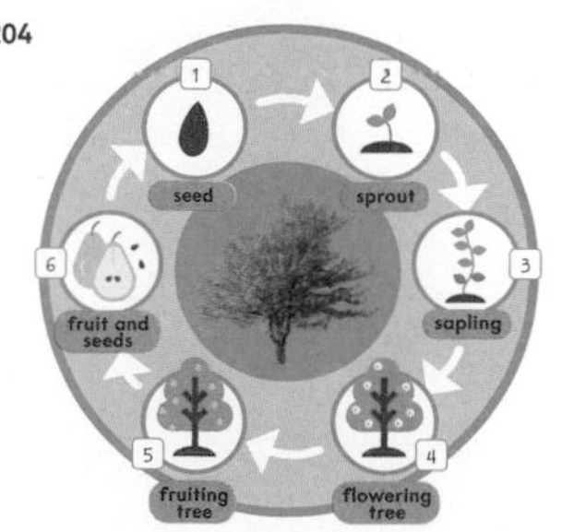

p205

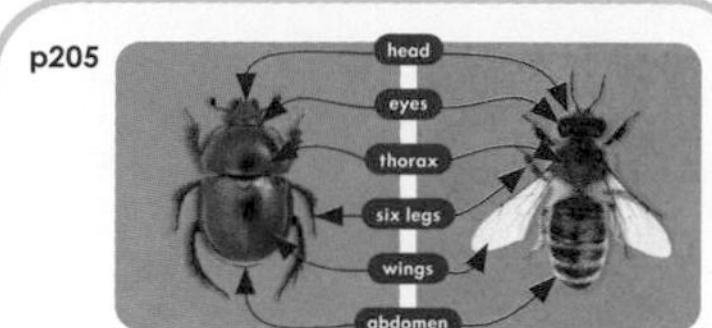

p206

A butterfly lays an egg.
The fully grown caterpillar spins a chrysalis around itself.
It comes out of the chrysalis as a butterfly.
The egg hatches into a caterpillar.

p207

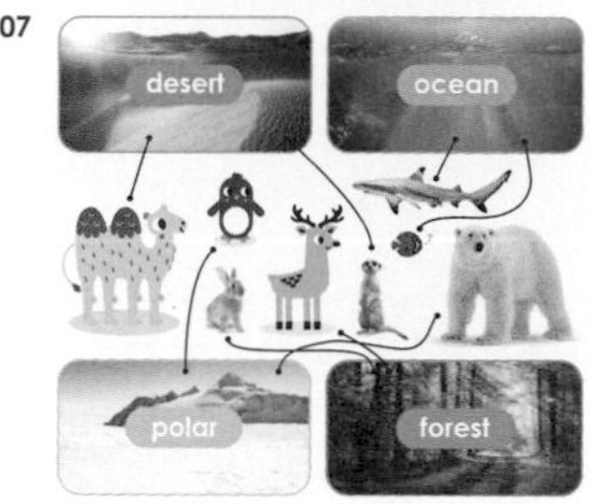

p208 algae > fish > seal > shark
owl
big fish
lion

p209

p210 4 1 3 2

p211 L L S
S L
S L

p212 F B B
E E F
E F B
B F E

SOCIAL STUDIES

p218 1 **C** 2 **B** 3 **A** 4 **D**

p219 smaller
bigger

p222

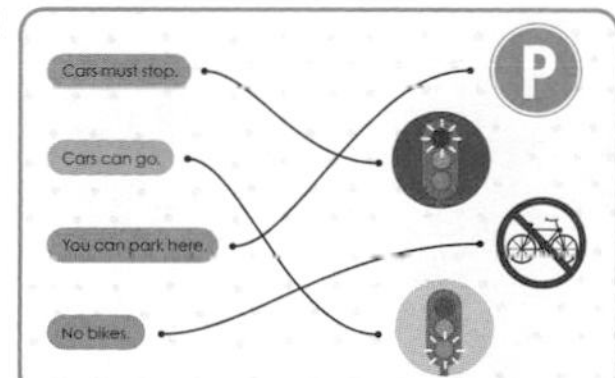

p223

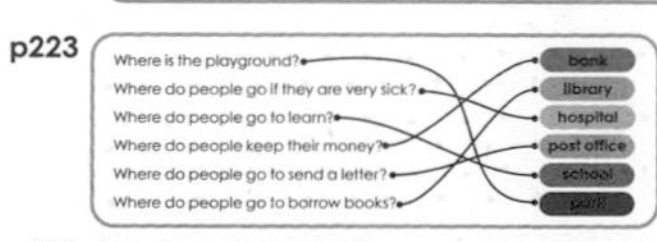

p224 (answers may vary)
doctor: helps people when they are sick/ helps people to feel better
librarian: helps people to choose and loan books at the library.
firefighter: helps protect people and buildings by putting out fires
teacher: helps children to learn at school

p226

hospital
school
train station
airport

p227

p228

p229

Human-Made Objects	Natural Objects
plastic	icebergs
clothes	stone
glass	wood
paper	sand
paint	feather

p230 toy: **good**
bread: **good**
shoe repair: **service**
package delivery: **service**
car: **good**
house cleaning: **service**
cupcake: **good**
car repair: **service**

p231 3 2
4 1
producer
consumer

p232 N N W W
N W W W
N N W W
N N W N

p233 Littering: **negative**
Cutting down forests: **negative**
Cleaning lakes, rivers, and seas: **positive**
Pollution from cars: **negative**
Recycling plastic: **positive**
Growing your own vegetables: **positive**
Protecting endangered animals: **positive**

p234 paper and card: **newspaper, cardboard box**
glass: **jelly jar, glass bottle**
plastic: **soda bottle, yogurt cup**
compost: **carrot tops, apple**
metals: **empty can, aluminium**
clothes: **old sneakers, dress**

Congratulations!

Good Work Award!

Name: ....

has successfully completed the

Grade 1

Jumbo Workbook

Date: ....

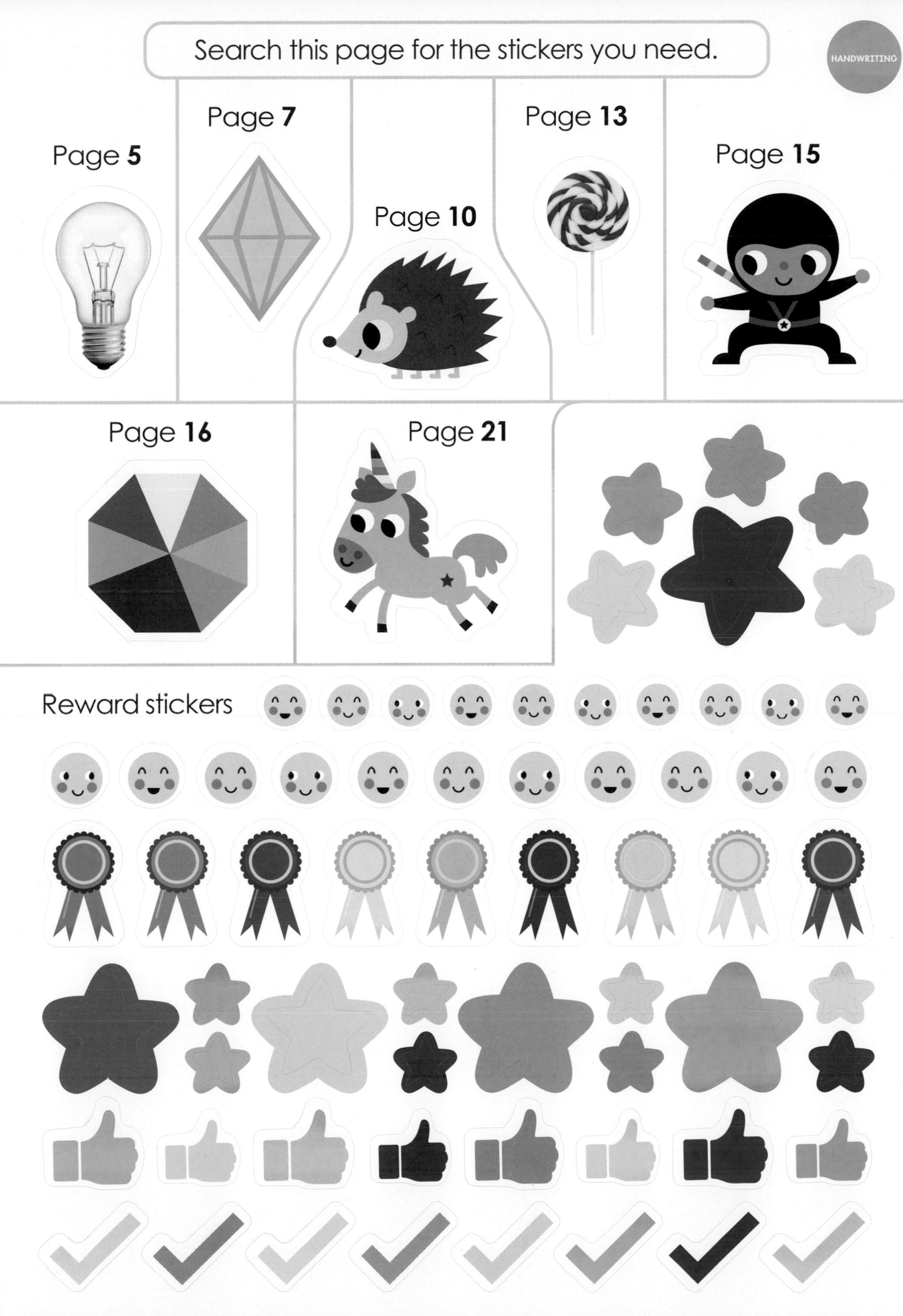
Search this page for the stickers you need.
HANDWRITING
Page 5
Page 7
Page 10
Page 13
Page 15
Page 16
Page 21
Reward stickers

Search this page for the stickers you need.

Page **26**

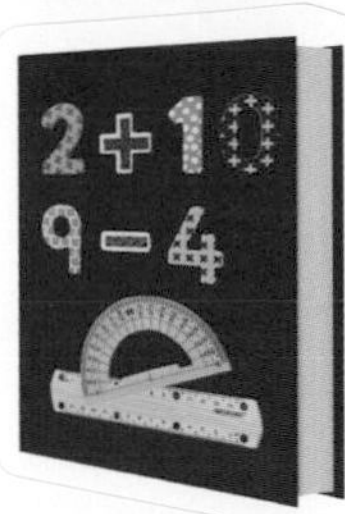

Page **29**

Page **30**

Page **35**

Page **37**

Page **40**

Pages **42–43**

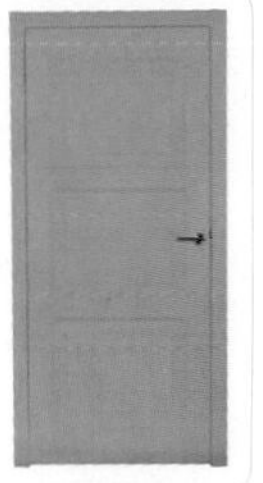

Reward stickers

         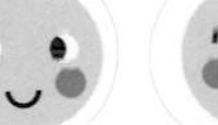

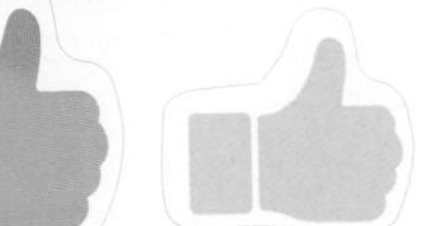 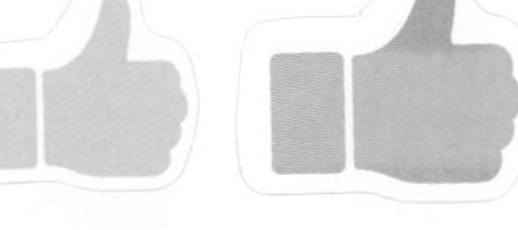 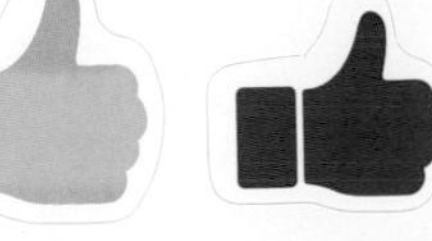  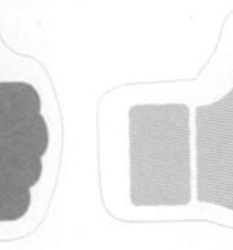   

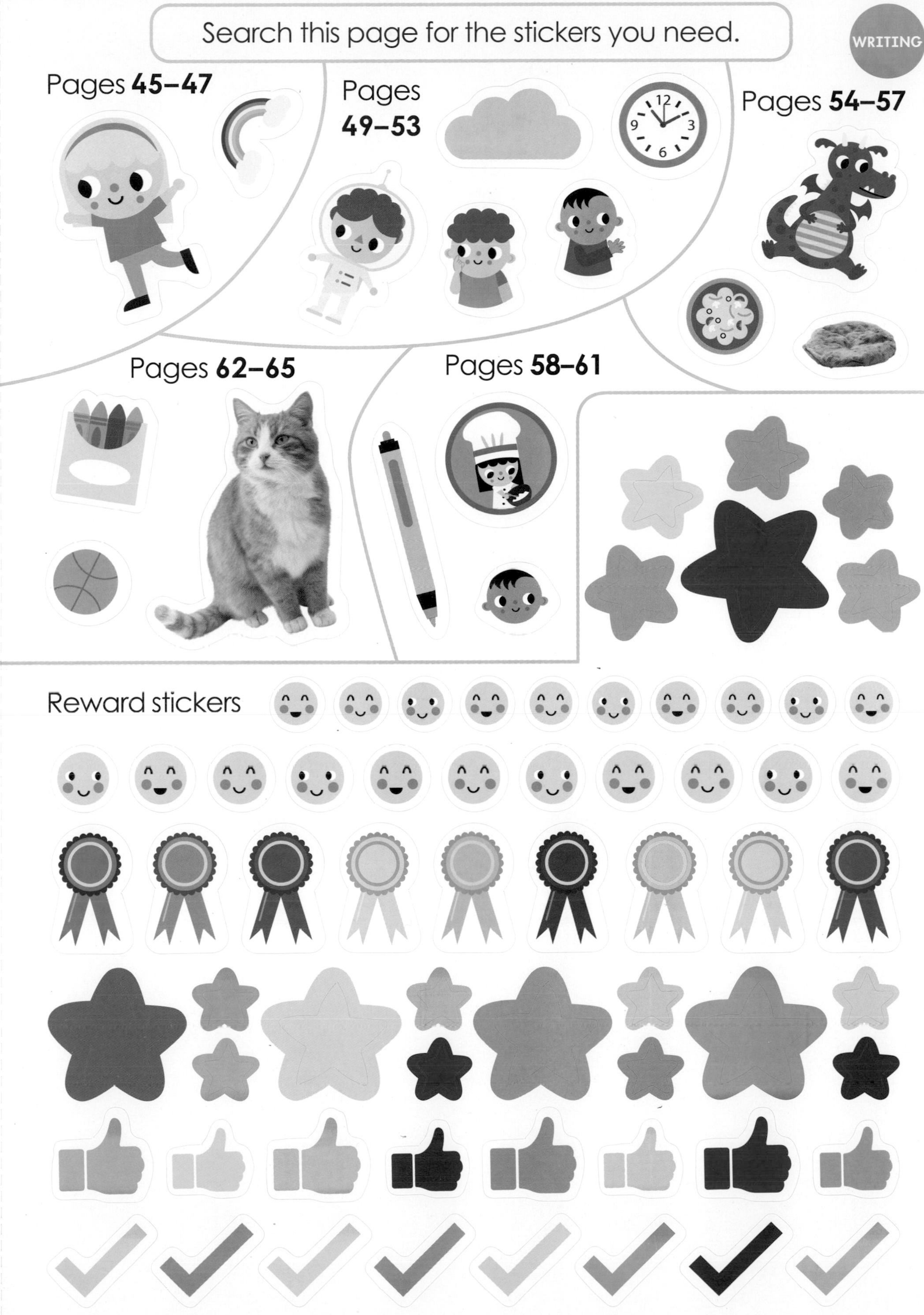

Search this page for the stickers you need.
WRITING
Pages 45–47
Pages 49–53
Pages 54–57
Pages 62–65
Pages 58–61
Reward stickers

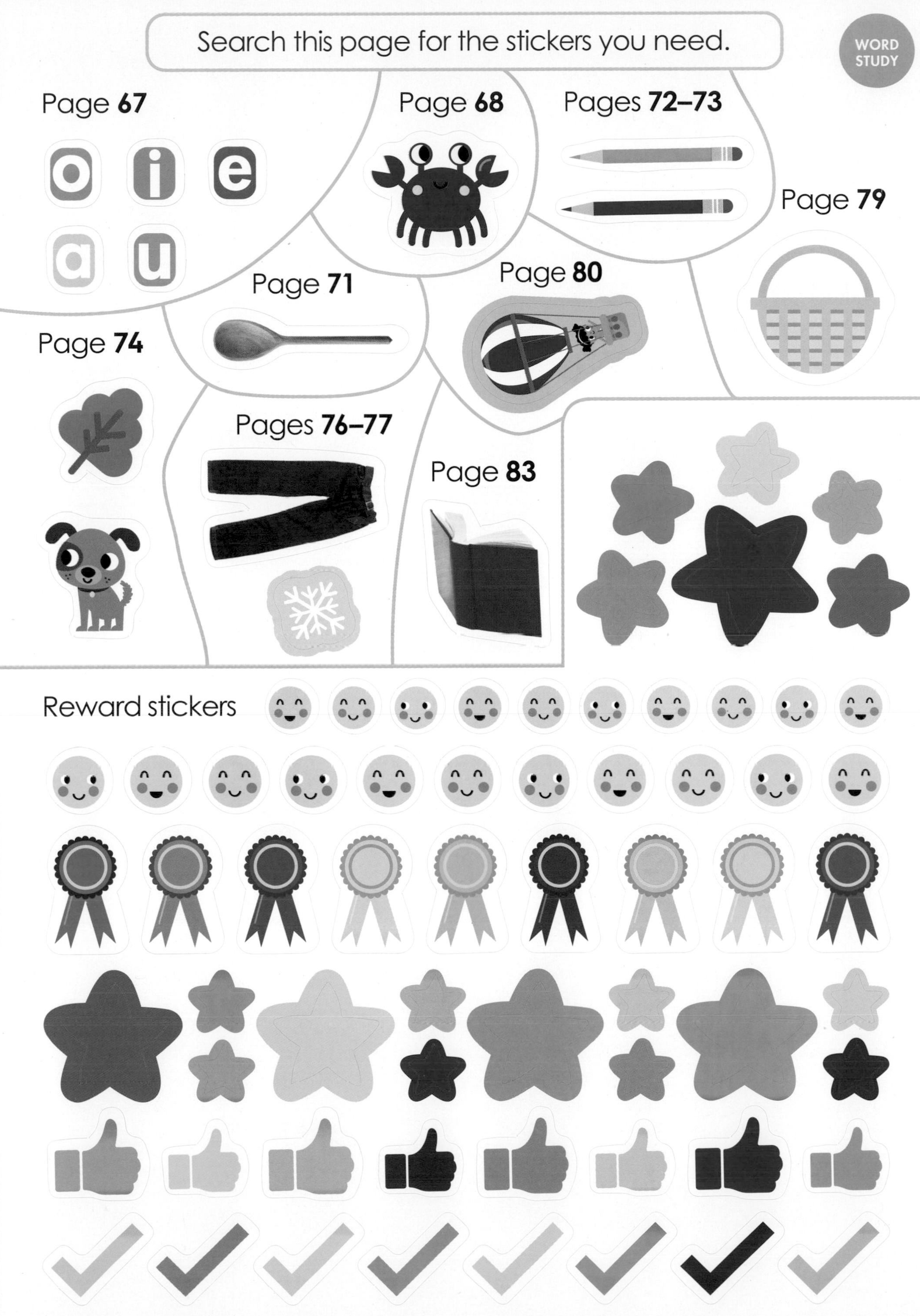
Search this page for the stickers you need.
WORD STUDY
Page 67
o
i
e
a
u
Page 68
Pages 72–73
Page 79
Page 71
Page 80
Page 74
Pages 76–77
Page 83
Reward stickers

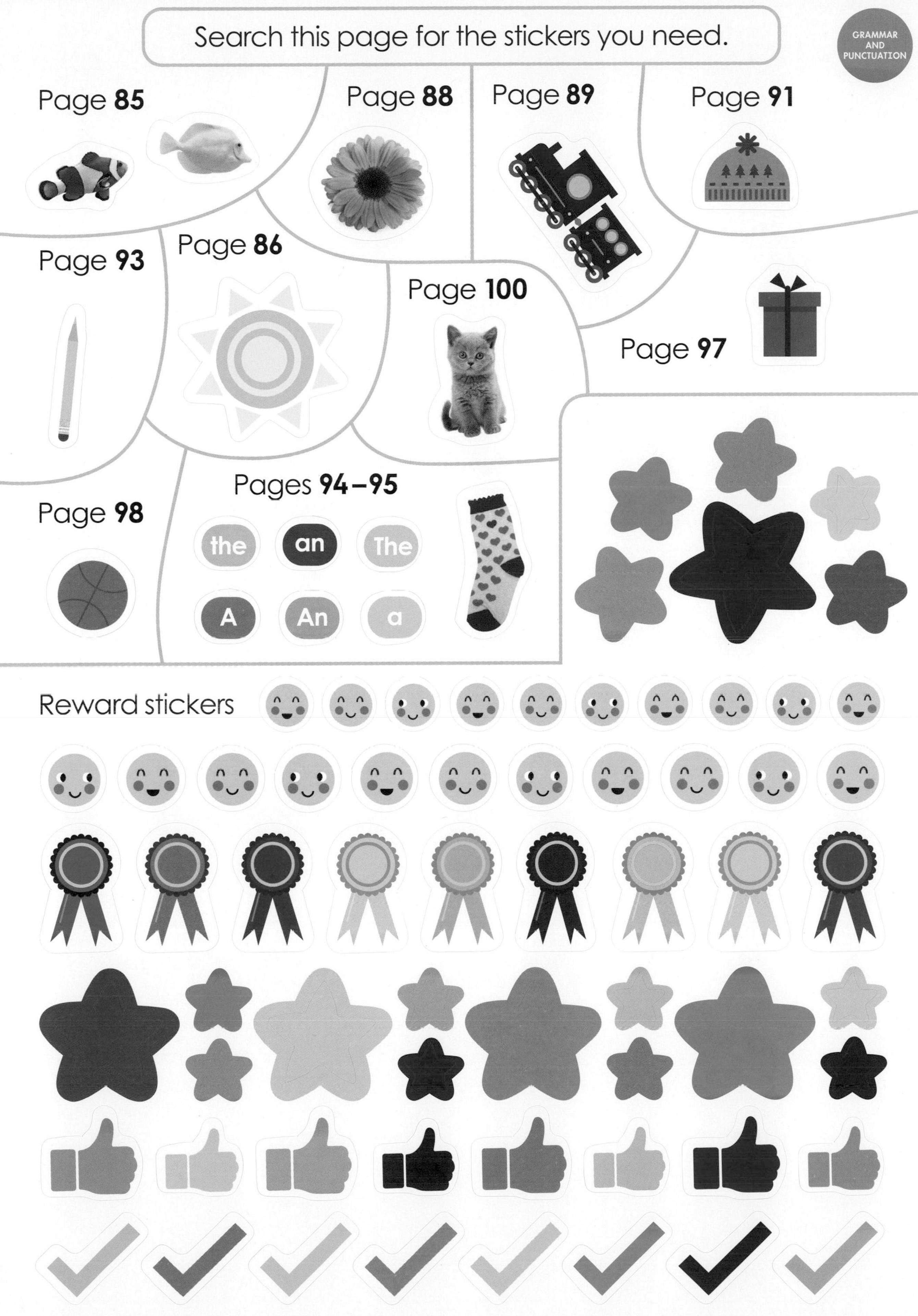
Search this page for the stickers you need.
GRAMMAR AND PUNCTUATION
Page 85
Page 88
Page 89
Page 91
Page 93
Page 86
Page 100
Page 97
Pages 94–95
Page 98
the
an
The
A
An
a
Reward stickers

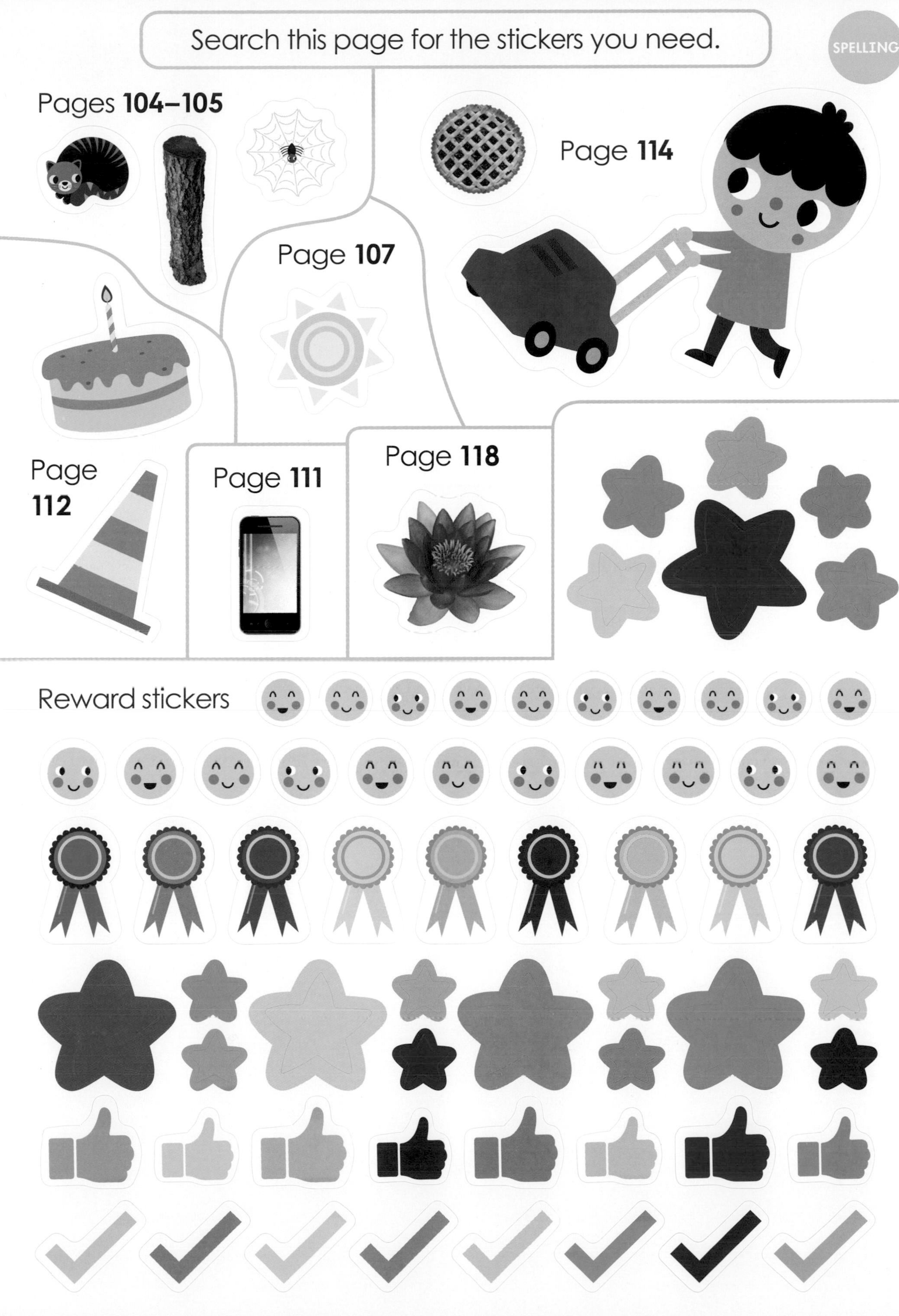

Search this page for the stickers you need.
SPELLING
Pages 104–105
Page 114
Page 107
Page 112
Page 111
Page 118
Reward stickers

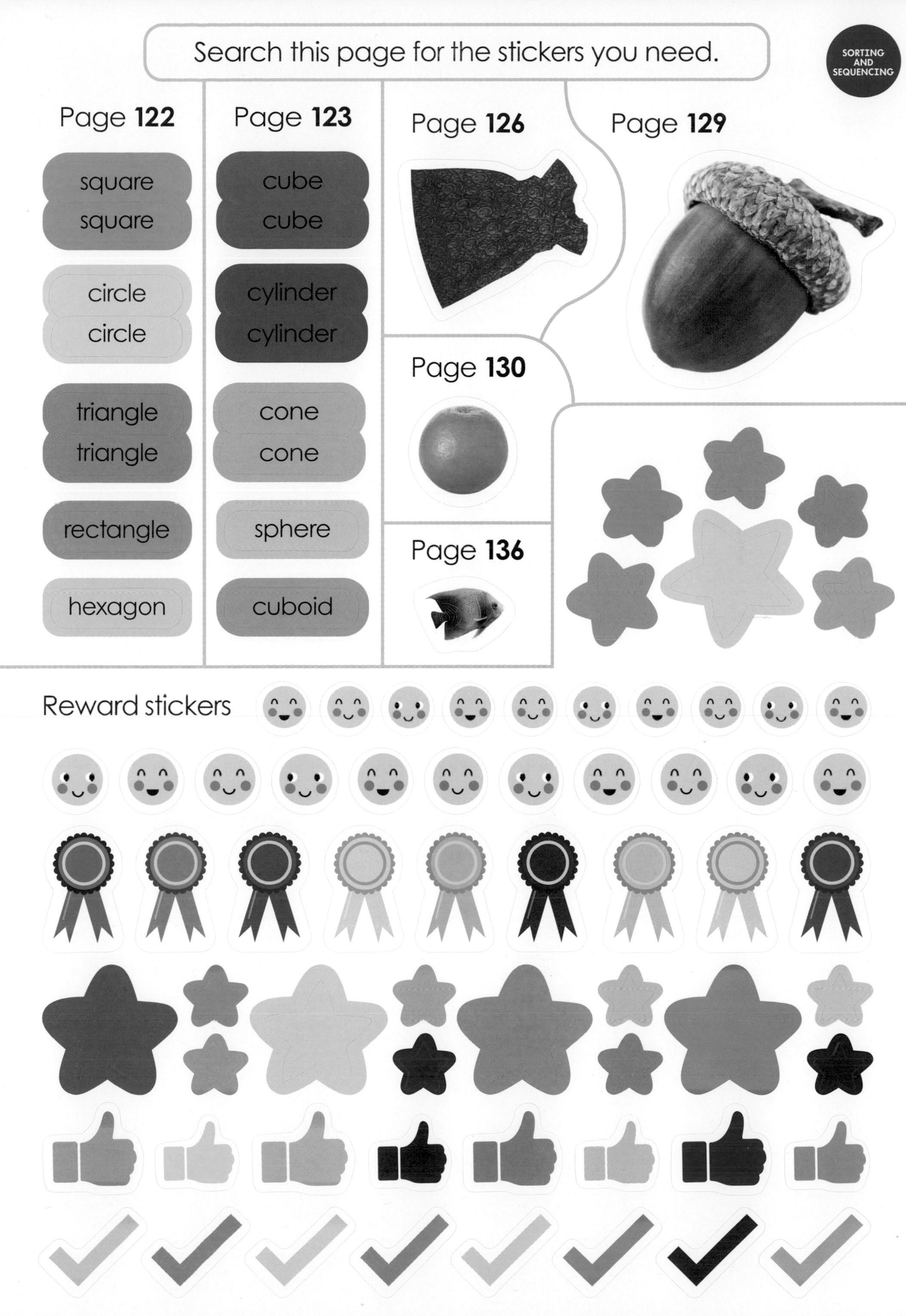
Search this page for the stickers you need.
SORTING AND SEQUENCING
Page 122
square
square
circle
circle
triangle
triangle
rectangle
hexagon
Page 123
cube
cube
cylinder
cylinder
cone
cone
sphere
cuboid
Page 126
Page 129
Page 130
Page 136
Reward stickers

Search this page for the stickers you need.

NUMBER SENSE

Page **140**

Page **141**

Page **142**

Page **147**

Page **149**

Page **156**

Page **159**

Reward stickers

Search this page for the stickers you need.

Pages **168 – 169**

Page **170**

Page **175**

Page **176**

Pages **178 – 179**

Page **177**

Reward stickers

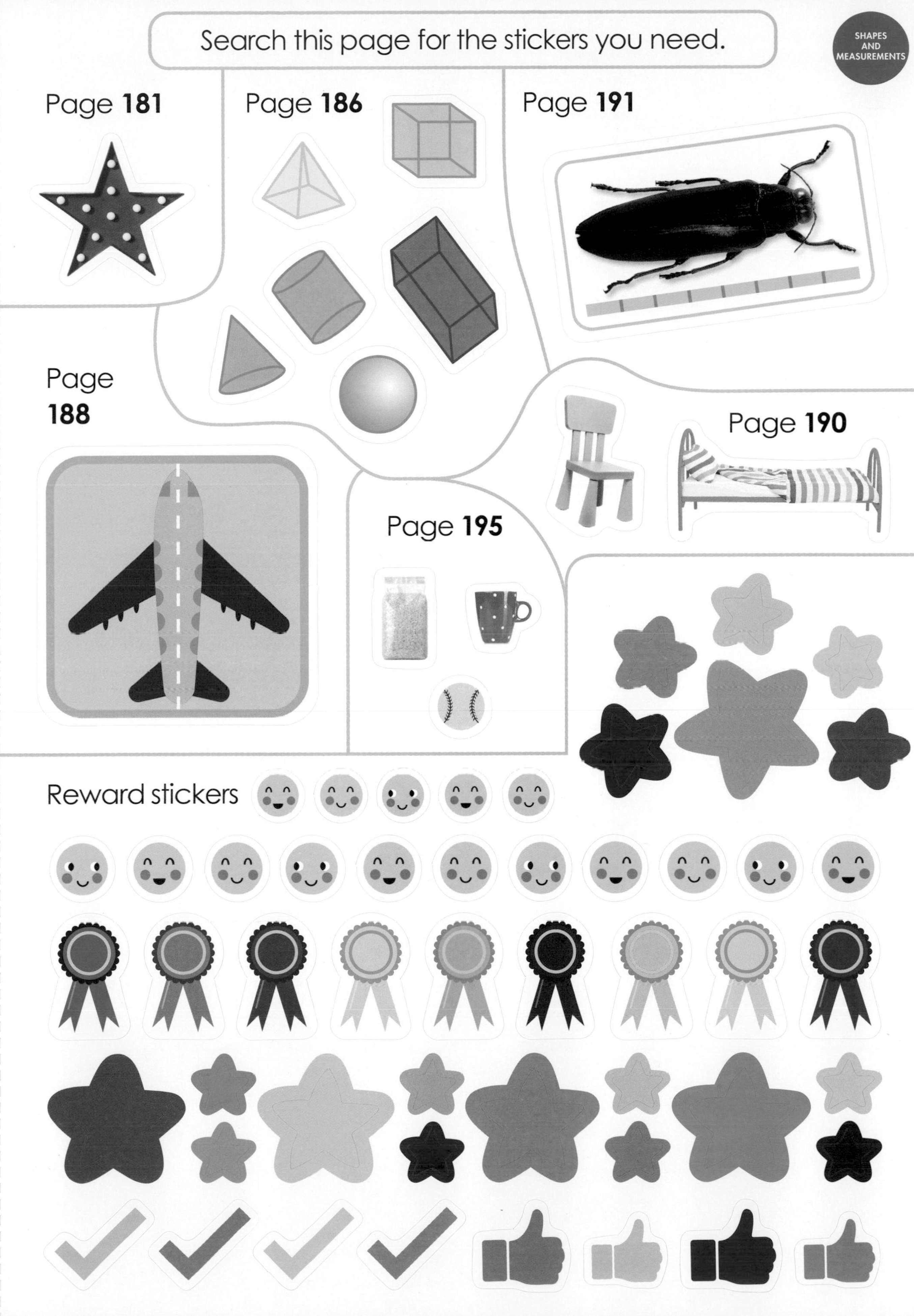
Search this page for the stickers you need.
SHAPES AND MEASUREMENTS
Page 181
Page 186
Page 191
Page 188
Page 190
Page 195
Reward stickers

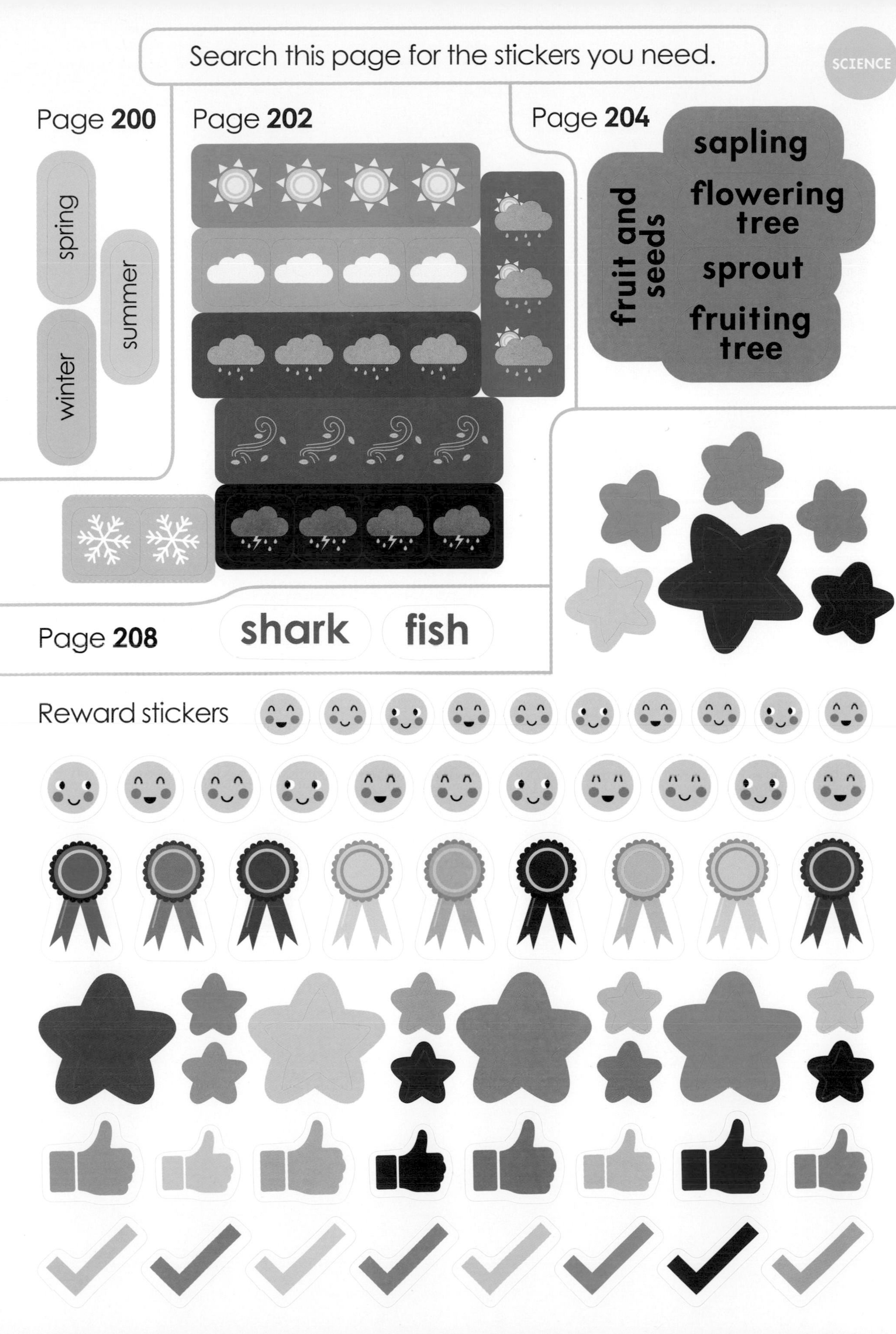
Search this page for the stickers you need.
SCIENCE
Page 200
spring
summer
winter
Page 202
Page 204
sapling
flowering tree
fruit and seeds
sprout
fruiting tree
Page 208
shark
fish
Reward stickers

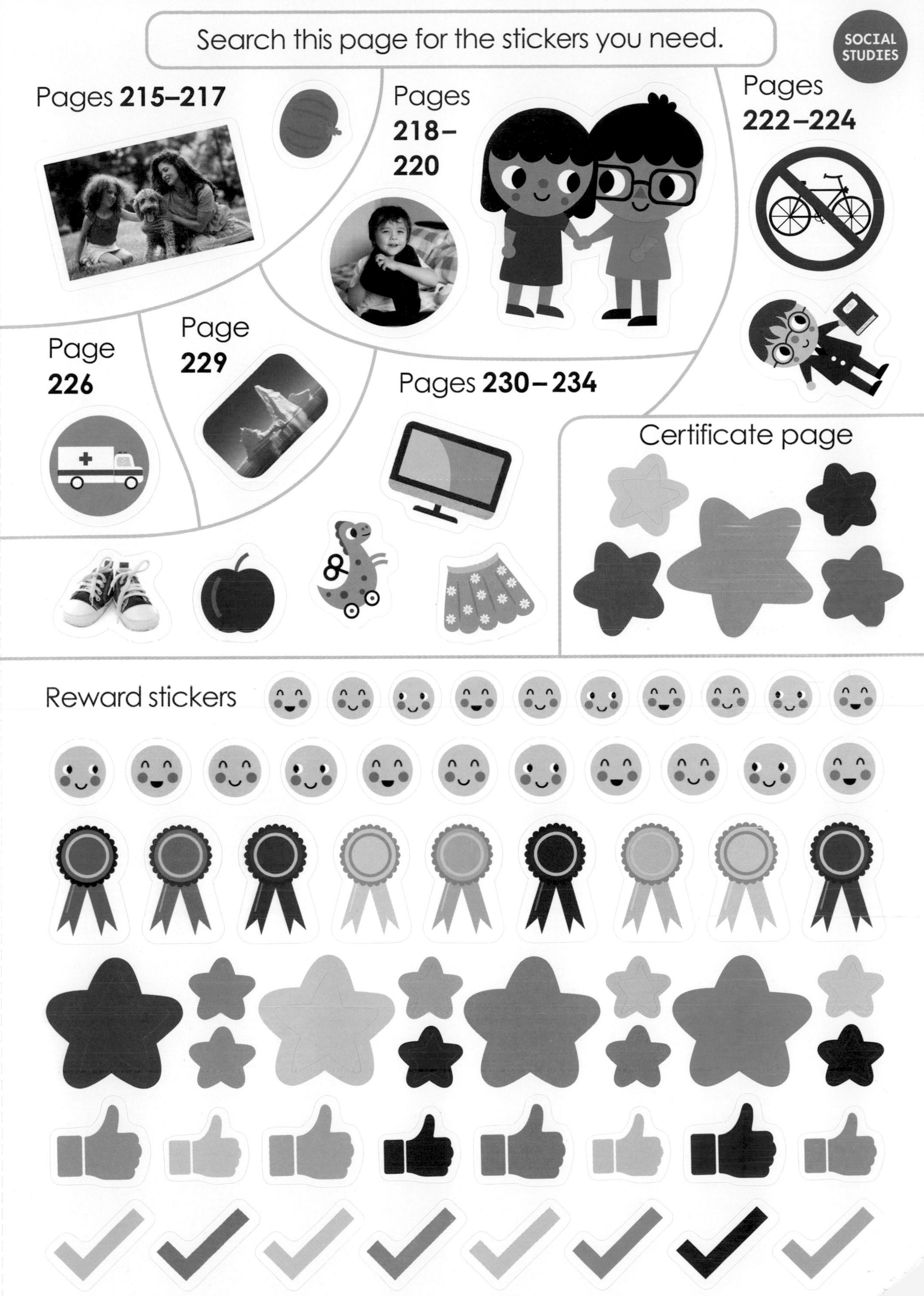
Search this page for the stickers you need.
SOCIAL STUDIES
Pages 215–217
Pages 218–220
Pages 222–224
Page 226
Page 229
Pages 230–234
Certificate page
Reward stickers